CW00548670

CULLODEN
(*CÙIL LODAIR*)

GREAT BATTLES

CULLODEN
(CÙIL LODAIR)

MURRAY PITTOCK

OXFORD
UNIVERSITY PRESS

Great Clarendon Street, Oxford, OX2 6DP,
United Kingdom

Oxford University Press is a department of the University of Oxford.
It furthers the University's objective of excellence in research, scholarship,
and education by publishing worldwide. Oxford is a registered trade mark of
Oxford University Press in the UK and in certain other countries

© Murray Pittock 2016

The moral rights of the author have been asserted

First Edition published in 2016

Impression: 2

All rights reserved. No part of this publication may be reproduced, stored in
a retrieval system, or transmitted, in any form or by any means, without the
prior permission in writing of Oxford University Press, or as expressly permitted
by law, by licence or under terms agreed with the appropriate reprographics
rights organization. Enquiries concerning reproduction outside the scope of the
above should be sent to the Rights Department, Oxford University Press, at the
address above

You must not circulate this work in any other form
and you must impose this same condition on any acquirer

Published in the United States of America by Oxford University Press
198 Madison Avenue, New York, NY 10016, United States of America

British Library Cataloguing in Publication Data
Data available

Library of Congress Control Number: 2015960786

ISBN 978–0–19–966407–8

Printed and bound by CPI Group (UK) Ltd, Croydon, CR0 4YY

Links to third party websites are provided by Oxford in good faith and
for information only. Oxford disclaims any responsibility for the materials
contained in any third party website referenced in this work.

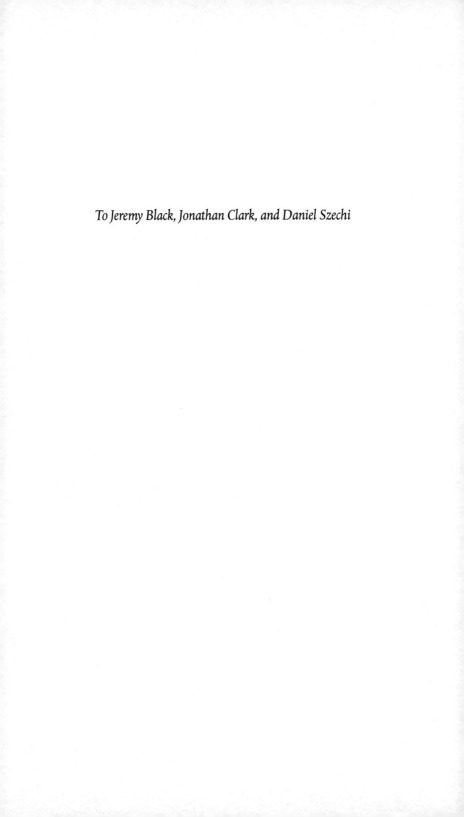

To Jeremy Black, Jonathan Clark, and Daniel Szechi

FOREWORD

For those who practise war in the twenty-first century the idea of a 'great battle' can seem no more than the echo of a remote past. The names on regimental colours or the events commemorated at mess dinners bear little relationship to patrolling in dusty villages or waging 'wars amongst the people'. Contemporary military doctrine downplays the idea of victory, arguing that wars end by negotiation not by the smashing of an enemy army or navy. Indeed it erodes the very division between war and peace, and with it the aspiration to fight a culminating 'great battle'.

And yet to take battle out of war is to redefine war, possibly to the point where some would argue that it ceases to be war. Carl von Clausewitz, who experienced two 'great battles' at first hand—Jena in 1806 and Borodino in 1812—wrote in *On War* that major battle is 'concentrated war', and 'the centre of gravity of the entire campaign'. Clausewitz's remarks related to the theory of strategy. He recognized that in practice armies might avoid battles, but even then the efficacy of their actions relied on the latent threat of fighting. Winston Churchill saw the importance of battles in different terms, not for their place within war but for their impact on historical and national narratives. His forebear, the Duke of Marlborough, fought four major battles and named his palace after the most famous of them, Blenheim, fought in 1704. Battles, Churchill wrote in his life of Marlborough, are 'the principal milestones in secular history'. For him, 'Great battles, won or lost, change the entire course of events, create new standards of values, new moods, new atmospheres, in armies and nations, to which all must conform'.

Clausewitz's experience of war was shaped by Napoleon. Like Marlborough, the French emperor sought to bring his enemies to battle. However, each lived within a century of the other, and they fought their wars in the same continent and even on occasion on adjacent ground. Winston Churchill's own experience of war, which spanned the late nineteenth-century colonial conflicts of the British Empire as well as two world wars, became increasingly distanced from the sorts of battle he and Clausewitz described. In 1898 Churchill rode in a cavalry charge in a battle which crushed the Madhist forces of the Sudan in a single day. Four years later the British commander at Omdurman, Lord Kitchener, brought the South African War to a conclusion after a two-year guerrilla conflict in which no climactic battle occurred. Both Churchill and Kitchener served as British Cabinet ministers in the First World War, a conflict in which battles lasted weeks, and even months, and which, despite their scale and duration, did not produce clear-cut outcomes. The 'Battle' of Verdun ran for all but one month of 1916 and that of the Somme for five months. The potentially decisive naval action at Jutland spanned a more traditional twenty-four-hour timetable but was not conclusive and was not replicated during the war. In the Second World War, the major struggle in waters adjacent to Europe, the 'Battle' of the Atlantic, was fought from 1940 to early 1944.

Clausewitz would have called these twentieth-century 'battles' campaigns, or even seen them as wars in their own right. The determination to seek battle and to venerate its effects may therefore be culturally determined, the product of time and place, rather than an inherent attribute of war. The ancient historian Victor Davis Hanson has argued that seeking battle is a 'western way of war' derived from classical Greece. Seemingly supportive of his argument are the writings of Sun Tzu, who flourished in warring states in China between two and five centuries before the birth of Christ, and who pointed out that the most effective way of waging war was to avoid the risks and dangers of actual fighting. Hanson has provoked strong criticism: those who argue that wars can be won without battles are not only to be found in Asia. Eighteenth-century European commanders, deploying armies in close-order formations in order to deliver concentrated fires, realized that the destructive consequences of battle for their own troops could be self-defeating. After the First World War, Basil Liddell Hart developed a theory of strategy which he called 'the indirect approach', and suggested that manoeuvre might substitute for hard fighting, even if its success still relied on the inherent threat of battle.

The winners of battles have been celebrated as heroes, and nations have used their triumphs to establish their founding myths. It is precisely for these reasons that their legacies have outlived their direct political consequences. Commemorated in painting, verse, and music, marked by monumental memorials, and used as the way points for the periodization of history, they have enjoyed cultural afterlives. These are evident in many capitals, in place names and statues, not least in Paris and London. The French tourist who finds himself in a London taxi travelling from Trafalgar Square to Waterloo Station should reflect on his or her own domestic peregrinations from the Rue de Rivoli to the Gare d'Austerlitz. Today's Mongolia venerates the memory of Genghis Khan while Greece and Macedonia scrap over the rights to Alexander the Great.

This series of books on 'great battles' tips its hat to both Clausewitz and Churchill. Each of its volumes situates the battle which it discusses in the context of the war in which it occurred, but each then goes on to discuss its legacy, its historical interpretation and reinterpretation, its place in national memory and commemoration, and its manifestations in art and culture. These are not easy books to write. The victors were more often celebrated than the defeated; the effect of loss on the battlefield could be cultural oblivion. However, that point is not universally true: the British have done more over time to mark their defeats at Gallipoli in 1915 and Dunkirk in 1940 than their conquerors on both occasions. For the history of war to thrive and be productive it needs to embrace the view from 'the other side of the hill', to use the Duke of Wellington's words. The battle the British call Omdurman is for the Sudanese the Battle of Kerreri; the Germans called Waterloo 'la Belle Alliance' and Jutland Skagerrak. Indeed the naming of battles could itself be a sign not only of geographical precision or imprecision (Kerreri is more accurate but as a hill rather than a town is harder to find on a small-scale map), but also of cultural choice. In 1914 the German general staff opted to name their defeat of the Russians in East Prussia not Allenstein (as geography suggested) but Tannenberg, in order to claim revenge for the defeat of the Teutonic Knights in 1410.

Military history, more than many other forms of history, is bound up with national stories. All too frequently it fails to be comparative, to recognize that war is a 'clash of wills' (to quote Clausewitz once more), and so omits to address both parties to the fight. Cultural difference and even more linguistic ignorance can prevent the historian considering a battle in the round; so too can the availability of sources. Levels of literacy matter here, but so does cultural survival. Often these pressures can be congruent but they can also be divergent. Britain enjoys much higher levels of literacy than Afghanistan, but in 2002 the memory of the two countries' three wars flourished in the latter, thanks to an oral tradition, much more robustly than in the former, for whom literacy had created distance. And the historian who addresses cultural legacy is likely to face a much more challenging task the further in the past the battle occurred. The opportunity for invention and reinvention is simply greater the longer the lapse of time since the key event.

All historians of war must, nonetheless, never forget that, however rich and splendid the cultural legacy of a great battle, it was won and lost by fighting, by killing and being killed. The Battle of Waterloo has left as abundant a footprint as any, but the general who harvested most of its glory reflected on it in terms which have general applicability, and carry across time in their capacity to capture a universal truth. Wellington wrote to Lady Shelley in its immediate aftermath: 'I hope to God I have fought my last battle. It is a bad thing to be always fighting. While in the thick of it I am much too occupied to feel anything; but it is wretched just after. It is quite impossible to think of glory. Both mind and feelings are exhausted. I am wretched even at the moment of victory, and I always say that, next to a battle lost, the greatest misery is a battle

gained.' Readers of this series should never forget the immediate suffering caused by battle, as well as the courage required to engage in it:
the physical courage of the soldier, sailor, or warrior, and the moral
courage of the commander, ready to hazard all on its uncertain
outcomes.

HEW STRACHAN

PREFACE

In the book that follows, there are some questions of nomenclature. The Jacobite claimant is described as James VIII and III, and his elder son as Prince Charles Edward. Many European powers accepted James's title, and its Scottish numbering was frequently used in anti-Union declarations and other Scottish documentation. The term 'Old Pretender' (descended as it is from the *pretended* Prince of Wales') is not neutral (see, for example, An Act for the Attainder of the pretended Prince of Wales of High Treason (13 & 14 Gul III n.3) *Statutes of the Realm* 7, 1695–1701); *Pretended Prince of Wales Born, 1688*, Royal Collections), while 'Chevalier' or 'Young Chevalier' reduces a major monarchical claim to a minor status conferred by the French Crown. To name James 'James Stuart' is to suggest that no question of rank or title is involved at all, so one is left with adopting either the title accorded by continental European powers or the various titles (Pretender, Pretended Prince of Wales, Prince of Wales, Chevalier) adopted in Great Britain. The former is chosen as it was consistent and recognized James's legitimate claim, and it was not based on a lie concerning his birth. The army his son Charles Edward led is called the 'Jacobite Army'; there is a case (which others have advanced) for terming them 'Scottish', but although the 'civil war' analysis of Jacobitism is tendentious and leaves much out of account, to term his force a national army is too strong a claim, albeit it did possess national qualities. Its self-description as a 'Highland Army' (in English) was not a geographical, far less a linguistic one, but a statement of commitment to the values of an older, patriot Scotland, defended by the martial spirit of its core north of the Forth, and, yet better, north of the Tay. I follow Reid in describing the government forces as the British Army: that is what they were. Other constructions of their nature or title are arguably manipulative, in that they are confined to the engagements of 1745–6 alone and designed to have us read them in a particular way: why the 'government' or 'Hanoverian' army at Culloden, but not at Fontenoy, Dettingen, or elsewhere, where a number of Cumberland's regiments had seen service? Indeed, by comparison with British forces deployed on the Continent, which had many soldiers from outwith the British Isles in their ranks, Cumberland's army was all but completely British. Barely a third of those who fought with Wellington at Waterloo were British, but they have long been adopted as such, while the British Army who fought with Cumberland are not usually even permitted the name.

The personalization of regimental commands is an early modern convention and should not lead us to personalize the struggle at Culloden, or to render it clannish, dynastic, or a matter of divided families on either side. Such things were part of it, as they have been part of many wars: but Culloden was a conflict between the emergent imperial power of Great Britain and the looser, more plural multi-kingdom monarchy of its Stuart predecessor. The power of the former already clearly lay in the south-east of England; the support for the latter was often to be found in the British peripheries. In that sense, Culloden was a thoroughly modern battle. It speaks to the present without the need for presentism.

Among the commanders on both sides, nomenclature is usually straightforward. There are two deliberate decisions. The first is to term the Jacobite quartermaster and adjutant general Sullivan not O'Sullivan. While recognizing that these forms are to a great degree interchangeable, John Sullivan is what the man called himself. The second is to use the form Iain Ruadh Stiùbhart for 'John Roy Stewart', as the Jacobite colonel in question was a well known poet in his native Gaelic, and to a great extent that is the means by which his name survives today.

MURRAY PITTOCK
Stirling 2015

ACKNOWLEDGEMENTS

Culloden is an apparently simple battle, but such simplicity is deceptive. Although it was well described and depicted at the time and subsequently, the symbolic importance of the outcome, and its strong framing in a particular way for the purposes of collective, cultural, and social memory, have led over the centuries to many misleading accounts. In *The Myth of the Jacobite Clans* (first published in 1995) I argued that on the basis of the archival evidence the Jacobite Army was conventionally armed and drilled. In the last few years, these findings have been borne out by the battlefield archaeology of Tony Pollard. Pollard's careful analysis, together with that of ex-serviceman Stuart Reid, has helped us to understand better the scope and scale of the encounter, the nature of the landscape of the battlefield in 1746, and the importance of the British dragoon action.

This book therefore owes a debt to Tony Pollard, director of the Centre for Battlefield Archaeology in Glasgow, whose pioneering work on Culloden battlefield has made an outstanding contribution to our recovery of the ascertainable facts of the day. Thanks are also due to my colleague Nigel Leask, to the Principal of the University, Anton Muscatelli, to Neal Juster his deputy, and to other colleagues at the University of Glasgow who have supported the book's development. I also owe much to Frank McLynn, who was an early influence on my career and development as a scholar of the Jacobite Army; to Harry Dickinson, who was always a better friend to my ideas than might be suspected from his own approach; and to Frank O'Gorman and Jeremy Gregory, for asking me to give the 44th British Society for Eighteenth-Century Studies Annual Lecture on 'Objects, Conflict and Memory in the State' in 2015. I am also grateful to Anndra Grannd MacCoinnich, property manager at National Trust for Scotland Culloden for his frank insights into the current state of interpretation of the battle and the challenges ahead, and to the staff at the National Library of Scotland and to Matthew Cotton at Oxford University Press for locating so many of the illustrations. Thanks too to my copy-editor Rowena Anketell for her suggestion of incorporating a reference to Alexander McQueen in Chapter 6. This book is dedicated to three friends and fellow historians: Jeremy Black, whose *Culloden* (1990) was the first truly modern study of the battle, and who was a great mentor and support to my career for many years; Daniel Szechi, for so many conversations on Jacobite military capability and its potential in 1715 and in 1745; and Jonathan Clark, my friend for a quarter of a century, who has done so much to make another eighteenth century possible.

My thanks are also due to Calum Colvin OBE for permission to reproduce his triptych on the aftermath of Culloden in Chapter 6. Many thanks also to the Royal Collections, the British Museum, the National Galleries of Scotland, the National Museums of Scotland, the National Library of Scotland, the Hunterian Museum at the University of Glasgow, the Foundling Museum, the McManus Museum and Art Gallery Dundee, the Bridgeman Art Library, and the National Army Museum, for permission to reproduce material in their collections. My thanks are due to my wife Anne for her love, support, and patience in the creation of this book, and for taking the battlefield photographs on location in the early spring of 2015. The faults that follow are my own.

CONTENTS

LIST OF FIGURES

LIST OF MAPS

1

Introduction

Tha 'ghaoth sguabadh Chu[a]il Lodair
Le sgal craingidh fuar
's na cuirp ghle[a]-gheal air dubhadh
mur b'e tuireadh Iain Ruadh

The wind scours Culloden
With a chill, piercing blast—
The whitened corpses would have turned black
Were it not for John Roy's lament.[1]

Some talk of Alexander
    And some of Hercules
Of Hector and Lysander,
    And such great men as these
But of all the world's great heroes
    There's none that can compare
To the gallant Duke of Cumberland
    And the British Grenadier.[2]

The Battle of Culloden is one of the decisive battles of the world, and one of the most powerful in its continuing influence on cultural memory. This is a claim which can seem strange or overblown for many reasons. First, it was a small battle in an eighteenth century where there were very many bigger ones: no more than 15,000 men were engaged on both sides of Culloden and its aftermath, fighting for the King and the British Army on one side, and on the other for the largely Scottish forces of Prince Charles Edward Stuart. Secondly, the tactical objective of the battle was nugatory: smallish forces met on open moorland on the edge of Europe for possession of the road to a small town, Inverness,

1

no more than one-hundredth the size of London. Thirdly, the strategic goal of the insurgents can seem anachronistic: to replace one dynasty on the throne by another at a time when parliamentary government and bourgeois institutions were on the rise in the British Isles. Fourthly, the battle has seemed to some no more than a police operation, rendered necessary by previous military incompetence—like the Battle of Ulundi brought about by the failure at Isandlwana in the Zulu Wars. Fifthly, even those who rate the significance of the Jacobite threat much more highly than this can rightly point out that had the result at Culloden been reversed, the eventual defeat of the 1745 Rising was assured. This was because the element of surprise and the chance to advance on London had been lost (though there is a minority view which suggests that victory at Culloden could have allowed the Jacobites to hold out for a stake in the peace settlement, which eventually came in 1748). Lastly, those with an interest in the wider picture in the War of the Austrian Succession (1740–8) can point out that the whole Jacobite campaign was a sideshow, which the French spent far less on supporting than they gained from Maréchal de Saxe's (1696–1750) capture of Brussels in February 1746—a victory rendered easier by the withdrawal of British troops to face the Jacobites.

And yet Culloden *is* a decisive battle in the history of the world. It was the last pitched battle on the soil of the British Isles fought with regular troops on both sides; it was the last domestic contestation of the Union state, the resolution of which helped to propel Great Britain to be the dominant world power for 150 years. Even if victory would not have reversed the outcome of the Rising, defeat was cataclysmic for its cause. And what was that cause? It was not just a narrow dynastic struggle which would have attracted little public sympathy or military support, but also a battle between two visions. These visions were inconsistently held with differing emphasis by the coalitions ranged on both sides, but each side's vision was strongly distinct. On the British side, the fight was for a centralized state, an alignment with the Protestant interest in Europe, the national debt as an engine for war, and the marginality of Scotland, Ireland, and above all Catholicism. Scottish supporters of this cause stressed the religious dimension: Presbyterianism established in the face of Catholic and Episcopalian threat was guaranteed by the Union, which the Jacobites threatened.

Just as Scottish supporters of Hanover and Union were marginal to the powerful if latitudinarian Anglican state with its alliance of landed and business interests and increasing room for Dissenters in the latter camp, so the English supporters of Jacobitism were marginal to the wellsprings of support for its cause. They were also much less military use to the Jacobite Army than were their Scottish Whig and pro-Union counterparts to the British forces. English Jacobites had an assortment of grievances: the marginalization of the Tory interest under the Georges, the dilution of traditional Anglican Stuart values, and the perceived waning of power of the landed interest. They also disliked the uncomfortable world of the national debt and stock markets and the frequent Continental conflicts driven by opposition to France and by the apparent ascendancy of the interests of Hanover under George II in particular.

Scottish and Irish Jacobites usually had simpler but more powerful priorities. For Scots, the restoration of the native dynasty was closely allied with the end of the Union and a restoration of Scottish sovereignty within a looser confederal British state ruled by a single sovereign, but with different royal capitals and parliaments. Historian Chris Whatley notes

> the popular appeal of the 1715 declaration of Jacobite leader John Erskine, sixteenth earl of Mar, that his objective was to break the Union, and of his claim to be fighting in the cause of Scotland's ancient liberties.[3]

Many sought the restoration of Episcopalianism in Scotland, and a resumption of the trends of 1660–88: the detachment of moderate Presbyterians from the extremes of Covenanting fanaticism, which might, given more time, have created a political centre ground, as it had begun to do in Edinburgh. For their part, Catholic Scots had little to expect officially, but might hope for more of a blind eye, if not indeed toleration, in the event of the restoration of a co-religionist.

Irish Jacobites also sought a confederal kingdom, a Catholic king who would yield—as James II had reluctantly done—to a native Irish agenda, an end to or at least relief from the penal laws and toleration for the Catholic religion, together with some reversal of the extensive Ascendancy and Presbyterian land-grab from which native Irish and Old English families suffered. Unlike English Jacobites, many Irish and Scots were serving abroad in foreign armies: in the case of the Irish, the armies of the Catholic powers opposed by the rising British Empire.

The battle is described in detail in Chapter 3: it lasted no more than an hour, the forces engaged were small, and in that sense it is a story soon told. Yet its implications were great. Given that a Jacobite victory at Culloden might well only have been a staging post on the road to ultimate defeat, it is nonetheless understandable that the battle itself is used as a synecdoche for that defeat, assured as that may have been following the retreat from Derby in December 1745. And what would have been the consequences of a Jacobite victory in the 1745 Rising as a whole? To some extent, that depends on an assessment of the power that a British monarch could wield in the mid-eighteenth century, boosted by the prestige factor of having regained a throne by force of arms. The maximalist case would have been the restoration of a confederal British state on the late seventeenth-century model with some religious toleration (more possible in 1750 than 1690). There would have been a looser association of nations seeking detente with France which in its turn would have precluded the 1756–63 global conflict and the rise of British power in Canada and India. The presence of French forces in Quebec would have been a powerful disincentive to any revolt in the American colonies in the 1770s. France would have been less likely to overreach her budgets in military competition with the British Empire, and in the absence of financial crisis in the French state, the Revolution of 1789 would have been less likely. Of course, domestic British antipathy to France might have made all this much more difficult (though Charles II did manage an extensive if secret rapprochement at a time of much greater sectarian tension), but it is easy to construct a case which presents a Jacobite victory as a globally significant event, given the critical juncture at which the balance of world power stood in the late 1740s.

Moreover, Culloden was no colonial war like that against the Zulu: a careless comparison, it is true, but one made, implicitly at least, by many distinguished historians. As we shall see in Chapter 5, British historians have long framed the conflict as a clash between the old and the new, the traditional and the modern, the backward and the advanced, the tribe and the state, the autocrat and the constitutional monarch, the Catholic and the Protestant, the swordsman and the musketeer, the warrior and the soldier, the amateur and the professional, the brute and the civilized, the divisive and the unified, the Highlander and the stranger, the Celt and the Saxon, and many other binary oppositions of doubtful historical though compelling rhetorical value. However, Jacobitism was itself a variant form of modernity and the Jacobite army was a much more modern fighting unit than it is given credit for. Nor was Jacobite modernity modern in the sense claimed by the historian Steven Pincus, a form of contemporary European autocracy, and in that sense a modern and effective alternative to states with multiple centres of power.[4] It was much more complex than that and indeed much more friendly to such multiple power centres.

The book that follows is a military and a cultural history of the battle, and it will be laid out to a design which encompasses both historiographical and other theoretical approaches. This introduction will specify my approach in the chapters that follow before considering the history and context of the battlefield's development by the National Trust for Scotland and the theoretical approach to memory which I shall be using in Chapter 6 of the book.

Chapter 2 will provide an account of the Jacobite campaign in the 1745 Rising and of the nature of the armed forces deployed. Recognizing that this is a story often told, the story of the campaign will be fairly straightforward, but in light of the controversy that attends certain episodes in the Rising, strong historical disagreements or conflicting evidence will be foregrounded where relevant. Chapter 3 will address the battle itself, which is frequently partially or inaccurately described. I will use contemporary sources where possible, backed up by the recent battle-field archaeology which has done so much to endorse the revisionist views of the Jacobite Army which I advanced using archival evidence in *The Myth of the Jacobite Clans*. The customary historical narrative, with its more or less explicit celebratory anaphora regarding the superiority of the British forces and their inevitable victory, is not only now open to question, but also in many areas demonstrably untrue.[5] Chapter 4 will examine the aftermath of the battle, in particular examining the charge of 'attempted genocide',[6] the occupation of Scotland by the British Army, and the building of Fort George. Chapter 5 will analyse the his-toriography of the battle, beginning with its crucial role in helping to formulate the stadial history model of the Scottish Enlightenment, which, with its assumptions of a perpetual movement towards more 'progressive' forms of politics and society, did so much to engender the whole Whig historiographical tradition in its modern form.[7] This chapter will examine the historiography of Culloden under three key headings: Jacobite ideology and the causes of the Rising; the character-ization of its supporters, organization, and weapons; and lastly the use of the character of Charles Edward Stuart as a measure of the credibility of the Jacobite cause.

Chapter 6 will address the memorialization of the battle and its devel-opment as a *lieu de mémoire*, inscribed with meaning and memorials by succeeding generations, and the representation of Culloden by film, television, and the Internet, before concluding with some possibilities as to what may lie ahead for the continually changing world of the bat-tle's interpretation and place in cultural memory. Memory theory is a complex area, and the rest of this introduction will lay out the theoret-ical approach I have adopted.

Culloden arguably remains as a battle in the sphere of what the cul-tural theorist Marianne Hirsch has called 'postmemory': the 'imagina-tive investment, projection and creation' by which more recent generations engage the 'catastrophic history' of 1745.[8] As we shall see in later chapters, strong counter-narratives, purporting to present the 'facts', have been used repeatedly to keep at bay the imaginative power of Culloden and to limit the space it can occupy in history and memory to one separated from all contemporary application.

At the same time, Culloden is not the memory of an event only, but of a place. It is arguable that in his famous definition of what constitutes a *lieu de mémoire*, the historian Pierre Nora does not sufficiently distinguish between events and places: both can be *lieux*. Yet the *locus amoenus* or *locus horribilis* has always carried a heavier freight than this, for we love and fear places and people more than the dead and their disembodied histories. The actors of the battle have vanished; their landscape has not.

Certain places associated with the Stuarts and the 1745 Rising obtained a reputation which survives in memory at an early date: Boscobel Oak, where Charles II hid after the Battle of Worcester, is only the most obvious. Culloden itself—though today we think of it as powerful and atmospheric, an entirely suitable landscape for a tragic battle, a kind of objective correlative to the bleakness of suffering to which it bears witness and the condescension of sentiment through which it is remembered—was for early generations after the battle simply a place of victory, and often hardly worth visiting. What had been accomplished there was self-evidently 'right', complete, and needed no re-examination. For Thomas Pennant in 1769, the battlefield was simply the place to which 'North Britain owes its present prosperity'. More detail on these early responses will be found in Chapter 6.[9]

By the beginning of the nineteenth century—the great age of centenaries, commemorations, and the visible signing of nations through the statuary of their famous citizens—Culloden had become a largely empty space in historical memory. In the era when the tombs of Milton and Robert the Bruce were opened, at a time when monuments to Robert Burns, Walter Scott, James Watt, and others were erected in celebration of a new era of secular sainthood linked to the French Revolution, Culloden remained a largely unremembered spot, perhaps too close a conflict to the present for comfort, although a sense of excessive brutality and regrettable sacrifice seems to have been increasingly present among visitors to the battlefield.[10] The primary language of public memorialization was triumphalist and in essence British and Whig: between 1794 and 1823, Parliament voted to create thirty-six monuments in St Paul's to the British leaders of the French Wars.[11]

Perhaps one trigger for the memorialization of Culloden was a living monument, former sergeant major Patrick Grant (c.1714–1824), whom George IV met as part of his orchestrated visit to Scotland in 1822, and who was introduced to the King as 'his majesty's oldest enemy'. Grant was painted by Colvin Smith in tartan trews, bonnet, and sword, framed as a living survivor of a previous age, whose presentation to George IV at last brought closure to the Jacobite era (Figure 1).

Two years later, the Act of Parliament 5 George IV c.59 restored many of the Jacobite titles to their rightful owners. It was a symbolic finale to the issue. Jacobitism had passed from real threat to remembered threat to sentiment, and in the 1830s it began to be recalled sentimentally in the minds of its visitors to the battle site: 'a sense of sacrifice had taken hold even for those not overtly subscribing to romantic Jacobitism'. By 1836, bones were being taken away as souvenirs in a manner reminiscent of the raid on Milton's tomb forty years earlier, as 'material vestiges of the celebrated dead'.[12]

The centenary of the battle in 1846 attracted a crowd of 3,000. A memorial narrative began to emerge on the site which stressed the battle as a Scottish conflict against England. Peter Anderson's 1867 guidebook, in print for more than half a century, presented a Scottish prince and emphasized the atrocities connected with the battle. The centenary event itself was followed by a dinner at the Caledonian Hotel chaired by Mackintosh of Mackintosh (Chief of the Name), at which the prospect of a memorial cairn was discussed. A foundation stone was laid on 19 September 1849—an event which incidentally coincided with the 'annual meeting of the Highland Games'—for what was to be a cairn with a 'weeping woman and her child'. The shape of the memorial had become much simpler and more masculinized by the time Duncan Forbes of Culloden erected a 6-metre cairn in 1881, inscribed to 'the gallant Highlanders who fought for Scotland & Prince Charlie'; as the historians John and Margaret Gold remark, 'this inscription thereby

Figure 1 Colvin Smith, *Patrick Grant* (1822). The old Jacobite, festooned in patriot tartan, leans on the broadsword he can no longer use, but whose presence indicates his consistency and loyalty to the cause.

appropriated the Stuart dead for the cause of Scotland and Scottish national identity' (Figure 2).[13]

Forbes 'also commissioned headstones for the clan graves' (or what purported to be such) at roughly the same time. These monuments

Figure 2 The Forbes Memorial.

bore only the most tenuous relationship to who (if anyone) was actually buried under them, but the battlefield's long-standing status as a gravesite and visitor interest has continued to lend them credibility, though stones bearing inscriptions such as 'Mixed Clans' clearly demonstrate the somewhat arbitrary nature of the enterprise. The stones have in any case been moved on numerous occasions. The 'Field of the English [dead]' was marked in an undifferentiated fashion, and today, with the changing framing of the battle as a civil rather than a national war, it is downplayed; it is in any event unlikely that the British forces are buried there.[14]

Forbes's monument was consistent with Culloden's role as both a gravesite and the locale par excellence for the cultural memory of the battle as the tragic but in the end beneficial defeat of an outmoded way of life by modernity. In exploring Culloden as a locale of memory, it is worth focusing on both of these interpretations, which are both elegiac in tone and remove the battle from all contemporary relevance. Distancing Culloden from contemporary Scottish politics remains especially important for many who remember it today, and in such a context graves can be a very powerful symbol, at least for those anxious about ethnocultural chauvinism. As the anthropologist Clifford Geertz puts it: 'Nationalist ideologies built out of symbolic forms drawn from local traditions...tend, like vernaculars, to be psychologically immediate but socially isolating.'[15]

Culloden has enormous psychological immediacy: it makes visitors uncomfortable. There has thus unsurprisingly been an effort through sentiment and through the model of the battle as the culmination of an outdated conflict to disrupt the potential of this immediacy to speak as a symbolic form of national loss. Interestingly, the only period in which Culloden was framed as a 'national' conflict was in the 1832–1945 era: the period of Scotland's closest integration into Great Britain. I will be discussing this further in Chapter 6.

As the historian Daniel Woolf argues, the development of a strongly articulated 'Whig' historiography was a feature of the early modern period. The creation of 'an increasingly homogenized...national sense of the past' in England, and the modification and marginalization of 'local memory' (a process begun by the Reformation, as the historians Eamon Duffy and Alexandra Walsham point out), were part of a process which regarded personal testimony, oral report, and local tradition as secondary. The Whig tradition by contrast associated documents with social order much as contemporary statutes were engaged in the 'progressive circumscription of prescriptive rights'. 'Institutions' and 'archivists' have selective memories just as much as individuals who tell stories, and the intense structural framing of this battle in rural northern Scotland—amid its 'hill-grazing', farmsteads, and rigs—into a conflict between antiquity and modernity, the rural periphery and the urban centre, the future and the past, and kings and parliaments, helped to make Culloden a decisive battle of the world in memory.[16]

The history of the battle that follows is inevitably also an act of memory: its conclusions will be based on the evidence of the day and of the time more broadly, and of the material traces which it has left. I suggest neither that memory and historiography are the same thing, nor that they are completely distinct, but that to understand their relationship is to understand what brings these strange bedfellows together and how they might both be associated and distinguished in understanding the past.

2

Conflicts and Armies

The Rising of 1745

Jacobitism remains a major topic in British history, although until recently it was often confined to a Cinderella status in many accounts of the eighteenth century: a tale more important for its narrative and the lessons that narrative conveyed than for any examination of the primary evidence in a fresh or sophisticated fashion. Jacobitism and the Jacobite Risings were embedded elements in the account of the growth of stability in the eighteenth century: anachronistic irritations to the development of a sophisticated and modern British body politic, worth lingering on only for those more interested in romance than in a serious examination of the past. Culloden was, as we have already begun to see, central to this: a battle foregrounded in history because of its apparently belated qualities and its representational value as the defeat of an entire way of life, subsumed under the framing narrative of an outdated dynastic struggle, where it was to become the sacrifice rather than the politics that mattered.

Jacobitism bore its dynastic allegiance in its name, being the name of the supporters of Jacobus (Latin for James) after his exile and deposition in 1688–9, and of his successors. In that sense its politics seem simple. Its badge was the white rose or cockade of the House of Bourbon, who often treated its exiled royalty sympathetically—the symbolic echo of the Wars of the Roses seems obvious. The Stuart badge was also the white rose; although this has on occasion been dated back to the 1340s, extensive use of it does not seem to have begun until the Exclusion

Crisis of 1679–82. At this stage the symbolic reference to Scotland (Albania) as the 'White Land', and its dynasty's association with white in the earlier seventeenth century, was combined with the white rose's reference to the legitimate claims of the House of York. As heir to the throne, James was both Duke of York and Duke of Albany, and thus doubly associated with the colour.

Following King James II and VII's exile in 1688, the Jacobite cause, unlike many other dynastic conflicts, lasted for over seventy years. It left a lasting cultural legacy in both Scotland and Ireland. Enduring dynastic conflicts often have a regionalist or nationalist dimension (such as the Carlists of Navarre or Catalan support for the Habsburgs rather than the Bourbons in the War of the Spanish Succession) and Jacobitism was no different.

In England, Jacobitism was associated with a range of religious and national prejudices: dislike of foreigners, such as Dutch William or German George, with their foreign courtiers, commanders, and supporters; suspicion of the dual loyalties of the Hanoverians, and their need to consider the interests of their militarily vulnerable German Electorate of Hanover; and High Anglicanism, which had a strong distaste for the Calvinism of William and the Lutheran antecedents of the Georges. Naturally, Catholics often supported the Stuarts also for religious reasons and hopes of better treatment.

The collection of English (and Welsh—for Jacobitism in Wales was largely limited to the anglophone and Anglophile gentry, such as Watkin Williams Wynn) Jacobite prejudices was initially reinforced by the long exclusion of the Tory Party from office between George I's accession in 1714 and that of his great-grandson, George III, in 1760. Hanoverian agents had reported widespread Jacobitism in the Tory Party to George, and he himself saw them as the friends of France and betrayer of the Allies at Utrecht. The Tories has also refused 'to pay arrears due to the Hanoverian troops in 1714'. The leading figures associated with the 1710–14 Tory Government—Bolingbroke, Harley, and Ormonde—fell under suspicion of Jacobitism, and in two of the three cases there is no doubt that they were active Jacobites. There were no more than fifty to eighty identifiable Jacobites in the parliamentary party in 1714, but the purge reached far beyond this group. Places in government, military, or ecclesiastical service—including county lieutenancies—were removed from the Tories, while as historian Eveline Cruickshanks tells us, 'Tory merchants could no longer get government contracts, or directorships in the Bank of England'.[1]

Although the exclusion of the Tory Party from office on a prolonged basis naturally did not serve to diminish Jacobitism among some of its members (historian J. C. D. Clark estimates that at least 56 of the 140 Tory MPs were still involved in Jacobite conspiracy in 1741–5[2]), others moved along a political spectrum which by the era of the patriot Whigs in the 1730s had begun to adopt aspects of an English patriotic discourse once used by supporters of the Stuarts. George II's son, Prince Frederick (1707–51) seemed more English than his predecessors, and the foreignness of the dynasty and its entourage was less and less manifest. Robert Walpole, prime minister until 1742, sought to unite opinion against a frequently invoked Jacobite threat. At the same time, High Anglican political power was eroded by the steady creation of Whig and latitudinarian bishops who were more easily secured as tools for the ministry, beginning with Hoadley at Bangor in 1716. Although the War of the Austrian Succession in the 1740s led to Tory anxiety that British foreign policy was favouring the interests of Hanover, and isolated individuals made contact with the Stuart court in Italy, there was—despite the high claims such gentlemen made in order to be taken seriously—little evidence of military capacity or even the capacity for a *coup d'état* in England. This was no surprise: in 1651, Charles II had gained only a few hundred English recruits on his march to Worcester, and almost a century later his great-nephew did no better en route to Derby, if not much worse.

The case in Ireland and Scotland was very different. In Ireland, the large-scale conflict between James and his supporters and the Williamites in 1689–91 involved tens of thousands of men, with French and Swiss-Italian troops fighting for King James and Dutchmen for William. The surrender of Limerick by treaty, which ended the war, saw thousands of

Irish soldiers leave to enter the service of France, while the Protestant Ascendancy in Ireland in the eighteenth century depended on the penal laws which followed a Williamite victory. Ireland's—and later Northern Ireland's—whole history as a state or statelet governed by 'a Protestant parliament for a Protestant people' rested on the defeat of King James in 1691. Jacobites in Ireland sought the end of the penal laws, rights for Catholics, restoration of Catholic landownership, and a sovereign parliament: they hoped that Continental Catholic powers would sweep the Saxons out of Ireland, and bring back the Stuarts, who, officially descended as they were from the High Kings in Irish lore, were legitimate monarchs of the island in many Catholic eyes. Even after the end of Stuart hopes, the language of Jacobitism continued to flourish within Irish political rhetoric, up to and including the 1916–21 era. Many of the leaders of Irish Catholic opinion in the nineteenth century had Irish Jacobite links: Daniel O'Connell, for example, had had relatives serving in the Irish Brigades in the service of France, who before 1789 were pledged to a Stuart restoration, and anti-O'Connell cartoons in the 1820s could still identify the Repeal cause with Jacobitism.

In Scotland, an initial rising in favour of the Stuarts in 1689 had attracted support among the West Highland clans and some others, but it was on a small scale compared to the resources on which the Jacobites could call after the unpopular Union with England in 1707, while the Episcopalian Church of Scotland, whose clergy had been expelled by the restoration of a Presbyterian establishment, remained an enduring bedrock of support. Nonetheless, the Union was the transformative element in the popularity of Jacobitism, and crucially made it more important in the eyes of foreign observers, to whom the Scots could be seen as looking forward to 'throwing off foreign rule'. In 1715, perhaps 20,000 men participated in a rising to restore James and an independent Scotland under the Crown; in 1745, almost a lifetime after his grandfather had lost his throne, Charles Edward had an army that reached 14,000, of whom over 12,000 were Scots. Both these forces were raised in a context where the maximum fencible strength available in Scotland for any purpose did not exceed 30,000.[3]

Strategically, however, the nationalist dimension which rendered Irish and Scottish Jacobitism so potent presented a problem for Continental supporters of the Jacobites. The best opportunity to destroy Great Britain as a state (which remained a clear French policy goal for many years, indeed into the 1790s) was to commit major military resource to Ireland, something France always failed to do. Scotland was difficult to reach and far away from London. It was also quite effectively policed by the Royal Navy and its remote western points of access for ships had limited security for the storage of materiel, as the Spanish expeditionary force of 1719 found when its magazine at the sitting target of Eilean Donan castle was destroyed by British warships and their crews. In 1740, Lord Lovat's private coach took more than four weeks to get from Edinburgh to London; the movement of a substantial artillery and supply train down the long bad roads from the Scottish border was a huge challenge. Generally, French planning focused on a short Channel crossing for Irish and Scottish troops in the French service, with one or two brigades landing on the south coast and marching on London. Militarily, this could have led to victory in 1745 if communications had been maintained with Charles Edward's army on its march south, but rapid lines of communication and intelligence between two armies separated by a powerful enemy were an insurmountable logistic challenge in the eighteenth century, and indeed much later. (In the early weeks of the Spanish Civil War in 1936, Franco and Mola found them difficult enough in the early electronic age.)

The Rising of 1745 was born out of its abortive predecessor, the planned French invasion of 1744. After many years of caution, indifference, or hostility towards Jacobite hopes, an approach was made to James by a group of Scottish noblemen in 1739, and this was followed by contact from English and Welsh Jacobites. It was, however, the death of Cardinal Fleury in January 1743 which opened a window of opportunity in French policy, one forced wider by the mixed fortunes that France was experiencing in the War of the Austrian Succession. This war had begun in December 1740, when Prussian forces violated the territory of Maria Theresa, the Habsburg monarch, on a pretext underpinned by her perceived weakness as a female ruler, seeking concessions which would weaken Austria and strengthen Prussia. Austrian forces fell back in the face of the highly drilled Prussian Army, which, joined by the French and Bavarians, pushed deep into Austrian imperial territory, taking Prague at the end of 1741 and appearing before Vienna in 1742, although the Austrian counter-attack regained Bohemia (in the present-day Czech Republic) in the same year. In 1743, Great Britain joined the war, winning a major victory with Hanoverian and Austrian support at Dettingen in June, where George II commanded, 'wearing the yellow sash of Hanover'—a disturbing indication to some of where his primary loyalty lay. The protection of Hanover from the Prussian threat seemed to some to be more at stake than the interest of Great Britain, although the opportunity the war presented to French power would have made it difficult for Great Britain (already engaged in war with Spain) to remain aloof.[4] Spain joined France and the Netherlands and the Kingdom of Sardinia joined the British side; French forces left the German front for the Dutch frontier. What had begun as an opportunistic grab of Silesia by Prussia was now a major European war, with the combatants bogged down everywhere. The prestige of French arms was at stake.

As Louis XV was acting as his own prime minister following Fleury's death, the pressure of war bore on him especially heavily, and the opportunity presented by a memorial from leading English Jacobites seemed to him worth exploring. A French 'fact-finding mission to England' in late summer led to an unduly positive assessment of the strength of the Jacobite cause, no doubt one reinforced by widespread feelings among Tories that George II's conduct of the war placed undue emphasis on the protection of Hanover. To many people, the British-Austrian-Hanoverian-Hessian army that fought at Dettingen (only 40 per cent British) was fighting a war to protect a vulnerable German state rather than those of Great Britain. Whether or not this discontent amounted to real militant enthusiasm for the Stuarts in England was quite another matter, as the next two years were to demonstrate.[5]

In consequence of these and related political developments, in 1744 the French prepared a major invasion fleet to attack England and restore the Stuarts, with up to 15,000 troops.[6] Bad weather and British intelligence blocked the crossing, and French interest switched to the Dutch front and the Austrian Netherlands. Victory for the French with decisive Irish Brigade support at Fontenoy on 11 May 1745 was followed by defeat at Louisbourg in Cape Breton, but French forces continued to carry all before them on the Dutch front.[7] At this point, Charles Edward Stuart sought to force the French government's hand by a speculative landing which—if converted into a full-scale rising on behalf of the Stuarts—would inevitably draw French military support. It would also lead to the repatriation of British forces from the Low Countries to defend the homeland, resulting in the total victory of Maréchal de Saxe and the French Army in western Europe. By early 1746, Brussels had fallen to the French, and the subsequent course of the war continued a pattern of French victories in the Netherlands which was not significantly reversed before the Treaty of Aix-la-Chapelle in 1748. French help did come during the 'Forty-five, but not nearly as much as Charles Edward had hoped for. The cost to France of aiding the rising was to be less than the booty gained from the fall of Brussels alone. Sir James Steuart—with John Law the greatest economist of the Jacobite movement—calculated that France had spent £213,000 sterling on the Jacobite Rising. On the other hand, the booty from Brussels totalled £1 million, while 'French privateers' were able 'to seize £700,000-worth of British shipping' as Royal Navy protection was withdrawn to guard British coasts from the landing of French troops and supplies and from the threat of a general invasion.[8]

The projected invasion of 1744 was an investment in regime change. By contrast, French support in 1745 was limited and diversionary, although argument still rages over whether France would have committed a major force to support a successful Jacobite military advance in southern England.[9] One indication that they might have done this was that in the end 1745 cost France more than 1744 had done; on the other hand, the gains France could make in the war after Fontenoy arguably justified a greater investment, though it could equally be argued that France had little spare military capacity, as she was fighting a war on several fronts. Initially the French government supplied little, and the 'Forty-five began looking almost like a private affair, although some of its aspects also suggested a deniable special operation with covert French support.

The 1744 plans had cost 900,000 *livres*, with substantial additional funds promised by English Jacobites as collateral.[10] Charles Edward was given a pension of £1,800 a year in 1744 from the French government and his 30,000 *livres*' personal debt was liquidated. In 1745, his pension was raised to £3,000, and he also raised money from the Paris banker Waters 'to hire ships, arms and men from Irish shipowners to whom he was introduced by Lord Clare', a distinguished Irish Brigade officer. King James agreed to cover the initial 40,000 *livres*' debt and so Charles Edward was able to extend credit lines to 120,000 *livres*. With this he 'scraped together enough for two ships, 3,500 stand of arms, 2,400 swords, 100 or more men and 4,000 *louis d'or* to pay them and his future recruits'. The Earl Marischal secured another 41,000 *livres* from the Spanish ambassador as a down payment; James secured 200,000 *scudi* from the Papacy and associated sources, some £50,000.[11] On 5 July 1745, Charles Edward, his materiel (which now included twenty artillery pieces), and two companies of Franco-Irish marines sailed in the sixteen-gun privateer frigate *Du Teillay* and the sixty-four-gun ex-Royal Navy *Elisabeth* for Scotland. On the ninth, HMS *Lion* (an old fourth-rate with fifty-eight or sixty guns, originally launched in 1709 and rebuilt in 1738) damaged the *Elisabeth* so badly that it could not even draw alongside the much lighter *Du Teillay* to transfer materiel, and had to return to Brest with 300 casualties. Nonetheless, Charles Edward went on with almost no men and very little money or equipment, making landfall at Eriskay on 23 July with the 'Seven Men of Moidart': William Murray, Marquis of Tullibardine and in Jacobite eyes *de jure* Duke of Atholl, who was to be a lieutenant general in his forces; Colonel Francis Strickland, a northern English Catholic; the banker Aeneas MacDonald, who was there to win over MacDonald support, including that of his brother, Donald MacDonald of Kinlochmoidart; Sir Thomas Sheridan; George Kelly; Sir John MacDonald, a Franco-Scottish cavalry officer; and John

Sullivan, a French regular and later quartermaster general and adjutant general (QMG/AG) in the Jacobite Army.[12]

There was little initial enthusiasm for a rising against the entrenched and well-funded British government. The situation was not helped by the refusal of Macleod of Macleod and Sir Alexander MacDonald of Sleat to join any insurrection, in part because 'they were being blackmailed by the authorities' over their practice of kidnapping tenants for sale in America. But MacDonald help did in the end arrive, and proved crucial. Tradition has it that when Donald MacDonald of Kinlochmoidart refused the Prince at their interview on 29 July, his younger brother Ranald pledged his life to the Stuart heir. Shamed into acceding, Donald allowed his house to be a store for the materiel from France. Charles Edward's discussions with Lochiel, Chief of the Name of Cameron, also bore fruit. On 14 August, MacDonald of Keppoch forces intercepted British reinforcements en route to Fort William; two days later, MacDonell of Tirnadris and barely fifty Glengarry men defeated the 1st Foot at Highbridge and Laggan. On the nineteenth, an initial gathering of 400 men from the MacDonald fighting tails (the feudal obligation to fight that could be called on by the Chiefs of the Name, barons, or Lords of Parliament in time of war) round the standard at Glenfinnan was swelled by the later arrival of over 800 men under Cameron of Lochiel's command. Charles Edward was proclaimed prince regent, and 'Prosperity to Scotland and no Union' was shouted by the troops.

At the end of August, George II returned from Hanover. By this time, Charles Edward had acquired over 1,000 additional troops, and the MacGregors had defeated two British companies at Inversnaid. Macpherson of Cluny, one of the most senior figures in the government Independent Companies in the Highlands, had been captured on the twenty-eighth and joined the Rising. General Cope's British forces, assembled at Stirling in the first half of August, had moved to intercept the Jacobite Army at the Pass of Corrieyairack, but failed to do so. Disappointed in his promise of support from the allegedly 'well-affected' in Scotland, Cope marched to Inverness and thence to Aberdeen. On 3 September, the Jacobite Army reached Dunkeld and the next day entered Perth without resistance, being joined there by the Duke of Perth, Lord George Murray, Viscount Strathallan, the Earl of Airlie, and Oliphant of Gask. The Duke of Newcastle expressed concern to Cumberland that Charles Edward might call an independent parliament if he reached Edinburgh. He is still sometimes criticized for not doing so, but militarily the Rising could only have succeeded through rapidity and military force: it was not a moment for constitutional forms.[13]

On 15 September, the Jacobite Army arrived at the capital, and two days later, as the militia tasked with defending Edinburgh melted away, the gate to the city was left open long enough to let in Lochiel's men. The guard dispersed immediately, and the Lord Provost, Archibald Stewart, was long suspected of complicity, despite being acquitted of the charges against him on this score two years later. There was in any case no resistance, and by the time the Prince entered the city, a 'crowd of up to 20,000 greeted his entry...which was accompanied by strongly nationalist symbolism'.[14]

Cope meanwhile had sailed from Aberdeen, disembarking at Dunbar (20 miles south of the capital) hours before Edinburgh fell. Moving north, his forces (about 2,200 men) took up a position north of Tranent Meadows, on open land without cover, some of which was a recently harvested cornfield. This space measured about 2.5 by 1.25 kilometres. To its north and his left was the sea and 'the villages of Port Seton, Cockenzie, and Prestonpans'; half of its western flank was covered by the walls of Preston House, while to the south and his right was the marshy meadowland ground sloping upwards to the mining village of Tranent. On the east, the position was 'comparatively open, excepting for the enclosures surrounding the ruins of Seton Tower, and the cottages of Seton village'.[15]

In the small hours of 21 September, the Jacobite Army were guided through the approaches from the south and west by a local sympathizer, Robert Anderson of Whitburgh. Coming to within 500 metres of Cope's forces, they had to deploy across the British Army's front. A dragoon picquet was sent to prevent this, and was sufficiently effective to divide the divisions commanded by the two lieutenant generals, the Duke of Perth and Lord George Murray. This left Perth and Murray facing the dragoons on Cope's wings while his infantry front largely had no enemy to oppose them; Perth did, however, out-flank the British right by 80 metres. A dragoon regiment covered each flank of the British Army. Cope's returning dragoons reinforced his right, though in a somewhat disorganized fashion. Four or six coe-horn mortars (small high-firing howitzer-type weapons which fired explosive charges short distances, which used relatively little powder, and were light and easy to transport) and six 1½-pounders (which fired a 5-centimetre ball up to 800 metres) were placed on Cope's right. One of them was fired as a signal and 'there was nobody to reload it', so it was not used in combat.[16]

Both Jacobite wings attacked simultaneously in the dawn light. Their order and organization struck British observers, Lord Drummore noting that 'every Front Man covered his Fellowes…though their Motion was very quick, it was Uniform and Orderly'. Clearly, even before developed drilling, the military habits of the Jacobite forces were conducive to regular military combat, despite the sneer that 'Charles Edward's men had never learned to march in a straight line'. Jacobite gunfire drove off the dragoons on the wings ('the volley had been so close that the wads of their charges flew among the enemy troops') and the British centre was swept away as its uncovered wings were rolled up before the artillery could fire more than a single volley from its remaining five 1½-pounders and coehorns. The complex platoons' firing system collapsed in chaos. The secure British position became a deathtrap, as many of Cope's troops could not escape, and were either cut down or taken prisoner: 1,500 British troops fell into Jacobite hands, and a good number—at least 160—joined the Perth Regiment or the 'Edinburgh Regiment' under Iain Ruadh Stiùbhart.[17]

On 24 September, Lord George Murray asked his brother, William, the Marquis of Tullibardine, to raise three battalions to 'gather the cess in Perthshire, Angus and Fife'. The campaign was more than a lightning strike: gradually Scotland, its burghs, taxes, and recruiting

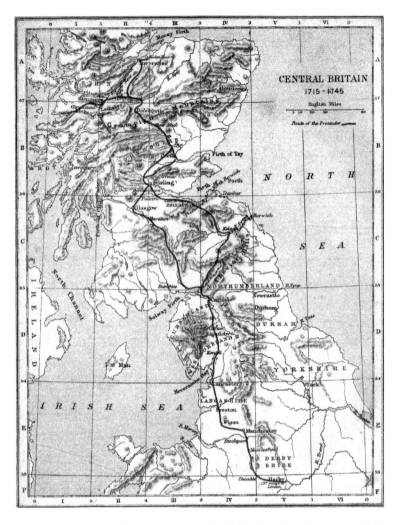

Map 1 The route south and retreat north of Charles Edward Stuart and the Jacobite Army in 1745–6. Courtesy the private collection of Roy Winkelman. FCIT.

grounds were coming under Jacobite control. Aberdeen fell on 25 September: James Moir of Stoneywood raised a battalion in the city without serious resistance, and the government cause crumbled from within.[18]

The British government, committed on the Dutch front, was alarmed. A financial crisis was in prospect, as a run on the Bank of England began on 28 September, and the government had to rely on wealthy merchants and City loans as many had stopped paying the land tax. Six thousand Dutch troops were brought in, but diplomatic wrangling with France prevented their use. Ten battalions under Sir John Ligonier were withdrawn from the war on the Continent, and after Prestonpans eight more, together with nine cavalry squadrons, all under the Duke of Cumberland. On 11 October, Major General John Campbell, Earl of Loudoun and the remnant of his Scots who had fought at Prestonpans reached Inverness, to receive there command of the eighteen independent Highland companies that Duncan Forbes of Culloden was in the process of raising; Loudoun also raised the 64th Highland during the process of the Rising. On 15 October, Lord Lovat declared for the Jacobites by trying unsuccessfully to capture Forbes.[19]

Although the Jacobites had control of most of Scotland, the rapidity of their advance had been secured by a force of little more than 2,500 men, quite inadequate as an invasion force for marching into England. Reinforcements, drill, and better arms were all necessary. Charles Edward's administration began to be developed in the localities, where the Jacobites set up—where they did not already control—local administrations. Here they raised taxes and recruits: in the end, up to 15,000 men were under arms for the Jacobite forces, probably more than half of the effective national fencible resources of Scotland (the number of men who could in practice be raised to fight). Lord Lewis Gordon in particular had success in reviving the traditional Scottish fencible system.[20]

Lord George Murray, briefly a regular lieutenant before the 1715 Rising in which he served as a Jacobite lieutenant colonel, took charge of drill in Edinburgh. Murray was a capable general organizationally, but with limitations too often overlooked by many histories of the Rising, which, following the hardly neutral assessment of his ADC, Captain Johnstone, regard him as a military genius thwarted by a captious and foolish prince. Assessments of Lord George frequently exaggerate his infallibility, minimize the role of the Duke of Perth, his fellow lieutenant general (Tullibardine held that rank more by courtesy than in the way of meaningful command), and discredit the role of John Sullivan, the quartermaster general and adjutant general.[21] Sullivan's influence was no doubt obnoxious to some of the Scottish noblemen engaged in the Rising, but he was a career French regular, and knew how to handle French regulars. He also had a reputation in irregular warfare gained in Corsica and on the Rhine. Sullivan was held in respect as an Irish officer in the service of France, and had a substantial French Army career. Sullivan's depiction as a blundering adventurer and the exaggeration of Lord George Murray's military experience and brilliance are two distortions in the historiography of the Rising which military historians such as Stuart Reid began to tackle in the 1990s. Their case is unanswered, though it would be unfair to deny Lord George's high degree of competence and occasional brilliance as a tactical commander. However, as the military challenges he faced moved along the spectrum from those of a field officer to those of a commanding general, his competency ebbed.

Meanwhile, Charles Edward sought to consolidate his political support by issuing two declarations on 9 and 10 October: the first stated the Union to be at an end and that a British Parliament was 'unlawful'; the second opposed the Act of Settlement, on which the Union was consequent. Charles Edward took care neither to repudiate the national debt nor to confirm the disestablishment of Presbyterianism.[22]

It was in the end decided to march on England by a single vote, the narrowest of all possible margins—the correct decision strategically, but one which placed as a secondary objective what was for many the primary aim: as Chevalier de Johnstone put it, 'to dissolve and annul the union', which 'would have given infinite pleasure to all Scotland'. Although proclaimed, this was not prioritized as much as many in the Jacobite leadership would have liked.[23] Many of the Jacobite leaders disliked and distrusted the English, and would have preferred a national restoration in Scotland; others had doubts about the

'Womanish Railing, vain Boasting, and noisy Gasconades' of the English Jacobites. Posterity, with a few notable exceptions, has borne out this judgement, which was hardly a new one: in 1690 Defoe commented that 'all they [the English Jacobites] have done ... is to stay at home, and drink for him, swear for him, rail and snarl at those they dare not oppose'.[24]

On 30 October, the ageing General Wade's forces, reinforced by Dutch troops from the Flanders front, reached Newcastle. Wade's subsequent attempts to cross the Pennines in a bad winter were ineffective, but the Jacobites decided to evade rather than confront his army. The same decision was made by Charles II's Scottish forces in 1651 on the march to Worcester; in 1745, as in 1651, few English recruits joined an invading Scottish army. Whatever the politics of Englishmen, many saw Scots as aliens, and propaganda prints played on this.[25]

About 5,500 men in two divisions—'five-sixths of them excellent material'—crossed into England on 8 November, leaving many of their heavy guns behind: the artillery train on the march south comprised an unmounted iron gun in a cart, six Swedish 4-pounders of French supply, and the six 1½-pounders captured at Prestonpans. This was all battlefield artillery, with no capacity for siege warfare, but big guns would have meant many horses and a slow, easily bogged-down artillery train; as it was, the baggage train was improvised and there was a persistent shortage of horse and wheeled transport. Jacobite cavalry was also much weaker than it had been in 1715, the Hussar squadron under Colonel John Murray, the Prince's secretary, being the most effective.[26]

With little prospect of immediate relief, Carlisle surrendered to Charles Edward on 14/15 November; on 23 November, Lord Derby abandoned the defence of Manchester; on the twenty-sixth, the Jacobites entered Preston. For some at least of the 18 or so miles from Preston to Wigan, the road was lined with supporters, who nonetheless declined to be combatants. On 29 November, the Jacobite Army was at Manchester, where a regiment was raised, and the Jacobites engaged in target practice behind what is now Deansgate; on 3 December, the

Duke of Devonshire withdrew from Ashbourne, and on the fourth the Jacobites arrived in Derby. As Maxwell of Kirkconnell noted:

> From Manchester to Derby the country seemed pretty well affected. As the army marched along, the roads in many places were lined with numbers of country people, who showed their loyalty by bonefires, acclamations, white cockades, and the like.[27]

Others in the Jacobite Army seem to have been more sceptical.

The Council of War at Derby led to retreat, much against Charles Edward's wishes. He had promised at Preston that help would have come in by this time from Sir Watkin Williams Wynn and the Duke of Beaufort. Its absence, combined with the lack of effective French help (despite the promissory presence of the Marquis d'Eguilles), and the fact that the Jacobites had raised only some 400–500 English recruits, led to the decision to withdraw. The fact that Lord John Drummond had landed at Montrose on 22 November with French regulars (the French Royal Scots (*Régiment Royal-Écossais*) and picquets from the Irish regiments) was also a factor underpinning the argument for a return to Scotland. Frank McLynn, in *The Jacobite Army in England* (1983), followed suggestions first made in the 1950s in arguing that the crucial intervention came from the double agent Dudley Bradstreet, who was introduced into the council to claim (falsely) that one and possibly two armies stood between the Jacobites and London. Since McLynn wrote, this very dramatic intervention has had its supporters, not least Christopher Duffy. It has also appealed to media presentations of the Rising, such as *What If? The Jacobites* (2000) and *The Battle That Made Britain* (2006). The evidence rests on Bradstreet's self-serving memoirs and a claim forwarded on his behalf from an ally in Lancashire, but it may never have happened as advertised: the matter is not mentioned in a letter of 4 December to Newcastle, while Johnstone stresses the key role played by news of Lord John Drummond's landing with a French force in Scotland, and Maxwell likewise does not mention Bradstreet.[28]

Whether or not Bradstreet's good story about himself was wholly true, the way to London lay open when the Prince's forces retreated.

Cumberland was at Lichfield, and could not have reached the capital in time, though some of his forces might have made Northampton, had the Jacobites proceeded in that direction. At Finchley Common, there were four battalions' worth of infantry and a dragoon squadron barring the route to the capital against three times their number. Many of the field pieces were defending the Tower, but the Jacobites would not have laid siege to anywhere when they entered the city, but would have relied instead on speed, terror, and an aura of invincibility.[29]

Whether or not that would have succeeded remains a significant 'what if?' in British history, and is one of the key questions which ensured that cultural and popular memory would revisit the 'Forty-five as no other failed insurrection against the state has been. Culloden may have been a small battle rhetoricized in its apparent belatedness into one of the great turning points of British history, but this would not have been the case had it been—like Glenshiel—the local and rapid suppression of insurgents on the 'Celtic Fringe' by British forces. The fact that the culmination of the Rising of 1745 was its only defeat was crucial, as was how close it came to victory—at least in the minds of its enemies.

This is the reason why 'What if the Jacobites had marched on London?' retains its resonance as one of the great counterfactuals of British history. Historians remain divided: Eveline Cruickshanks notes that 'the psychological advantage of Charles Edward and his army at this stage was enormous', and many more recent historians accept this view. If the Jacobite Army had marched on, its record to Derby suggested that opposing militia would have melted away: it could only have been faced down by a substantial force of regulars, and recruitment was becoming difficult for the government, who were planning to introduce a draft.[30] It is therefore odds-on that the Prince's forces would have swept aside the limited opposition on Finchley Common (Hogarth's *The March of the Guards to Finchley* (1750) (see Figure 3), with its gloomy and trepidatious soldiery, suggests little else) and entered London. It is unlikely that this would have triggered a general English rising—England was demilitarized and largely indifferent—although some more English Jacobites could have been expected to come in. Would the government and the

Figure 3 William Hogarth, *The March of the Guards to Finchley*. Hogarth's famous and much-reproduced painting evinces the chaos, anxiety, and apprehension felt by the weak British forces tasked with defending the Jacobite approach to London.

anti-Catholic London mob crumble? Would the Tower? The Jacobites would very likely—as in Edinburgh—have seized a city without being able to capture its strongholds or lay effective siege to them, although they would have taken some heavy guns. In London, there would be fewer sympathizers than in Edinburgh and a much larger population to control. In 1780, the government almost lost control of the City to Lord George Gordon's Protestant Association, which was outraged at the restoration of limited rights to Catholics; it is hard to see 6,000 Jacobite insurgents without control of major public buildings holding back anti-Catholic violence when a Catholic king was at the point of being restored, but possibly the presence of military force would have held back civic violence. Charles Edward also had the advantage of speed and apparent invincibility, and his opponents had no time to organize; a collapse in morale could have—possibly would have—delivered him the City's strongpoints, or some of them, and the mob would not have benefited from the extended neglect from the authorities which allowed Gordon's association to develop.

But would Charles Edward have had time? Cumberland (had he missed Northampton) would have dashed for London with 6,000 men from Staffordshire, and would have been only forty-eight hours behind. Could he have held his army together, with the Stuart Prince Regent in the capital? Probably, in which case there would have been another and worse Worcester, with total Jacobite defeat, as dissipated forces tried to hold a huge and largely hostile city which was ready to side with the determined and concentrated advance of the British Army. The Jacobites had struggled in Dunkeld in 1689; they were not good streetfighters (which is only one reason why the idea that they could have fallen back on Inverness rather than fight Culloden is unsustainable), and it is hard to see what could have held dragoons and infantry pushing steadily down the main arterial routes to wherever the court and command centre of *Tearlach Ruadh*—the fair, fertile, and ruddy Prince Charles Edward—was located in urban and alien London.

Three things could have happened. The first is the collapse of British Army morale in the face of losing the capital—unlikely in forty-eight hours, but possible. The second is the tendency of crowds to side with the victors, which could have compromised London's hostility: did not Paris cheer Pétain on his visit of 28 April 1944 as the Allies were to be cheered only a few months later? The third is the possibility that, with British command structures and the Royal Navy in disorder, French regulars—predominantly Irish and Scottish forces in Louis XV's service—would have landed in large numbers in Essex. In this scenario, Jacobite control of London might have been sustained. But some of these possibilities depended on each other. If Cumberland had held his army together, he would have been too fast for any French landing; also the French might have dithered or sent insufficient forces, as they usually did when victory was possible (as in Ireland in 1798). The evidence is that the first wave of the French force assembled to sail was of seventeen battalions, of which six were Irish and three Scots: about 7,000 men. This might have been enough to be effective, but it is hard to see how a sustainable restoration could have taken place with Irish Catholic troops in the French service controlling London. Foreign invasion of England did not have a good track record, nor was control of London everything, as Northumberland and Lady Jane Grey found out in 1553. There would have had to have been a collapse in morale and a lot of opportunistic English Jacobites.

There might have been: a major French invasion was expected both by government and by the general population, and it was not until late January that it was clear that one would not come.[31] It all comes down to timing and morale. One would have to be more optimistic on behalf of the British forces than the facts warrant to imagine that the Jacobites would not reach London with a further victory at Finchley, and indeed possibly also at Northampton, where only three dragoon regiments and at best as many foot could conceivably have made it in time. After that, everything is an 'if', based on morale and the sequence of events. The likelihood is that the Prince would still have lost; but it is not certain. And beyond that, there stretches a whole sequence of conditional results from a Stuart restoration: rapprochement between Britain and France; no war in Quebec and consequently no independence for the American colonies, which would have been unable to play the powers off against each other; local independence for Scotland and Ireland, with a loose and multi-kingdom monarchy more like Iberia in the first half of the seventeenth century than the centralized Great Britain of a hundred years later. Ireland would have been both more independent and more integrated; Catholicism might have been tolerated, together with Dissent, in a pliant and politicized High Anglican–Episcopalian hegemony, possibly with bishops engaged in government. France might have remained the prevailing imperial power in loose alliance with England as in 1670–88, with fewer military engagements leading to a better economy and no 1789 Revolution; consequently, no rise of German nationalism in response to the threat from the French Republic and its Napoleonic successor. The 'what ifs' are intoxicating. If all the dominoes had fallen into place, then victory for Charles Edward Stuart might have completely changed the British state and the whole of European and world history. Unlikely as all this may have been, it is why the Rising of 1745 should remain a critical moment in history, on a different scale from Lewes, Shrewsbury, or Towton.

Charles Edward's strategy was the right one: to take London as rapidly as possible. It was his great-grandfather's failure to do this in 1642–3 that had in the end doomed the King's forces. Once retreat from Derby had been forced on Charles Edward, however, there was no real strategy left, only tactics. Many of the Jacobite leaders were no doubt tacitly accepting eventual defeat in retreating, misleadingly supposing that they could go to ground in Scotland and the storm would pass, as in 1715; others had what only ever seems to have been a vague idea of keeping operational in their heartlands with the now substantial northern Jacobite Army while the French drip-fed them support until they could negotiate something. It was this lack of strategic vision which meant that Lord George Murray's brilliantly managed retreat, which beat off the British advance guard at Clifton on 18 December and delivered clear-cut victory against up to 10,000 regulars (though some estimates are much lower) under Hawley at Falkirk a month later, was ultimately purposeless, though the Jacobites called the battle 'Bannockburn Muir' to bring to mind an older national success.[32] After Falkirk, Lord George exaggerated the numbers of deserters to push the case for retreat rather than try to reoccupy the south of the country. The sometimes brilliant attacks on government-held towns and strongholds in February and March were likewise those of a senior field officer and not a general. Murray was no traitor as his detractors claimed, but his advocates have long been more interested in taking sides than looking at the evidence, which does show a degree of limitation, albeit in very challenging circumstances.

It was indeed difficult to know what to do. Once the decision to retreat had been taken, no strategic objectives remained. Whatever France's commitment had been, there was no doubt that it would become tokenistic in the wake of any retreat from England. Even such support as could be landed depended in large part on the evasion of a Royal Navy blockade and continuing Jacobite control of the main east-coast ports, which, although initially sustained by Murray's division, finally disappeared with retreat from Aberdeen on 23 February—indeed, a French ship arrived a couple of days later with 650 troops, and had to withdraw. France also understood, as some in the Jacobite leadership perhaps did not, that the sinews of financial power available in London meant that, unless rapid victory was achieved, the fiscal military force of the Hanoverian state would obliterate its domestic opponents. Great Britain's national debt was large; when the Jacobites were marching south, the debtor's creditworthiness was under threat, as many feared that the restored Stuarts would repudiate financial obligations largely entered into since 1689 in order to prevail over French interests. As the Jacobites retreated, Great Britain's interests demanded and secured additional financial resources to ensure the containment and defeat of the threat and to prevent any recurrence. The fatal tokenism of leaving a Jacobite garrison at Carlisle was Charles Edward's responsibility, and it indicated a serious underestimation of the nature of the forces facing him: it was an emotional gesture made with men's lives. By the end of January 1746, as the Duke of Cumberland took command of the British Army, the net was tightening round the Jacobites.

In this sense, Jacobite victory at Culloden might have changed little. Yet in the months running up to the battle, much—in the end illusory—local success had been achieved in Scotland, despite the reoccupation of Edinburgh by Ligonier and four regiments on 14 November. While the Prince's army marched south, the Jacobites had been recruiting steadily in the north, reinforced by Lord John Drummond's *Royal-Écossais* and those Irish picquets in the French service who had got through the Royal Navy blockade. On 7 October, 2,500 firelocks were landed at Montrose; six cannon followed and six heavy guns came on 24 November. In all, 'upwards of 4000 French muskets and an equal number of bayonets and swords were landed in Montrose'. On 23 December, Loudoun's forces had been defeated by the Jacobite troops of Aberdeen and Angus at Inverurie, reinforced by French regulars.

Lord Lewis Gordon commanded in the counties of Aberdeen and Banff, James Moir of Stoneywood the city of Aberdeen's regiment—a battalion in Gordon's brigade. Colonel Sir Alexander Bannerman commanded in the Mearns, Sir James Kinloch in Angus, and the Earl of Cromartie raised the cess in Fife; Lord Lovat escaped from Loudoun's custody in December, and three battalions of Frasers were raised for the Stuarts and Scotland, for Lovat was a profoundly patriotic Scot if a most unreliable ally.[33] More recruits came in, and together with them supplies: 250 carts had been landed at Stonehaven in October, and France continued to supply the east coast ports. As a result, Charles Edward could field an army of 10,000 or even more by January, in addition to other troops guarding the localities. Most of these were effective, even though the main army's victory at Falkirk on 18 January over General Hawley's British forces changed less than it might have done. And supplies continued to come in. One squadron of Fitzjames's Horse got through to Aberdeen on 21 February (three were captured) and a company-strong picquet of Berwick's was landed at Peterhead four days later. In March, however, a second picquet in *Le Prince Charles* was captured at Tongue on 25 March with up to £15,000 in gold, and in April, Cromartie's regiment, sent to recover it, was defeated by British forces. On 2 May, a further £38,000 was landed by two more French frigates at Loch nan Uamh, but it came too late to be of effective military use.[34]

The minor actions in February and March protected Jacobite interests to the south and east of the Spey for a time. A direct hit by a mortar shell on the magazine at Fort Augustus on 5 March and the successful raid launched from Major General Lord John Drummond's command at Fochabers on that of Major General Humphrey Bland at Keith on the twentieth were in the end illusory victories. Arguably far more serious was the loss of the Jacobite magazine at Corgarff on 28 February. Cumberland reinforced his forward base at Huntly, and Colonel (Acting Brigadier) Mordaunt moved to Oldmeldrum on 23 March, thence to Turriff on 8 April; Lord Sempill's 4th Infantry Brigade moved up to Inverurie. The net was tightening on the Jacobites drilling on the northern coast, and it was through poor intelligence that Perth and Lord John

Drummond were surprised at Fochabers on 12 April and failed to contest the Spey with their division; this was critical, as the Jacobite high command in Inverness had been relying on delaying and making costly any fording of this river by the British Army. Sullivan was further alarmed when the Jacobites continued to fall back, as the British came through Forres. On the fourteenth, Drummond's forces left Nairn, screened by four troops of Jacobite cavalry. Their retreat was only slowed by some of Fitzjames's and half a picquet of Berwick's, who continued to skirmish up to 8 kilometres beyond Nairn as the British forces advanced.[35]

With Inverness the only major burgh under its control (with a population of about 5,000), the Jacobite Army had to defend it or retreat into the glens. It had too many Franco-Irish and Franco-Scottish regulars to do that, not to mention the large numbers of Lowland volunteers who were still in the ranks of an army that—except in the early stages of the Rising—was never more than half from the area now identified as the 'Highlands'. Many of those who were would not have countenanced such a war either: their leaders had significant real estate and landed assets to protect in their localities. Moreover, the army had almost no money and very little in the way of supplies. Opportunistic guerrilla resistance would entail the dissolution of the army. That point was brought home forcibly by the abortive night attack on Cumberland's camp at Nairn on 15 April, when the gap between the columns reached up to 3 kilometres: irregular warfare on rough ground would not have been possible for what was in most respects a conventional field army. Whatever the myths of its primitive, romantic qualities, however fascinated the nineteenth and twentieth centuries would become with the futile swordsmanship of the Children of the Mist in the face of modern firepower, despite the quixotic construction of the Rising in cultural memory through the condemnation of its leader's folly combined with sympathy for the dupes of this idle Stuart dream, in reality the Jacobites were too much of a normal army to do anything but fight at Culloden. They still had significant recruitment potential—with Cromartie's and Lovat's battalions, Glengarry and Skye MacDonald reinforcements, and the Macphersons absent—but they had no food and no money. For his part, Cumberland too needed—if less urgently—to fight, as too many British forces were being deployed at home, and the French forces in the War of the Austrian Succession would be entering on a new campaigning season in the spring of 1746.[36]

Although the popular image of the 'Highlander' might equate in some minds to groups like the Maroons, who had resisted British forces in the Jamaican interior throughout the early eighteenth century,[37] the Jacobite Army was in reality composed very differently. The 'Highland clan' forces were regional light infantry militia raised by local magnates, whose ability to exert feudal control in relatively remote geographical areas was stronger than that of their counterparts in England, or indeed in Lowland Scotland, which nonetheless in the end provided as large a part of the army.[38] They had marched far and fast; they were short of heavy guns and horses for their cavalry, of trained artillerymen, equipment, and food, but at Culloden they appear to have fired two balls from their French and Spanish musketry for every Brown Bess ball in reply. As on many other eighteenth-century Continental battlefields, there was much Jacobite musketry in evidence at Culloden, a feature almost entirely missing from traditional accounts of the battle. Before turning to the battle itself, I will examine afresh the evidence for the conventional organization, arms, and drill of the Jacobite Army in 1745–6, so that the reader can engage with accounts of the battle and its memorialization with a very different view of the nature of the threat finally defeated by the British Army near Inverness on 16 April 1746 from that which we have inherited.

Prince Charles Edward's forces were—perhaps even more than their Jacobite predecessors of 1715, and certainly more than the army of 1689—organized along conventional lines. Most were single battalion regiments; three (Lochiel's, Glengarry's, and Ogilvy's) had formal grenadier companies. These were the companies of the strongest and most physically imposing soldiers, originally armed with grenades, and often used for assaults on emplaced and fortified positions. In the British Army, the grenadier company flanked the firing line of its battalion and might be held for reserve fire. There might be fewer companies in a battalion than in its British equivalent (although Jacobite battalions were not always smaller), and multi-battalion regiments after the French model were more common on the Jacobite side. Jacobite forces were strongly disciplined, with a combination of British and French deployment, tactics, and drill: in particular, 'French tactical doctrines, calling for rapid movements in column formation, and an emphasis on shock tactics rather than firepower, were well suited to the Jacobites'. Jacobite columns also presented a narrow front of about 4 metres, not the 10 metres more normal in the wide front British Army marching formations. Jacobite infantrymen on the defensive fired volleys by ranks and then *feu à la billebaude*, fire at will 'dropping shots'; on the attack, they volleyed at 40–50 metres and used bayonet, pistol, and sword at close quarters. Mobile reserves were deployed in column in the French fashion, with company integrity apparently preserved. There were no 'firings' in the Jacobite Army.[39]

The Atholl Brigade was the largest unit, comprising four Perthshire battalions, with a peak strength of about 1,200 men (including MacLachlan's and Robertson of Struan's). Other large units were MacDonell of Glengarry's (two battalions of up to 1,200, including the Grants of Glenmoriston), Cameron of Lochiel's (a peak of 1,050 in the 1st and 2nd battalions), Fraser of Lovat's (three battalions of up to 900), Lord Ogilvy's Forfarshire regiment (two battalions of up to 900), Lord Lewis Gordon's (three battalions of up to 800, including Stoneywood's Aberdeen battalion), the Duke of Perth's (two battalions of up to 750, including Pitsligo's Foot), and the Royal Scots (two battalions of up to 400). Monaltrie's and Balmoral was a weak two-battalion regiment of about 300.

The single battalion units with between 200 and 500 men at peak included Cromartie's Ross-shire regiment, Gordon of Glenbuchat's Donsiders, MacDonald of Clanranald and of Keppoch (including Mackinnon levies), MacGregor of Glengyle, Lady Mackintosh's, MacLean's, Macpherson's, Stewart of Ardsheal's, John Roy Stuart's, and the Manchester Regiment. Smaller units such as Bannerman's

Mearns battalion (maximum 160), Chisholm's (maximum 150), the Irish picquets, and MacDonalds of Glencoe were sometimes brigaded with larger ones as the campaign proceeded.

Cavalry was weaker than in 1715, with the strongest unit being the Life Guard Squadron of Elcho, Balmerino, and Kilmarnock, up to 220-strong. Due to the loss of horses during the campaign, Kilmarnock's troop was reformed as the Foot Guards in February, and turned into a battalion by the addition of some weaker or broken units such as Bannerman's, who had been forced to retreat from their native Mearns. Forbes of Pitsligo's Foot had up to 200, Fitzjames's Horse (four squadrons were sent from France but only one got through) had no more than 130, and Murray of Broughton's Hussars and Strathallan's Perthshire Horse were only by courtesy squadrons, each numbering eighty horse at best. Grante's Artillery, of some sixty men at best reinforced by three of Perth's companies, completed the picture of the army. In all there were some 12,800 foot and 800 horse in the field at one time or another (with some more in the localities), but the Jacobites never successfully managed to deploy more than 9,000–10,000 in the field at any one time, because of desertion, turnover during the Rising, and the role their forces had in guarding the localities they controlled. Thus the Jacobite Army was unable to deploy maximum force at any point: the need for rapidity of movement on the one hand and to raise funds from the localities on the other, divided the army, while I have already noted that heavy guns could not be taken on the dash to London.[40]

The Jacobite Army on campaign, even more than its predecessors in 1689 and 1715, was uniformed in tartan. This signified its patriotism on behalf of true Scotland, which was held to be the north of the country: Alba, its original core beyond the Forth. The wearing of tartan in no way implied that the Jacobite forces were 'Highland' or Gaelic-speaking: though they termed themselves (in English) a 'Highland Army', this was an ideological as much as a geographical expression. Even the Manchester Regiment wore tartan, and 'Plaid Breast-knots, Ribbands and Garters' were much in evidence among female sympathizers in the city.[41] The only exceptions appear to have been 'the French regulars' who 'wore their own uniform' (though even they wore tartan on occa-sion), and the Life Guards, who had 'handsome blue coats with red fac-ings'. Many of the rank and file soldiers wore the plaid, a rectangle of cloth some 4 by 1.5 metres; although their officers often wore trews, their similar uniform served as a badge of solidarity with their men.[42] The saltire was frequently used as a badge: Charles Edward wore one in his bonnet, and many of the surviving banners (for example that of the 2nd Battalion, Ogilvy's, preserved in Dundee Museums, the Stewart of Appin standard, captured by Monro's 37th Foot, and even the standard of the Royal Scots) bear it prominently, thus symbolizing the primacy of the national cause.[43] Most Jacobite flags involved the saltire. As the historian Stuart Reid notes, in this and other visible features, the Jacobite Army of 1745 was 'to all intents and purposes the last Scots army...fighting for Scotland'.[44]

Tartan signified the colours of old, martial Scotland—a symbol of the Jacobite defence of Scottish nationality. Bright-coloured tartan—using expensive imported dyes—symbolized wealth and status, and there were district and to an extent family or 'clan' tartans even in 1745, though on nothing like the systematized scale that ensued. Charles Edward had already started to wear it in this guise from the 1730s on, and in the after-math of the Rising he was frequently depicted in a harlequin-like check tartan (possibly a deliberate caricature, as will be discussed in Chapter 5), which may derive from 'the uniform of an officer of the Scottish highlanders with a multi-coloured checked costume' which the Prince wore for the January 1741 ball at the Palazzo Pamphili in Rome.[45]

One of the lasting myths of the 'Forty-five, and of the Jacobite mili-tary threat in general, is that the Prince's troops were largely armed with swords rather than firearms. This suited contemporary Hanoverian propaganda and the heroic traditions of Gaelic verse alike. Yet the idea that a fully armed Highlander should carry firelock, pistol, sword, and dirk was recognized by the arming of the Independent Companies in the Highlands (who carried a pistol each), nor was any great change being initiated thereby in Scottish arms. Muskets and pistols were wide-spread in Montrose's army in 1644–5 (his cavalry were reported to be carrying a carbine and four pistols a man on entering Aberdeen), while in 1668 the Marquis of Atholl protested against arming Perthshire men 'with matchlocks, as they were "altogether unacquainted with the use of any other gunne but fyrelocks"'. The standard weapons technology of English musketeers in 1640 was regarded as outdated in central Scotland a quarter of a century later; even in the islands, the Macleans in 1679 surrendered half as many guns as swords, and had barely any Lochaber axes—a weapon of which there is no secure record after Prestonpans in 1745, although it makes an appearance in David Morier's famous painting of *An Incident in the Rebellion of 1745* as a sign of the 'primitive' quality of the army (see Chapter 5 for further discussion of this highly influential depiction). The Lochaber axe was usually a long curved blade (though other shapes of axe head were possible) mounted on a 2–3-metre shaft which was itself topped with a hook. In use from at least the beginning of the sixteenth century, the Lochaber axe was an obsolete weapon by 1745, though witnesses attest to it being carried early in the campaign. Rather than characterize the Jacobite Army of 1745 through such weapons, we might do better to heed the words of Daniel Defoe, who in *A Tour Through the Whole Island of Great Britain* noted that the inhabitants of the Highlands, 'who are named....as if they were barbarians, appear at court, and in our camps and armies, as polite, and as finished gentlemen as any from other countries, or even among our own ... outdoing our own in many things, especially in arms and gallantry'.[46]

This was unsurprising: after all, the multilateral conflicts of the Wars in the Three Kingdoms required armies who could compete with each other militarily. It was the same in 1745. In 1724, General Wade's comment on 'Highland' arms stressed the presence of muskets and pistols as well as swords and dirks, while surviving contemporary pictures of Jacobite soldiers from 1745 show them carrying muskets. At Prestonpans, the Jacobite Army was still not well armed (about 75 per cent had muskets and swords and about 20 per cent only one or the other, while a small minority had neither),[47] but this changed substantially following their captures of materiel on 21 September and the subsequent landings at the east coast ports. Two and a half thousand or slightly more French and Spanish muskets, which shared a 0.69 inch, 17.5-millimetre bore (firing a 16.5-millimetre ball), were landed at Montrose and Stonehaven in October 1745, 2,500 more at Barra in October and November. Jacobite soldiers frequently carried the bayonet, which could be fixed in action.[48]

Pistols were usually made of imported iron, and could carry Celtic designs. Many Jacobite pistols were made in Scotland, by gunsmiths such as McNab of Dalmally and Caddell of Doune; these were all-metal guns, often with a ramshorn butt. Star and rose decorations, symbolic of the Stuart cause and its heirs, were common. Barrels were around 25–36 centimetres (short 16-centimetre barrels are known in the heart butt pattern), bores 12–16 millimetres. The Doune pattern pistol, widely used by officers and cavalry, had a ramshorn butt and 25-centimetre barrel. Cheap pistols might cost less than £1 sterling the pair, but ornate ones were of course very much more expensive. Pistols usually weighed about 1.25 kilograms. Although Doune was the centre of the trade, a wide range of pistols was made in Edzell, Brechin, and Leith, most with bores of around 13–14 milimetres, with some ranging as high as 19. Buchanan of Glasgow's pistols had 28-centimetre barrels and were of 12.7-millimetre bore. Heart-butted rather than scroll-butted pistols were more usual on the east coast.[49]

Tacksmen (landholders under a feudal superior), bonnet lairds (petty landowners), and professional men who were volunteer officers all usually carried the sword, either the *claidheamh mòr* (claymore or broadsword) with a double-edged blade of 70–96 centimetres or the similarly sized backsword, *claidheamh cuil*, with one sharpened blade only. The broadsword was a sword with a basket hilt made of vertical bars or panelled bands and two cutting edges, known from before 1600. Designs including thistles, hearts, and lozenges are found: the Allans of Doune carried out particularly fine work. The broadsword was largely carried by officers, as in the British Army, though its use was more widespread. The traditional claymore, the double-handed sword drawn over the shoulder, which could be up to 1.8 metres long was last used at Killiecrankie (1689), though one was surrendered by the Inverness armourer Robert Low in 1715. The term 'claymore' was retained to sig-nify the beginning of a charge, at the close of which officers would raise their broadswords, which now became described as 'claymores'.[50]

The dirk (some of which were made from converted claymores, either broken or no longer fit for use), was a long stabbing knife or short sword with a 45-centimetre blade, often a shortened sword blade, known from at least the sixteenth century. Dirks were customarily held in the left or targe hand, to stab an adversary at close quarters once the targe had deflected the bayonet.

Many if not most Jacobite troops initially carried the targe. This was a small round shield some 50–70 centimetres across and weighing from 2–3.5 kilograms depending on whether or not it had metal studs or nails, with an 8-centimetre brass central boss and a spike, which stood in the boss. It was usually made of wood with a leather covering, and had been carried by Scottish troops for a very long time: it is known from the fifteenth century. The targe—following Henry Fletcher's description to Andrew Fletcher of Saltoun in January 1716—was com-posed of animal skin with hair on it, a steel plate on which the handle was fixed, wool, and cork, with leather over the cork nailed on with brass-headed nails (silver in decorative targes) in a circular pattern, thicker towards the boss, from which a spike might protrude. Another description identifies the targe (probably a cheaper version) as 'formed of two pieces of thin oak or fir boards laid across each other for strength and covered in cowhides' (or sometimes deer or goatskin or cork and steel) with 'raw wool' or 'moss' padding between the boards, after which a steel plate might be added, with a skin behind it with a handle. Targes were sometimes coloured. Other patterns including radiating lines from the boss, stars, semicircular panels, lozenges, and roundels are known, while the surface leather itself was also decorated, embossed, and indented with various animal, plant, or heraldic designs, possibly depending on the originating workshop. The boss might be unscrewed to reveal a brass cup from which the soldier might drink. During the 1745–6 campaign, the prices per targe from the same supplier could vary from over 5s. sterling per targe to 2s. 3d., these latter being made of

43

wood, leather, and skin only. The very best targes might cost over 10s.: this was an item of military equipment which varied widely in quality. Targes were manufactured throughout the campaign.[51]

The 1745–6 campaign was the last in which targes were extensively carried, though they were technically available for a few years more in the British Army. It is likely that most of them had been abandoned or lost before the Battle of Culloden itself. Despite intermittent claims that targes could repel musket balls (made from the 1690s on) there is very little real evidence for this, and their ineffectiveness may account for their progressive abandonment in the 1745–6 campaign. The assertions of their bulletproof qualities can probably be accounted for by expensive targes, which with a plate of iron or steel (horn seems also sometimes to have been used) behind the leather or brass studs on top might indeed deflect or stop a ball nearing the end of its effective range. Glenbuchat's targe, carried by Lord George Murray, was supposed to have done service at closer quarters at Clifton: it, unusually, had a second plate of steel on the front of the targe.[52]

Commissions were granted in the name of 'James the Eight by the Grace of God King of Scotland, England, France & Ireland',[53] thus using the Scottish regnal number of the king, associating the Jacobite cause with that of Scotland (although not using the older title 'King of Scots'). Patriotic symbols were common on the banners and in the propaganda of the Jacobites.[54]

There appear to have been two kinds and phases of army drill. Even at Prestonpans as we have seen, there were signs of 'uniform and orderly' motion in the Jacobite attack which 'surprized' politically unsympathetic observers such as Lord Drummore.[55] To develop and enhance this, there was 'a simple method of drill' devised by Lord George Murray at Edinburgh which accustomed volunteers and drafted men to the basics of military fieldcraft, including loading and firing the many muskets which were captured by the army at Prestonpans or came in afterwards. Reports at the time suggest that this was regularly and fairly intensively carried out: 'daily exercising' by the army is noted in a letter from mid-October 1745. It is also likely that a more sophisticated musket drill based on the 1727

British Army regulations was taught in some regiments, such as Ogilvy's, while the arrival of French regulars seems to have led to much more developed training in early 1746, with a stress on French habits of 'rapid movements in column formation, and an emphasis on shock tactics', with volley fire by four ranks followed by firing at will. These are probably the 'dropping shots' reported from retreating Jacobite units at Culloden. On the other hand, some Jacobite units in the localities seem to have continued with British Army-style training (for example, from Chelsea pensioner John Webster at Arbroath), and there is no surviving evidence of cavalry training. Orders were given in English (there is no evidence for Gaelic), despite the ideological use of the term 'Highland Army' to signify the patriotism of Charles Edward's force; passwords might occasionally be in or partly in Gaelic, such as 'Rie [Righ] James'.[56]

The 'Highland Charge' has long been seen as the basic battlefield tactic of the army. Historian David Stevenson argued that this tactic was first introduced from Ireland by Alasdair MacColla, who supplemented it with a single musket volley at 25–55 metres, after which the final charge would be through dense and obscuring smoke from the firing, with the front rank of officers/tacksmen often having sword in the right hand and the dirk in the left (hence no targe, useless at close range). The soldiers would charge forward, being almost horizontal behind their targes, before stopping to discharge their muskets, with the final attack being almost in column. A battalion ordered into action would thus move forward rapidly to within 50 metres of the enemy lines, fire a volley, then form into rough company-sized columns behind their officers (described by Hawley as 'True Highlanders'), so that they were '12 or 14 deep by the time they came up to the people they attack',[57] sometimes by this stage in a wedge formation to present a smaller target, though this must have been difficult to achieve; some in the rear ranks may also have held their fire until close quarters. The officers in the front line would use sword or dirk and pistol as they closed, while the weight of men behind them would break through the front line, which, pierced at several points, would be vulnerable to multiple flanking actions.[58]

The concentration of force required to widen and turn a breach in the British front line became a handicap at Culloden, because the second-rank regiments were close to the front line and moved up quickly to deny the Jacobites space, so they may have stood thirty deep but only able to return fire on a narrow front. At Prestonpans by contrast, Lochiel's 1st Battalion's attack on the artillery was carried out with a front of twenty men standing thirty deep, and overwhelmed its opponents.[59]

Supplies of 'shoes, targes, tents and other items of equipment' were ordered steadily almost from the beginning of the Rising, while at Perth in early September, Lord George Murray 'ordered that each man was to be supplied with a "pock"...so that a daily ration of meal could be issued and carried'. In Glasgow at Christmas 1745, 6,000 coats, 12,000 shirts, and 6,000 bonnets, tartan hose, and shoes were ordered. Income for continuing the Rising was largely drawn from the cess raised from Jacobite areas, and when the army's territory shrank, so did its income; the loss of the east coast ports again intensified this problem, by making it more difficult for French subventions to get through.[60]

The standard routine for the day for regiments on the march was as follows. The major or acting major received the orders of the day at 11 a.m. Each day, captains (company commanders) were in their turn responsible for submitting a muster roll and company report to the major. Captains were also responsible for giving tickets of leave; without these, being a mile from camp constituted desertion. Deserters were shot: this was the fate that befell Robert Munro of the 1st Battalion, Ogilvy's on Leith Links on 16 October. Sergeants were to 'cause the men to keep their arms clean, and qualify themselves for exercise'. Curfew was at 9 p.m. On the march, two captains marched in the rear and two lieutenants on the flanks of each battalion, to keep them in line. The battalions marched with a much narrower front than their British equivalents, aiding traversing rough ground: this approach dated back at least to the fifth century BC, being recommended to the Greeks by Xenophon in his *Anabasis*.[61] Each man was issued with twelve bullets, and carried his arms: it was the quartermaster's duty to see that arms were carried and not surreptitiously left on the wagons. It was clear from all aspects of daily order that firelocks not swords were seen as the 'primary weapons' of the army. Although the Jacobites were outnumbered two to one at Culloden, and some of them carried English Land Pattern muskets, an equal number of Franco-Spanish and British army ball was recovered from the battlefield in the 2005 excavation. At Culloden there were several intense firefights across the field, on the British left, between Leanach and Culchunaig, and to the Jacobite rear. Infantry firelocks predominated both in these exchanges and in the battlefield archaeology; only 8–10 per cent of recovered ball came from carbines or pistols. This was in keeping with military practice: pistols were only really effective at close quarters (under 10 metres), while cavalry doctrine had it that carbines slowed a charge and were in any case highly inaccurate fired from a moving horse.[62]

The Jacobite Army had at its peak substantial numbers of heavy weapons such as artillery at its disposal (up to eighty-five pieces), but found it difficult to obtain enough trained gunners. Moreover, additional to the general unwieldiness of transporting such heavy weapons over bad roads in a rapid advance was the fact that horses were absolutely indispensable to moving large guns. The Jacobite Army had persistent shortages of horses, and had to acquire them on the march: 180 were obtained at Manchester alone. For this reason, the Prince's forces entered England with only thirteen cannon: six 'Swedish' (in fact French) guns of 4-pound ball (the French battlefield standard rather than the British 3-pounder), with a high firing rate, and six 1½ -pounders captured from the British Army at Prestonpans. The guns that travelled south were battlefield weapons for close infantry support, and not even 6- or 8-pounders for cannonading infantry at range. The army had no transportable guns which could be used effectively in a siege,[63] so the Duke of Perth's order to the Edinburgh bookseller Gavin Hamilton on 22 October for Vauban's *Fortifications* and *Memoirs* was perhaps wishful thinking. On 24 November, a small 'siege train' was landed at Montrose, with two 18-, 12-, and 9-pound guns, while a number of 3-pounders captured at Fontenoy were also landed. Colonel Grante, the artillery commander, was wounded at the siege of Fort William, and his inability to exercise command at Culloden limited the effectiveness of the Jacobite artillery.[64]

Pay seems to have been in line with the last independent army of the Scottish state prior to 1707: much in Jacobite taxation and finance policy made it clear that they wanted to return Scotland to pre-Union norms. Interestingly, while Jacobite pay bears comparison with the Independent Highland Companies for NCOs, the gap between their pay and that of officers was much smaller in Charles Edward's army. Gentlemen volunteers in the cavalry received 2s. a day (24s. Scots at the standardized 1707 rate of exchange), sergeants 1s. 6d., and ordinary troopers 1s. Captains in the infantry had 2s. 6d. a day; first lieutenants and surgeons 2s.; ensigns 1s. 6d.; gentlemen volunteers 1s.; sergeants, pipers, and drummers 9d.; and privates 6d. By contrast, a British Army or Independent Company captain might have 10s. and a lieutenant 4–5s. including a small allowance for servants.[65]

In the Jacobite-leaning localities, business went in much as usual. John Webster, treasurer of the Town Council at Forfar, led opposition to taking the oaths to government in autumn 1745, arguing on 2 October that with 'the Capital itself' (i.e. Edinburgh) 'under the Government of an army fighting in opposition to the Regnant power', the time could hardly be right for subscribing to government.[66] The Jacobite administration in Perth was—even though the town was divided in its sympathies, and there had been a Hanoverian riot on George II's birthday—confident enough in January 1746 to order 1,360 palisades at 2d. sterling a piece for the defence of the town against siege.[67] At Brechin, the oaths were avoided and the minutes of the Town Council destroyed, while in Forfar in May 1746 the councillors explained to a sceptical British Army that they had not taken 'the Oaths of Alleadgiance and Abjuration' because they had been 'Overawed by numbers of Rebells'. Coffee house keepers, fiddlers, and town pipers were among those who joined the Jacobite Army; the public sphere in places like Aberdeen, Arbroath, and Dundee was very far from being a Whig phenomenon.[68]

Prestonpans was the last engagement in which the Jacobite army was not well armed. As one government source put it:

> Some of then seem, not to be Arm'd but 'tis reported they are all to be Armd out o' the Cargae imported at Monross [Montrose]. The rest seem All of them to be very well armd, Each having a Gun, a broad Sword, a side Pistoll & severall have each one, two—&some three pair side and packet pistols—besides Dirks, Target &c[69]

Even in retreat, the Jacobite Army seemed not to be short of arms (though bullets may have been another matter).[70] At Perth, although there were many orders for shoes and some for targes put forward by the Jacobite administration, the lack of orders for weapons (despite the relatively close areas of manufacture, such as Doune) suggests that the troops were on the whole well armed. As long as they controlled areas of eastern and central Scotland they seemed to be well fed also. Even as late as 4 February 1746, substantial sums were coming in to support the Jacobite administration of Perth under Laurence Oliphant, with £5,192 sterling being recorded as the total raised by the beginning of the month, with £5,038 in all spent: the Jacobite government of the town was solvent.[71]

The British Army was not so different or so superior as many might suppose. First of all it was—except in times of emergency when the Press Acts were brought into operation, as in 1704–12, 1745–6, and 1755–7—a small force. In 1739, it was composed of six troops of Household Cavalry, eight regiments of horse, fourteen regiments of dragoons, six battalions of Foot Guards in three regiments, forty-one foot battalions, and four artillery companies, together with a small force of Invalids; by 1748, it had expanded considerably to meet the challenge of war, with thirteen battalions of foot raised in 1745 alone. Half the foot were in Ireland in 1716–39, evidence enough of the concern felt for the Jacobite threat in that kingdom (although it was also cheaper to billet them there); in 1749–55, there were to be 'more battalions in Scotland than in the whole of the Americas', with most troops stationed on or south of the Great Glen. In comparison, the Jacobite

Army of 1715 consisted of forty-four foot battalions and nineteen cavalry squadrons; that of 1745, forty foot battalions and six cavalry squadrons. Nor were these units always of smaller size than their British equivalents.[72]

The morale and *esprit de corps* of the British Army could be suspect too, not least because of the complete lack of social cohesion between an officer class influenced by social rank and connections, where two-thirds of commissions were purchased, and a rank and file recruited from the poor, the desperate, markets, hiring fairs, or simple pressing, though there were some volunteers from a higher social background than the generality of infantry, and cavalry were another matter. The social gulfs were perhaps exacerbated at times of heavy and repeated pressing: in 1755, Lieutenant Colonel James Wolfe observed of the infantry that 'I know their discipline to be bad, & their valour precarious, they are easily put into disorder... they frequently kill their officers thro' fear, & murder one another in their confusion'.[73]

British soldiers occupying Scottish towns after 1746 were not infrequently ill-disciplined, and the brutality after Culloden has been attributed by some Sandhurst or British Army military historians to poorer quality recruits or pressed 'vestry men'. However, many units of the regular British Army had been extensively deployed against rioters and the dispossessed: at Trowbridge in 1726; at Manchester in 1739; at Stafford, Shrewsbury, Walsall, Birmingham, and Burton upon Trent in 1751–2; at London in 1733, 1736, and 1753; in Cornwall in 1726–7; and in many other places. Though volunteer units such as yeomanry could be particularly brutal (as in Ireland in 1798 and Manchester in 1819), the gentry of the unstable, violent, and often starving world of 'Augustan' Britain were quite willing to believe on occasion 'that the rule of dragoons and that of law were one and the same'. The idea that the regular army's reputation was undermined by the behaviour of a few 'bad eggs' among the poorer recruits, pressed 'vestry men', or ex-prisoners, is public relations not history. In the aftermath of Culloden, British soldiers were occupying what to them was conquered territory, and frequently behaved accordingly.[74]

Both infantry and cavalry in the British Army were organized into regiments. In the case of infantry, this usually comprised a single battalion for tactical operations, but sometimes multiple battalions. The regiment was commanded by a colonel, who was usually substituted by a lieutenant colonel. The colonel had a company in the regiment, which, if a single battalion, was composed of between eight and twelve (usually ten) companies including a grenadier company: these were 'grenadiers', other infantry soldiers 'hatmen'. Just as the colonel's regiment was in effect commanded by a lieutenant colonel, so the colonel's company was commanded by a captain lieutenant, all other companies being commanded by a captain. The grenadier company flanked the firing line of the other nine companies in two platoons, each platoon being commanded by a 2nd lieutenant; the other nine companies had a lieutenant as second in command and an ensign as third in command. Ensigns stood to the left of their company commander at the head of the company, lieutenants to the right, while the rightmost company was the colonel's company and so on to the most junior captain on the left. Sergeants stood in flank and rear. The Grand Division was a unit composed of 25 per cent of the hatmen in a battalion, comprising two to four platoons, effectively a double company, and about the same size as a modern company. Just as the battalion's hatmen were divided into four Grand Divisions, they were also composed (until 1764) of three firings (Bland suggests variations on this number), the platoons composing which were numbered and scattered along the division line: each fired at once, but they were not contiguously grouped. Grenadier platoons on the wings might be held for reserve fire. The key motivation of soldiers—to fight to be seen by and to support their friends and comrades—was diluted because the firings system mixed up the companies men usually belonged to. The mid-century move to 'alternate fire', by established companies rather than grouped fire platoons, may in part have been a response to faster rates of fire, as the reserve fire and repeat volleys of the firings were useful not least in addressing the slow loading of musketry with separate cartridges and wooden ramrods. The new system also provided additional benefit in that soldiers known to each other fought together.

The regiment varied in size between 300 and 500 men. Companies were much smaller than they became in the twentieth century (this is important because Jacobite companies have sometimes been considered to be unusually small by those using presentist standards), partly because the view was taken that forty-eight or so was the largest number that could be controlled by a single officer. The cavalry regiment was organized in two or three squadrons, each composed of two troops, while the cavalry squadron was operationally equivalent to the infantry Grand Division. Regimental staff might include an adjutant (usually a lieutenant or captain), a quartermaster, a surgeon, and a chaplain.[75]

The chief weapon of the infantryman was the Land Pattern musket (popularly the 'Brown Bess'). This was a muzzle-loaded smooth-bore flintlock of 0.75 inches (19 millimetres with a 17.5-millimetre ball) used by the British Army in a sequence of designs from the c.1730 to just before the Crimean War. The barrel was up to 117 centimetres in length (though it could be only 100 centimetres), and there was a 43-centimetre bayonet; 10 grams of powder were needed to fire the gun. The ball was typically 1.5 millimetres smaller than the calibre, though closer fitting balls would give better accuracy. The gun weighed 4.5–5 kilograms and at Culloden was used in short and long Land Pattern forms, the dragoon version being 10 centimetres shorter in the barrel.

The rifles that replaced it were estimated to produce 1 casualty from 16 rounds as opposed to the estimate of between 1 in 260 and 1 in 459 for Brown Bess, with its low muzzle velocity of 310 metres/second. As the historian Christopher Duffy notes, 'the crack and buzz of a rifle' was a much more threatening sound than 'the thump and whistle of a musket shot'. The musket was made from iron, brass, and walnut, ordered separately through the post-1715 Ordnance system, designed to prevent single suppliers producing shoddy weapons at high margins, and after 1722 to prevent regimental colonels profiting from supplying lower quality muskets. It was regarded by those who used it as superior to Continental muskets, the French guns of the Jacobites being seen as less strong, even if Brown Bess was heavier and frequently criticized for the quality and quantity of its ammunition.[76]

Accuracy was poor above 50–75 metres, especially in the case of volley firing on command, and there was no gunsight. The maximum possible range was around 225 metres, but the musket was almost completely ineffective at half that. At 60 metres, some 3 per cent of balls penetrated and caused vital injuries, though many more might penetrate a static target to some extent. The black powder produced a great deal of smoke, and this rapidly obscured the target in a firefight; the barrel also became hot under repeated firing, and after twenty to thirty rounds could not be held. The rate of fire was one shot every fifteen to thirty seconds using an iron or steel ramrod, but wooden ramrods were in use at the time of Culloden. Although the Prussians had introduced iron rammers in 1698, there were sceptics in the British Army: Hawley noted in 1726 that iron rods got bent or rusted without the correct admixture of steel. Wooden rammers, however, loaded 'very slow' on cold days, and in 1740 a marine subaltern noted that 'twelve rammers were broken in firing six rounds'. The conservative use of wooden ramrods (iron ones were introduced from 1724, but were not in the majority until the end of the Seven Years War, partly due to poor metallurgy) limited the effectiveness of the British Army.[77]

The firing pan was primed direct from a torn cartridge also used to load (a recent innovation which increased the rate of fire following the changes in the 1740 drill regulations), and was vulnerable to rain, though less so after the introduction of sealed cartridges. Before the 1730s, cartridges and primer were kept separately. Both metal ramrods and direct priming from the cartridge speeded the rate of fire (typically raising it from two to three rounds a minute), but it is easy to see how second-rate troops using older equipment might readily be overwhelmed by a charge. Under pressure in battle, the firing rate could fall and proper loading could be abandoned, with the butt thumped 'on the ground so as to shake the load down the barrel' and no ramrod used. Flints 'became blunt' and the 'touchole fouled', leading to 'flash in the pan'. If the rammer broke in the barrel, a loaded gun was reloaded without being discharged or if 'dirt or snow' blocked the barrel, the musket could explode. Board of Ordnance parsimony led to poor rates of weapon renewal, and many muskets were not in good condition, while cartridge cases were often poorly made as they were contracted for by colonels using government funds, who stood to make a profit if they ordered the cheapest option. The average infantryman only received enough powder for 60–120 shots a year, and could only fire two to four balls from the 'annual issue of shot' to a regiment. This increased in wartime (Cumberland's army carried 240,000 musket rounds), but leaving aside the condition of the guns and the presence of pressed men, lack of drill made speed of firing and accuracy poor. Modern tests show that Brown Bess would be fairly ineffective on infantry at 100 metres, but would be devastating at 20–5 metres, when the large balls would tear through human flesh, leaving major wounds.

At Culloden, British hatmen were told to fire at 30 yards (27 metres). The regimental firings would be locked at the command 'Make Ready', with the front rank kneeling, and the second and third moving apart to form a 'file interval' through which the rearmost rank discharged. British military doctrine called for heavy fire closely controlled by officers, and the maintenance of 'some part of the battalion's firepower' in reserve. General Hawley argued in January 1746 that the Jacobites would face inevitable defeat if the firings fired at complementary angles and held fire until 7-metre range or closer: 'at 3 deep to fire by ranks diagionaly to the Centre where they come, the rear rank first, and even that rank not to fire till they are within 10 or 12 paces... If the fire is given at a distance you probably will be broke.' This would require the kind of nerve and timing which at once identified such advice as purely academic. It was more frequently the case that small gaps appeared in the British ranks which widened as the Jacobites approached, while the ranks behind were often not drilled to cover. At Culloden, Cumberland's lines were tighter and the distance between the lines short.[78]

The infantry were also armed with the hanger, a short sword carried by the British Army infantryman. These were not regarded as of much use in the era of the screw bayonet and were not often carried on campaign. Cavalry on the other hand had both a shorter-barrelled version of Brown Bess as a carbine, and basket-hilted swords, with a blade of almost 100 centimetres. Both carbine and pistols were seldom used, the shock of a charge being used to break infantry, who countered this risk by tight formation of ranks.[79]

British Army drill could be varied by individual commanders (who had a share in their regiments through the commission purchase system), but in practice departures from normal practice were limited. Standard drill was important given the relative lack of professionalism of the armed forces, and the normal text was the *1728 Regulations*, prepared by a committee of general officers of horse, dragoons, and foot, allegedly at the command of George II, who on his accession 'Observ'd in his Review of the Forces, that the Regiments do not use One and the same Exercise'.

In practice, there had been pressure building for standardization for some little time. The *1728 Regulations* were not highly innovative, and drew on experience in the War of the Spanish Succession, together with Humphrey Bland's 1727 *Treatise of Military Discipline*. As usual with military expenditure, cost-cutting meant too few copies were issued to each regiment, and officers seem to have copied the most relevant parts of the *Regulations* into their commonplace books, or bought their own copies. After 1745, the *1748 Regulations* simplified the firings system: it was clear from the Jacobite Rising that the current rate of infantry fire could do with being increased (which is why battalion replaced platoon fire at Culloden), and indeed Cumberland (perhaps following Bland) modified the firings, while already intense drilling practice was increased. On the other hand, the Duke's famous bayonet drill, where the front-line infantryman was supposed to bayonet under the sword arm of the advancing Jacobite on his right rather than to defend himself directly and be deflected by the Jacobite targe, was parade-ground propaganda, 'so unrealistic as surely to be no more than a morale-booster'. Cumberland's steady, intense, and dull artillery drill was almost certainly exponentially more effective, especially in the context of Bland's excellent battlefield tactics, as was the use of the cavalry to break the enemy only when they were already wavering, rather than committing the dragoons early, as at Prestonpans and Falkirk.[80]

The British Army's artillery was comparable with that of the Jacobites, but the British Army was much better able to support the slow movements of an artillery train, and had a better supply of gunners and a greater variety of ammunition. At Culloden, both grapeshot (loose ball with a weight of about 100 grams each in a bag) and canister (packed into a container) were fired extensively by the British forces: about three times as much canister as grape has been retrieved from the battlefield. Roundshot of solid iron was also fired from 3-pounders, a standard British Army battlefield cannon, with an effective range of 300–700 metres, able to maintain a firing rate of up to two rounds a minute; below 300 metres, canister was preferable.[81]

Recruits were taught posture, then simple manouevres, then marching and speed of marching. Music was not used until the 1740s to maintain step, though drums had a long history, drummers typically marching 20 metres ahead of the front line. Pipes remained a key element of military communication for the Jacobite forces.[82] On the British side, Generals Bland and Hawley were innovative tactically in terms of varying the firings system to allow more concentrated ranks in battalion fire (Bland, used by Cumberland) and the use of dragoons (Hawley). Moving the dragoons ahead of the main British force before the battle had been tried at both Prestonpans and Falkirk however, and although their use was usefully delayed at Culloden, this may only have been because of the time needed to break down the enclosure walls at Culchunaig. We may thus give Hawley too much credit. For his part, Cumberland's monotonous and heavy drilling was—if unimaginative—effective in increasing morale and confidence.

The Jacobites' key problem was that they did not have a unified command structure which functioned in a harmonic or complementary way. Charles Edward was a fine strategist but a poor tactician, and tended to lose interest as the prospect of ultimate victory faded from view; he was also young, captious, and sulky. However, as Daniel Szechi

THE RISING OF 1745

has pointed out, the fact that the Jacobites had a member of the royal family in command may have eased tensions between rival factions.[83]

Henderson thought that Charles Edward 'had not one good officer along with him',[84] but posterity has judged the situation differently in generally valuing Lord George Murray as he rated himself. As already discussed, however, the case has been recently made that Lord George was a good tactician but a poor strategist; since he and Charles Edward were deeply divided over the priority to be accorded tactics and strategy, they were complementary in their strengths early in the campaign, but later distrustful and at loggerheads. The Duke of Perth and Lord John Drummond were effective and professional, but probably no more than that; Perth was also of a sweet nature and disliked forcing his own ideas into view. Sullivan had significant merits in arranging battle lines but was widely distrusted in the army, while Alexander Robertson of Strowan/Struan, Tullibardine, and Glenbuchat carried general officer rank more in tribute to their age and long service to the cause than any serious capacity to officer at this level—indeed, the aged Strowan (who had been in arms in support of the Jacobites as long ago as 1689) had gone home after Prestonpans. Viscount Strathallan was a major general by courtesy for his service in the localities while the army was in England. The Jacobites had fine battlefield commanders but their general command was divided and inconsistent in its approach. At Culloden, this was to leave them with no alternative to fall back on if victory were not secured by the front line.

3

Culloden Moor

The long-held view of Culloden is that the 'field of battle was ill-chosen, which gave the Duke of Cumberland great advantages, especially in his cannon and horse'. This interpretation originates in a dispute between the advocates of Lord George Murray, lieutenant general and veteran of the 'Fifteen and 'Nineteen, and John Sullivan, quartermaster general and adjutant general of the Jacobite forces in the 'Forty-five and a respected French regular.

On 13 April, as it was clear the British Army was approaching, Murray sent Colonel Ker to reconnoitre 'a hollow that reached into the higher ground south of the Nairn-Inverness highway near Dalcross Castle' (OS 4878),[1] 5 kilometres from the final battlefield, where there is a ravine just north of the castle towards Croy. Sullivan advised against this battle site the next day, as the landscape obstacles did not exceed musket range, and would also impede a Jacobite attack; if they are those between the castle and the old chapel site, where there is a plateau on which the Jacobite forces might have been drawn up, they do not exceed 50 metres (Figures 4 and 5).

If the British Army were able to occupy a secure defensive position, their superior firepower could win the day, unless the Jacobites withdrew.

Sullivan's original site at OS 4575 was to the east of the final battle line. Early on the morning of 15 April, Sullivan

drew his army up in order of Battle upon a Spacious moor to the South of Culloden with some park walls to their right, and their left towards the descents that go down to Culloden. Their front was straight East.

Figure 4 A picture of what may be the planned Dalcross Castle site, with the brief ravine visible and a plateau for the disposition of the Jacobite Army beyond.

This position, with the army 'above Culloden House, in a position which effectively covered both roads into Inverness from the east', may have placed the Jacobite forces with their right at Culchunaig where they stood the next day, and their left close to the site of what has been known since Victorian times as the 'Cumberland Stone'. If their right had been much to the north of this, then their left would have been beyond the 'descents' which caused the wings of the army to lose sight of each other the next day. Lord Elcho describes the regiments as lining up roughly as they did the following day, but with some small alterations in the front line and in the dispositions of the forces in reserve.[2]

Murray was not content with this site, and sent Ker and Brigadier Stapleton (perhaps hoping that the senior ranking Irish officer would help his case with the Prince and Sullivan) at 'About Ten o'Clock' to examine a second site, which involved falling back 'across the River Nairn to the formidable heights on the right...near Daviot Castle': the rising

Figure 5 The Dalcross Castle site from the other direction.

land on the other side of Strathnairn from the battle, which itself took place 160 metres above sea level. On the southern bank of the Nairn, the land here rises to 330 metres within 1 kilometre from Nairn bank upwards to Meall Mór (369 metres) (OS 4073). This would have put the battlefield very near Daviot Castle; the slope is gentler further away (e.g. at OS 4374), and this may be a more likely site, as the reconnoitred battle site is described as being 'a Mile farther than the Moor they were upon'.[3]

Figure 6 Strathnairn battle site at Daviot.

This site on the right bank of the Nairn at OS 4073 provided good, open ground for a downhill charge, as at Killiecrankie. However, it presents tactical problems on a major scale (Figures 6 and 7).

Figure 7 Strathnairn battle site at Daviot, second view.

Afforestation makes it difficult to appreciate the condition of the ground in the eighteenth century, but today, despite the extensive number of tree roots, it can be very boggy in spring within 250 metres of the Nairn, seriously impeding a charge. This was the view taken by Ker and Stapleton on their return by 1 p.m., 'that the Ground was rough and rugged, mossy and soft'. The site is also overlooked by high ground on the other side and it would have been impossible for the Jacobite Army either to see the approach of British forces or to contest the road to Inverness. The opposing slope would also have been an ideal location for coehorns firing from 80 metres from above to explode mortar bombs among the forces ranged against them. Coehorns could fire up to 900 metres, so the Jacobite Army would have been well covered by British fire. Whether this or a site closer to the moor was the one chosen, there were clear tactical problems. Ker and Stapleton reported that 'no Horse could be of Use there', but Lord George was nonetheless convinced 'that the other Side of the Water should be the Place for the Army to be drawn up in Line of Battle next Day'.[4]

There were also strategic challenges to any site on the south side of the Nairn, whether at Daviot or closer to Culloden. The first of these was quite simply the problem of securing a decisive engagement which would successfully defend Inverness, the last major burgh held by the Jacobites, and the last source of regular food supply. It was alleged by Lord George Murray that there was food available in Inverness which could have been distributed more effectively, and which would have made the need for immediate battle less pressing. Both the inadequacies of the Daviot or any closer Strathnairn site (which made more sense as a location from which to withdraw south on to higher ground than as a way of withdrawing to Inverness or as a battlefield) and the impossibility of securing Inverness in the face of superior forces and artillery still tend to be overlooked in the long-standing framing of the Rising in terms which focus on the inadequacies of the Prince and his Irish advisers and the unquestioned excellence of Lord George. OS 4374 would have been better than OS 4073, but once again it did not contest the communication routes to Inverness. For all Lord George's protestations about the excellence of the site on the south of the Nairn, he received the response 'that it looked like shunning the Enemy...at a greater Distance from Inverness...a great deal of Ammunition and Baggage being left there'.[5]

Murray's ADC, Captain James Maxwell of Kirkconnell, placed the blame for the food shortage on the Prince's secretary, John Murray of Broughton,[6] though others suggested that John Hay of Restalrig, the other secretary, was the responsible party, and it is sometimes thought that Murray of Broughton's ill health affected provisioning. It is interesting, in the light of the view that there were provisions in Inverness while the army was starving, that Lord George seems to have preferred a battle site which would leave the route to the town open to the British Army.[7] The need to defend Inverness is why the option of a 'defensive action' was unrealistic, the Jacobites having neither artillery sufficient to deter an attack nor the cavalry to destroy units broken by that artillery.[8] Offence was the only option, and at OS 4073 and to a lesser extent OS 4374 there was an opposing slope to climb if the Jacobites did not want their backs to water. If the army formed up on the high ground beyond the river, it was at least 4 kilometres from any road to Inverness: the military road ran north of Croy. These roads could be defended from the Dalcross position, but not nearly so easily from Strathnairn. A British Army column flanked by dragoons could march straight past into the town, out of range of Jacobite musketry and cannon, even if these were in view of the enemy, which they could not be on the south bank of the Nairn by Daviot. It would have been more than unlikely that the British Army would have forded the Nairn to stand with their backs to the water to receive a downhill charge, but that is the only conceivable way in which victory could have been delivered for the Prince's forces at this site. Mackay had been forced to fight with his back to the water at Killiecrankie, but he had been surprised while on the march with no easy means of escape; moreover, he had only a few Scandinavian-style leatherbound guns, firing shot of 1-pound weight or so, and prone to disintegrate under heavy firing. The British Army in 1746 both had far better artillery, including the Coehorn mortars which had prevailed at Glenshiel, and had limited need to fight, although Cumberland did need to ensure troops were returned to the Continent to hold back French advances. The Jacobites were starving and short of money, and a British seizure of Inverness would put paid to the Jacobite Army as a significant force in the field, though substantial units could (and did) subsist in localities for months or even years after the end of the Rising. But two hundred men are a local menace; five thousand are a national threat.

If the British Army fought at all against a Jacobite force on the south of the Nairn, the result might be more like Wightman's at Glenshiel than Dundee's at Killiecrankie. In 1719 a significant if still-small Jacobite army, backed by a battalion of Spanish regulars, had held high ground on both sides of the glen. Wightman's artillery—not least his high-firing and easy-to-transport coehorns—and regular musketry, disposed so they were difficult to overwhelm at once, had continued to cause attrition until the Jacobite ranks frayed and an assault could be made.[9] It is hard to see the Prince's army on the slopes of Strathnairn withstanding steady artillery fire from the other side of the water: if they charged, they would charge uphill against guns (though less so at sites closer to Culloden Moor than Daviot), while the dragoons who would be on the flanks of the British line would destroy the Jacobites from the flank on the wrong side of the river, which they would in any event have to cross. If the Jacobites retreated, the way to Inverness was even clearer than before for Cumberland's forces, and the Jacobites had—as Maxwell observed—neither meal nor magazines. The army would disintegrate and the Rising as a major challenge to the British State would come to an end.[10]

The inevitability of retreat from such a position may have been suspected by some; and Sullivan was not keen on the Strathnairn site. Murray was highly adept at evading British forces and had done so repeatedly: he had also declined to march on London (as of course had many others) or to follow up Falkirk. Drawing up the Jacobites in such a way as to leave the road to Inverness open would invite the British forces to bypass them: Murray would have saved the army for another day, but the days were running out, and the fact that the British Army had pitched their camp across the Inverness road made their immediate objective very plain. Far from simply waiting to be taken prisoner rather than fighting a guerrilla campaign, as was alleged by Murray's party,[11] Sullivan saw the need to ensure that Cumberland was brought to battle. What Murray's favoured site—even according to his own account, it was not recommended by Ker or Stapleton—seemed to offer was the prospect of retreat into the hills for 5,000 starving men, and the inevitable dissolution of the army. A more humane end to the Rising perhaps, but hardly an alternative battle site. Sullivan has been scorned for centuries for choosing a better one.

The site on which the battle was finally fought was to a large extent decided by the lack of time available to the Prince's forces following their abortive night attack on the British camp. Nonetheless, some responsibility must remain with Sullivan for the site chosen, especially when 'snow and hail' started 'falling very thick' on what was probably already sodden ground, which Sullivan had perhaps not had time to check out adequately. Rain supervened by lunchtime, though at 1 p.m.—as battle commenced—the day seems to have grown fair. It should be noted that the judgement on the quality of the ground after rain was a challenging one even for great commanders—overestimating the condition of the ground after rain helped defeat Napoleon at Waterloo—but perhaps the chief adverse effect on the Jacobite Army was that their powder grew damp. As Tomasson and Buist noted fifty years ago, the British Army were now 'using cartridges, which were both quicker to fire and easier to keep dry', although they were still vulnerable to bad weather. At Culloden, the better clad British soldiers kept their cartridges under 'our coat laps' during the rain.[12] Sullivan's view that the enclosures at Culloden House (perhaps up to 1.8 metre high, as were the Culwhiniac walls on the Jacobite right) would protect from a flanking attack was not entirely implausible, but was undermined by the Jacobite Army's inability to protect its flanks, with weak cavalry and a weak reserve.[13]

The night attack, decided on after Elcho reported that the British camp at Nairn was 'quiet...and by all appearance they did not intend to move that day', was to some extent a solution to the unfortunate dilemma facing the Jacobite Army: whether to face the British on open and reasonably level ground to deny them the road to Inverness and risk their inferior numbers against Cumberland, or whether to take the high ground and run the risk of being bypassed, with the likelihood of disintegration to follow. They were in good spirits: the Duke of Perth had addressed each different corps on 15 April in preparation for the battle.[14] Still, attacking at night across country was nearly always a desperate venture; moreover, the Jacobite Army was without Keppoch's, Cluny's, Glengyle's, and most of Cromartie's regiments, while 'many of the recruits of Glengary and other regiments' had not yet come up, and others were going to Inverness to get provisions.[15] If the Jacobites were not successful in pressing their attack, they would have had little time for sleep and the disposition of their forces if Cumberland pressed on in the morning. So it proved.

The British Army were 'at Balblair on the outskirts of Nairn', some 10 kilometres away, with the cavalry beyond the Nairn river at Auldearn, 3 kilometres further off. The Jacobite forces divided into two columns to press their attack, with four brigades under Charles Edward, the Duke of Perth, Lord John Drummond, and Lord George Murray, moving along 'the axes of the present B9006 and B9091'. They had to delay marching as they would be in view of the Royal Navy until darkness fell: the tightening naval blockade in the Moray Firth, carrying 120,000 musket rounds (half of what Cumberland carried) and 640 shot and associated charges for field guns (half as much again as Cumberland), could easily see elements of Jacobite Army movement, as the land sloped steeply up from the Firth. On the 150-metre contour, the army was only 3 kilometres inland (Figure 8).

The night attack may have been further delayed by soldiers going off to search for food. Murray was to attack Auldearn from the south-east on the right bank of the Nairn, while Perth and Drummond's brigades made a frontal assault from the west. Both, led by Mackintosh officers and men from this Strathnairn country as guides, marched through Kilravock wood before separating, but in the dark soldiers began to get lost in the trees. The columns, originally 1.5 kilometres long, now separated: the regulars began to lag behind the more locally raised forces. Communication between them appears to have been very weak. At 2 a.m., Murray was still 6 kilometres away from Cumberland. He ordered a retreat, but Perth's men—ignorant of the fact—pressed on and almost reached the British forces. Some historians—including Christopher Duffy— think that an assault might have prevailed at this point, but most do not: there were perhaps only 1,200 men with Perth. Even so, Lord George would have had to have marched with the rest of the force and attacked from the west. Dividing the army into two columns was just too complex an additional risk to add to the mix in darkness, woodland, rough ground, and rain.[16]

Figure 8 Field of Culloden, showing how visible the Jacobite Army was to the Royal Navy in the Moray Firth.

Wearied by the abortive night march, the Jacobite Army returned to the environs of Culloden House, and their officers lay down there to sleep, while many went off in search of food; morale was low, and some in the army were reflecting on their leaders, up to and including the Prince. Squabbling over who was to blame for the failure of the night attack broke out between the Prince, Lord George Murray, and Colonel Cameron of Lochiel, while the Marquis d'Eguilles, the emissary of the French court, seems to have tried to persuade Charles Edward to fall back on the ground to the south of the Nairn or to retire to Inverness itself, and buy himself a little time by using his artillery to deter an advance.[17] Both courses were superficially appealing, but both had their serious difficulties: the first would, as we have seen, involve abandoning Inverness and all the army's remaining stores and provisions, while the defence of a town was at odds with the dynamic strength in mobility of the Jacobite Army, and would most likely lead to a severe—if delayed—defeat. Keppoch and Lochiel both declared against giving battle, but the die was rapidly cast. A guerrilla campaign was impractical without a secure base and supply lines, and the fact that 'any Proposition to postpone Fighting, was ill received' by Charles Edward was because there were no practical alternatives. Murray's Strathnairn site(s) were utterly impractical, and at least Sullivan's plan blocked access to the last major Jacobite base with a harbour. The battle site on which Culloden was fought was by no means the worst that had been reconnoitred, and it was in any case soon to be the only option available, given its contiguity to the command centre of the scattered and exhausted army at Culloden House. A cavalry patrol came in before 9 a.m. with news that the British Army was only 6 kilometres away, and this was confirmed 'by a Cameron officer, who had fallen asleep in Kilravock wood', almost 8 kilometres north of the Jacobite Army. When this information came in, only two or three battalions were ready for battle. There was no time for further discussion, or for the rewriting of battle orders. Cromartie's, MacGregor's, Macpherson's, one of the MacDonald, and two of the Fraser battalions were all in the north or south-east. Six battalions short, the exhausted Jacobites stood to arms. Some who slept through the battle only awakened to their deaths at the hands of the British forces afterwards. As Cumberland's men approached, it began to rain heavily.[18]

John Sullivan had, as at Falkirk, effective operational command. He drew up the army over 1 kilometre closer to Inverness than they had stood the day before, when a morass had covered their left: the position of the exhausted men and the command centre at Culloden House may have dictated this slight shift. The army faced north-east over common grazing land for the 'surrounding farms'.[19] On their right was the water of Nairn, up to 1,000 metres beyond their initial flank; on their left the Culloden Parks, around (given emerging evidence) 1,200 metres from the right at Culchunaig. The Jacobites did not break down the Culloden Park enclosures, as that would have disrupted the advance of the front line, on which they were heavily reliant. The Jacobite Army then formed into three lines, at a slant where the left of the hastily assembled front line lay initially 200–500 metres behind the right. There was little time to reconnoitre the ground in the morning, and so the 'boggy nature of the slight hollow' that the left of the army would have to cross in the event of an attack was missed, although an alternative view is that Sullivan thought it would impede British cavalry. Thus disposed, *L'Armée Ecossoise* awaited *L'Armée Angloise* as a contemporary cartographer put it (Map 2). It is important to note that in French eyes (as in the eyes of memoirists like James Johnstone), this was a battle between Scotland and England/Britain: this was certainly one of its dimensions and, as I will discuss later, the need to deny this is itself political.[20]

The battlefield as it is now presented by the National Trust for Scotland (NTS) covers a smaller footprint than it did for the

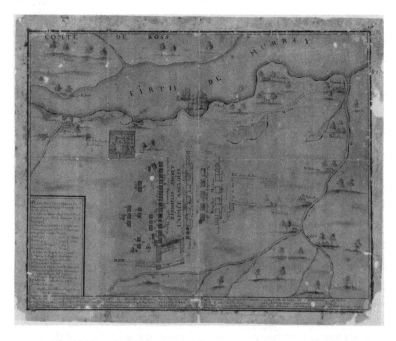

Map 2 French map of Culloden (1748), showing the battle as a national conflict. The Jacobite formation is too straight and regular, though the scattered nature of the second line is captured well.

combatants, and has the effect, as Tony Pollard has observed, of marginalizing the cavalry action (the current audiovisual display shows no cavalry whatsoever). It also marginalizes the second line's rearguard action; inevitably, the interpretation of the site has to an extent been driven by the area owned by the Trust which can be visited. The Jacobite line as marked on the field, although it has been moved recently, is about 100 metres or more too far to the east, being marked right on the boundary of NTS property. The British left has also been moved, but was still arguably beyond the marker for Barrell's on the current battle-field.[21] The Jacobite right stretched to Culchunaig by Culwhiniac Parks, with drystane dyked infields and open runrig land, a position which was 'difficult to outflank'. There was a farmhouse within the Culwhiniac enclosures, which were (and are still) good land, in agricultural use. At least one of the fields that dropped down to the Nairn was under cultivation at the time of the battle. Here,

> enclosures stretched (and still do stretch) all the way down to the water of Nairn, while forward of these particular stone walls a horseshoe-shaped turf-walled enclosure also bulged out onto the moor beside the farm of Leanach.[22]

Leanach Cottage, inhabited until 1912, has traditionally been supposed to have lain ahead of the Jacobite right; *lèanach* in Gaelic means marshy or sodden underfoot, so the name the cottage now bears may be a self-fulfilling prophecy of the outcome of the battle. A track from Inverness seems to have cut south-east across the moor in front of the Leanach enclosures and Barrell's regiment on the British left may have stood on it. Almost certainly there was nothing like the current building at Leanach, but a cluster of buildings, including a cottage termed 'ruinous' in 1868 which 'probably' forms the basis of the current structure. The 1994 NTS claim, that the cottage 'survived the battle being fought around it', is more romance than history, however, and has since been abandoned. The walls at Culloden Parks, Culwhiniac, and Leanach were all removed in the nineteenth century. Sullivan's position was vulnerable given British numerical superiority and the lack of Jacobite cavalry and reserves but, as the Sandhurst historian Christopher Duffy notes, it had 'tactical potential...if exploited properly'.[23]

If this was the case, the Jacobite right at the small settlement of Culchunaig (possibly slightly further from the Culwhiniac walls than is now the case) faced Barrell's at Leanach about 500 metres away, while the left at the Mains of Culloden Parks was at first up to 1,000 metres from the British front line, though this distance closed up before battle was joined. The whole line stood around 160 metres above sea level at the highest point, though on a slight slope. The field was mildly convex, the ground being 'lower and wetter' ahead of the left on the whole, with a boggy hollow ahead of the right at Culchunaig, which appears not to have been fully reconnoitred before the battle. Part of the right may have been barely able to see the British lines properly. In truth, however, anyone familiar with Scottish rainfall levels and drainage should have been able to guess that a convex site might drain to boggy ground at the extremes of left and right, which would impede the speed of a charge and its ability to roll up the enemy flank. In addition, since fertile land abutted on Culchunaig, it is likely that to the extent that the farmland was well drained, the land adjacent to it would be correspondingly wetter. The whole left of the line was both more distant and more exposed to British fire; the centre stood on the ridge of the old road, again slightly exposed, though it offered shelter to those behind it, and a route of attack for the centre and right. The further right lay beyond. The left and right could not see each other perfectly as they moved forward (Figures 9 and 10).[24]

Figure 9 The Jacobite right at Culchunaig. The left would not have been visible from here.

Figure 10 Culloden Moor, actual position of Jacobite centre right, taken at the beginning of spring. Poor ground is evident.

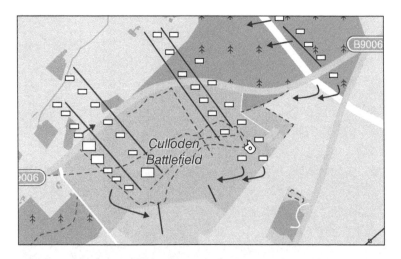

Map 3 The first phase of the battle. Kingston's Horse moves to support the British front, together with two third-line battalions. Shielded by walls at Culchunaig, the Atholl Brigade on the right form into column (shown by an expanded box, as with Iain Ruadh's and Lord Lewis Gordon's in the second line) as Ballimore's and the dragoons move to probe the defences on the right, with two battalions of Lord Lewis Gordon's detached to cover the threat, reinforced by a cavalry screen with support from Ogilvy's, moving right of the Culchunaig enclosure. Glenbuchat's in the Jacobite second line is being moved into the front line. The area marked 'Culloden Battlefield' is that in the care of the National Trust for Scotland.

On the left stood MacDonell of Glengarry's 1st and 2nd battalions, whose front-line firepower at Falkirk had been so effective. Their operational strength was barely above 500 men (their peak had been 1,200, and 'many of the [new] recruits' had not yet come up). Beside them stood MacDonald of Keppoch's regiment and Clanranald's, with some 400 men between them, with two 3-pounders screening Clanranald's and the 80–100-strong Chisholm company beside them. (There remains some debate as to the calibre of the Jacobite guns: the balance of evidence appears to be that the Jacobite gunners opened with 3-pounders and a solitary 4-pounder was brought up later.) All three MacDonald regiments had demonstrated the power of musketry at close quarters in

Falkirk only three months earlier. There was some bad feeling over the positioning of the MacDonalds on the left, but it has become mythologized.[25]

To the left of the centre of the front line were the remnant of Cromartie's regiment, most of whom were absent in an attempt to rendezvous with French supplies in Sutherland, and MacLean and MacLachlan's men: about 200–300 in all. In the centre itself, screened by three (or possibly five) 3-pounders, stood Monaltrie's and Balmoral's battalions, perhaps as few as 150–200, though up to 600–700 are reported in some sources,[26] and 350–700 of Mackintosh's regiment under Lieutenant Colonel Alexander MacGillivray. Beyond them on the right were one battalion of Fraser of Lovat's regiment, no more than 500–800 men under Fraser of Inverallochy, and Stewart of Ardsheal's regiment, 150–250 strong and behind two more 3-pounders. On the furthest right stood the two battalions of Lochiel's, another 600–700 men, and 400–600 of the Atholl Brigade's 2nd and 3rd battalions, screened by (probably but not certainly) four more guns. (It has been suggested that these troops were asleep near Culloden House, but this would have been a long way to come quickly if so—not least if there were only 1,000 men 'ready to take the field' when the alarm was sounded.) The Jacobite line presented a frontage of around 1,100 metres, with between eleven and thirteen guns (eleven according to Thomas Sandby's depiction, and probably the thirteenth is the 4-pounder brought up by Captain du Saussey after the battle began). Some depictions give the Jacobites only nine guns, which is the number Elcho reports on the fifteenth, and Wolfe thought that their 'very extended thick line' had only four. The Jacobite soldiers were probably 'drawn up 4 deep in accordance with French tactical doctrine', with 1 metre per file. If this was the case, there were either 3,600–4,400 men (the totals above allow for a range of 3,230–5,000) or (more likely) gaps in the front line to allow for the 1,100 or so metres between the flanking shelters of 'the Culwhiniac and Culloden park walls'. These latter were, as stated above, about 1.8 metres in height, but some may have been 'deliberately destroyed' to allow firing space for the Jacobite cannon. Grante's Artillery, composed of two companies of Perth's as gunners with an additional pioneer company, together with twelve French gunners and two artillery officers, had left many of its guns in the localities. Grante had been wounded at Fort William and the Jacobite gunners were—if not incompetents—not as well drilled or trained as their Royal Artillery opponents. Maxwell (who puts only six to eight cannon in the front line at the start of the battle) notes that the 'cannoneers...on the left could not be found', and that therefore raw volunteers manned the Jacobite guns at Culloden Parks, at the greatest distance from the British Army. These could not have been very effective.[27]

Almost all the strongest units stood in the Prince's front line. If the initial frontal attack should fail or only partially succeed, there was little in the way of reinforcements to deploy. In the event, however, second-line Jacobite strength proved crucial to saving many lives and enabling a phased withdrawal from the field.

In the second line, commanded by Brigadier Stapleton, stood the Perthshire Horse (seventy, though the practical total for all three units may have been only this) and Bagot's Hussars (twenty-six), possibly together with around a dozen of Balmerino's Life Guards on the far left. This small cavalry force therefore stood slightly apart from the rest of the line, and were almost the only units which could be rapidly deployed over the distance which separated the armies, which was initially up to 1,100 metres. With the 40 kilometre/hour gallop rarely being used by the eighteenth-century cavalry arm, these troops might be as much as four to five minutes away from the British front line: the trot was 15 kilometres/hour.[28] Sometimes the cavalry are portrayed as being in the third line, but they constituted a mobile flanking force rather than a reserve. Many of the cavalry had lost their mounts owing to the difficulties of the prolonged retreat, and had either been integrated into the infantry and had their remaining mounts cannibalized for other units (as with the Earl of Kilmarnock's Grenadier Troop) or had disintegrated altogether. The 1st Squadron of Fitzjames's Horse, on the far right of the second line together with Elcho's Life Guards, had the remainder of Kilmarnock's horses; the other three squadrons of

Fitzjames's had been captured, depriving the Jacobite Army of over 300 quality horse. It is possible that a third troop had been added to the squadron at Culloden, from the remaining elements of surviving cavalry units; in this case up to 165 cavalry troopers may have been stationed on the right, though it is fairly clear that some sixty-five of the 131 of Fitzjames's lacked horses and were thus likely to have stood with the picquets; numbers of cavalry on the right have been put as low as between forty and seventy.[29]

Between the two flanking horse squadrons stood the Irish picquets, now around 260–300 men, on the left (though Maxwell puts them more towards the centre, with Stoneywood's and Bannerman's battalions from Lord Lewis Gordon's command on the left). The picquets had the 1st Battalion of the Duke of Perth's regiment beside them, up to 900 including dismounted men from Fitzjames's, Glenbuchat's (200–300), and Kilmarnock's Foot Guards under Crichton of Auchengoul, Viscount Frendraught (200–300). At the centre of the second line were Iain Ruadh Stiùbhart (John Roy Stewart's) Edinburgh Regiment, perhaps now no more than the same strength (200–300), and to their right Ogilvie's 1st and 2nd battalions, some 350–500 men now that many had returned home or were otherwise active in the localities. Further right were the 1st and 3rd battalions of Lord Lewis Gordon's (450–500 at most); Frendraught's 2nd Battalion had probably been absorbed by this stage into Kilmarnock's. Beyond them, the 1st and 2nd battalions of the *Royal-Écossais* (Royal Scots—another 350) ensured that French regulars flanked both wings of the second line (again, Maxwell appears to place the *Royal-Écossais* more centrally and sees Ogilvy's and Avochie's command in Lord Gordon's to the right). Behind (although it seems to have moved from the front of the front centre of the second line to the rear when the Atholl Brigade moved into column before the battle) was Charles Edward's command post, with a detachment of about sixteen cavalry from Fitzjames's (or Balmerino's) surrounding the Prince, under the command of Colonel Robert O'Shea; it was not entirely out of range as Johnstone alleges, though it may have been for coehorns and the lighter cannon. Bannerman's regiment is depicted on the wings in some contemporary accounts,[30] the survivors of this never particularly large territorial unit from the Mearns being now either within Lord Lewis Gordon's command or incorporated into Kilmarnock's Foot Guards. The Jacobite second line was 2,386–3,139 men, and it is more than likely that many of these units were effectively below strength as men were absent on the day. Many of them may have stood as far as 800 metres back from the first line, and Lord Elcho certainly thought the second line had a divided and straggling appearance, as do some of the surviving plans of the battle. The lie of the land was also concealed by the distance, which made it harder for the Prince's command post to judge how the front rank was faring. Nonetheless, they had some potential, for the centre, round Iain Ruadh Stiùbhart, was in column, 'with a frontage of one to two companies', 'in order to act as mobile reserves, in accordance with French tactical doctrine'. Clearly, Jacobite drill now allowed for the possibility of deploying from column by single or paired companies. The combination of line and column and the distance of the second from the front line, combined with its low numbers, may have given it its ragged appearance.[31]

Colonel Ker was sent out to reconnoitre, and reported the British Army on the march from Nairn, in three columns 'with their cavalry on their left, so that they could form their line of battle in an instant'. According to the account in the *Gentleman's Magazine*, the British Army had set off in three infantry columns of five battalions each, with the artillery/baggage train in the rear and the cavalry flanking. Artillery and baggage followed the first column, while the fourth column of cavalry rode to the left, initially across fields, and the main army with the artillery took the road to Inverness until it veered off south-west to face the Jacobites, at which stage the condition of the ground worsened and progress became much slower. On arriving on the field of battle, the British forces noted the Jacobite Army 'behind some old walls and huts, in a line with *Culloden House*'.[32]

Cumberland had been informed by a Kingston's Horse picquet and skirmishers that the Jacobites were forming battle lines on Drummossie Moor. Taking care not to come too close in column,

Cumberland 'formed ... line at a great distance, and marched in battle-order' till within cannon shot. His men's morale was high and he encouraged them effectively, offering 'free pardon to any [British] soldier who quit before the fight'; his columns re-formed as line with a steady movement. The Jacobites could see them from 'about 12 o'clock' 4 kilometres away, and line was formed at 3 kilometres, far too distant for small cannon. In the broad daylight of 10–11 a.m., the sight of the British Army marching forward in full battle order and still out of range must have been intimidating, most particularly with '225 kettle-drums' beating and the Campbell pipes skirling. By contrast, the silence and gloom of the Jacobite Army was remarked on, although other accounts stress huzzas on both sides or British Army silence. It is possible at this stage that the Jacobite cannon were not fully in position, as it was difficult to move them 'for want of horses': in the end, two had to be left behind at Culloden House. The rest—possibly flanked by 'gabions—large cylindrical wicker baskets filled with earth' which, like sandbags, defended against light artillery fire—were moved up (with one exception) to the front line by the time that Cumberland's forces arrayed their artillery. The British Army moved its guns up to the front through the ranks once it was within 500 metres' range.[33]

Facing the Jacobite left, on the far side of the government right were the Royals under Lieutenant Colonel John Ramsay, with a strength of 401 (481 officially), with two guns to the front. Cumberland's command post lay between this and the second line, as he imagined 'the greatest Push would be there', as the Gentleman's Magazine put it. The 'Cumberland stone', placing him 800 metres behind his front line, is—he is alleged to have stood on it during the battle—a mute and unjustified implication of cowardice, as the historian Bill Speck observes. Cumberland was a brave commander, and there is some higher ground towards the British right which might in any case have made a better command post. Both Campbell's 21st (regimental numbers did not finally take precedence over the colonel's names until the 1750s) under Major Charles Colvill, and Cholmondeley's 34th under Lieutenant Colonel Charles Jeffreys with 399 (459 officially) and two guns stood inside the Royals, with Price's (304 (359 officially)) under Lieutenant Colonel Edward Gray and the Scots Fuziliers (358 (412 officially)) behind four guns at the centre. On the left, facing the Jacobite right, were Monro's 37th (426 (491 officially)) with two guns under Lieutenant Colonel William Deane and Barrell's 4th (325 (373 officially)), under Lieutenant Colonel Sir Robert Rich. William Keppel, Earl of Albemarle commanded the front line, with Lord Sempill as brigadier. The guns which stood between or between and forward of each battalion were two Royal Artillery 3-pounders, ten in all.

Stretching over an 1,100-metre front, the Jacobite front line initially had eleven or twelve 3-pounders (with just possibly some 1½- and 4-pounders in their number) facing ten 3-pounders on the British front (though again some sources give the British twelve guns). The Jacobite right outgunned the British left by six to two; Charles Edward was outgunned on the left. Jacobite troops may have outnumbered the opposing front line almost two to one, and certainly three to two, with a preponderance on the Jacobite right, which had the better ground.[34]

The Jacobite Army relied on its front line to carry the day, and that meant breaking the British formations and driving them off the field. As Maxwell put it:

> a general shock of the whole line at once…had that happened, it is more than probable that the first line of the enemy would have been routed, whatever might have been the consequences afterwards.[35]

The Jacobite second line contained good soldiers, but only the French regulars and Lord Lewis Gordon's had seen much action, although Iain Ruadh was an experienced regular officer, with a significant number of British Army deserters in his regiment. The line was also weak: despite its organization in column, the need to reinforce the battlefront as the conflict progressed meant that only the Royal-Écossais and Kilmarnock's Foot Guards were intact units as the British Army advanced.[36] The effective cavalry force on the flanks was barely more than 150–200 horse with mounts—far below the maximum cavalry muster of the

army, which could now barely feed its men, never mind its horses—
while the loss of mounts had also severely eroded the Jacobite artillery
train over the winter months. The cavalry could only realistically be
deployed to effect to drive broken formations off the field in a rout
achieved by the front-line battalions. Although it stood on the flanks of
the army, it was inadequate for attacking the flanks of the British forces
opposite unless they were already in chaos. Since cavalry are hardly an
effective defensive arm, the Jacobite horse were to all intents and purposes useless unless the government formations were destroyed by the
front line. Everything rested on them.

Charles Edward's army thus already stood exposed to critical risks:
there was only a limited effective reserve and no Plan B. But matters did
not end there, for the British second line, under Major General John
Huske, was as strong as the first, and moreover the second-line regiments were disposed to cover the interval between the first-line ones,
ensuring covering fire in the event of a Jacobite breakthrough.[37] On the
right were Howard's 3rd, the Buffs under Major Gerard Elrington or
Lieutenant Colonel Sir George Howard with 413 (464 officially), then
Fleming's 36th under Lieutenant Colonel George Jackson with 350 men
(full strength 415) and three coehorn mortars ahead of them, then
Bligh's 20th under Lieutenant Colonel Edward Cornwallis. Sempill's
25th (Edinburgh) under Lieutenant Colonel Sir David Cunynghame
with three more coehorns stood in the centre (officially 477), and
Ligonier's 59th under Lieutenant Colonel George Stanhope and Wolfe's
8th with 650 (official full strength 758–60) on the left, with the former's
regiment screened by the Leanach enclosures, forming a further obstacle to the Jacobite right. Some 50 metres divided the two lines, which
were drawn up much more strongly and densely than their Jacobite
opponents. In the event, the ability of the British second line to give fire
at effective musket range when the first was broken was to prove significant if not crucial.

The coehorns, with 116 artillerymen under Captain Lieutenant John
Godwin, standing in for Lieutenant Colonel William Belford who was
the Royal Artillery commanding officer, were thus concealed from the

Jacobite Army, which by contrast, had set out its stall with the transparent aim of carrying the battle by the first assault. With their high trajectory, the coehorn mortars could fire from the second line over the heads of the first, bombarding the Jacobite advance with mortar bombs. This is exactly what happened.

Beyond his second line, Cumberland had deployed a third line of Pulteney's 13th under Lieutenant Colonel Thomas Cockayne (probably 410 on the field (474 officially), Batterau's 62nd (354 (423 officially)), and Blakeney's 27th Inniskilling under Lieutenant Colonel Francis Leighton (c.300 (356 officially)). Lieutenant Colonel John Mordaunt was the brigadier (at this stage always a temporary rank) in command of this reserve of just over 1,000 men (1,253 full strength), with Kingston's Light Horse, round about 200 men (211 full roll), flanking on each side: these were to be brought up during the action. On the far left of the British forces stood a largely mobile reserve of perhaps 200 (though 140 was quoted in the *Gentleman's Magazine*) Argyll militia in four companies under Lieutenant Colonel John Campbell, together with three of the 64th and one of the 43rd. This was the Black Watch, renumbered as the 42nd in 1748. They had another 200–300 men, though there is some doubt here, as the *Gentleman's Magazine* noted that 'all our Highlanders were left to guard the baggage' except the 140 with Ballimore, and indeed the Black Watch had not been viewed as reliable on the Jacobite march south, in part because of their mutiny in 1743. A force of Cobham's 10th (effective 185 (full strength 276)) and Ker's 11th dragoons (full strength 300) under Major Peter Chaban and Lieutenant Colonel William Lord Ancrum respectively were with them (though a company of the 64th and the militia 'fell back to the rear'). The dragoons presented a cavalry concentration sizeable enough to hit the Jacobite right flank or lead the pursuit of a broken army, which is in fact what they did. Initially briefed to guard the baggage, this force—in combination with John Campbell's command—has traditionally been seen, from the first account in the *Gentleman's Magazine* onwards, as the most effective in securing victory, through a successful flanking action achieved by breaking down the Culwhiniac walls, which were lined by Lord Lewis Gordon's men in the run-up to the battle.[38] Sullivan had suggested that some of the huts could be used for concealed firing. In fact, Ballimore's could fire at the Jacobite right as it advanced, though the effectiveness of this may have been exaggerated.[39]

The British Army contained Scottish units numbering about 1,700–1,800 men: it has always been tendentious to say that more Scots fought against the Jacobites than for them at Culloden. The majority of these stood in the front line, possibly for reasons of historical contestation (Munros against Cromartie's Mackenzies) or simply on the principle of set a thief to catch a thief, which Wolfe and his commanders would put to good use in Canada a dozen years later.

By contrast with the Jacobites, the British Army's units had far more recent combat experience. Although Pulteney's had fled at Falkirk, they had been in Flanders since 1742, and had fought at Dettingen (where their 'rolling fire was so hellish') and Fontenoy. Cumberland had also practised extensive drilling at Aberdeen, holding courts martial and enforcing strict army discipline. Moreover, Commodore Smith's ships were in the Moray Firth, denying the possibility of further French support or seaborne escape.[40]

As Cumberland's forces formed line of battle, it was clear that the right was vulnerable, as 'When we were advanced within 500 yards … we found the morass upon our right was ended, which left our right Flank quite uncovered to them'.[41] Alert to the risk, Cumberland moved up the two squadrons (c.200) of Kingston's Light Horse on the right from the third- to the first-line flank, brought across a squadron of Cobham's 10th Dragoons (90) from reconnaissance as reinforcement, and moved Pulteney's—and later Batterau's—up from the reserve to extend the front lines. The government right was now reinforced at once by 600, and eventually by 1,000 men, more than a quarter of them cavalry, and stood far less chance of being overwhelmed. Cumberland appears to have manouevred along his front to try and outflank the Jacobites unsuccessfully for about 'half an Hour'. During this time, the Atholl Brigade and Lochiel's expressed concern regarding the possibility of being flanked on their right, and two battalions of Lord Lewis Gordon's moved to cover the wall of the Culwhiniac enclosures, which limited the potential of an attack from that quarter, but did not dispel it, as Cobham's and Kerr's dragoons had begun probing with Ballimore's men. Murray seems to have been reluctant to allow Stoneywood's and Avochie's battalions to flank Culwhiniac fully (he was possibly already concerned with the prospect of flanking from the low ground by Culloden Parks, given the growing strength of the British right), but they formed in a hollow and on a crest on the right with a company of Ogilvy's and some of Fitzjames's and Elcho's Life Guards from that flank to repel flanking

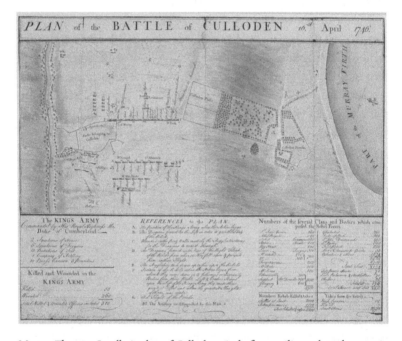

Map 4 Thomas Sandby's plan of Culloden. As befits a military draughtsman in the Ordnance Office, who was probably on Cumberland's staff at the time of the battle (he formally became Cumberland's draughtsman in 1750), it is more precise than the maps already shown. The enclosures protecting the Jacobite wings are clearly visible and delineated, as is the old road crossing the moor and the proximity of the Royal Navy. Cumberland has used his third line to reinforce his forward positions, and has extended his right.

by the dragoons, forming over a 100-metre front. Hawley's dragoons (under Bland's command, who may have had responsibility for the movement) moved to a wider 500-metre front, threatening (though too weak to perform) an envelopment on the Jacobite right, and deterred by the very visible forces on the crest whom they could not see past. It is alleged in Colonel Sullivan's narrative of events that Lord George was at this stage given an order to attack the British right, which he declined to do, but controversy surrounds this allegation. Murray certainly moved some of the right into column in preparation for an attack and to evade the obstacle of the Leanach enclosures ahead of Barrell's 4th, thus opening gaps in the line. In response to Cumberland's probing, the Jacobite forces also moved Perth's and Glenbuchat's to reinforce their left, while Iain Ruadh's Edinburgh Regiment moved up to the centre right of the front line to compensate for the right's move into column. Now, more than ever, hopes of victory rested on the Jacobite front line carrying the day: their reserve was now utterly inadequate.[42]

Unable to gain a compelling advantage through manoeuvre, just after 1 p.m. Cumberland sent forward Lord Bury (reputedly the target of an assassination attempt by a claimed Jacobite deserter) to within 100 metres of the Jacobite front to ascertain the strength of their battery (*Gentleman's Magazine*). This began the battle and the 'weather grew fair' almost immediately, as the three guns at the Jacobite centre opened fire with two successive volleys (though at least one account claims the government fired first, and there may have been small-arms fire almost simultaneously, as Hawley's dragoons moved to flank the Jacobite right and take them in the rear). Grante's Artillery had ceased to be an effective unit, and it seems that the cannon on the left at least were operated by rank and file from the centre regiments who were untrained and hence inaccurate, although some of the dragoons to Cumberland's left—probably Cobham's and/or Ker's—seem to have suffered casualties from the Jacobite right's artillery fire. The battery on the Jacobite left, ordered to fire at Cumberland's own position, did however score some near misses, including damage to his hat and the deaths of nearby dragoons.[43]

Despite these risks, Cumberland moved forward his front line with their paired cannon, and opened fire at what may have been less than 400 metres, and no more than 500 metres, from the Jacobite right and 600–700 metres from the left. The British left stood 'a little way short' of what is now the Well of the Dead, where Lieutenant Colonel Alexander MacGillivray died and where many on the Jacobite right no doubt were either killed in the attack or took brief and futile shelter until the British forces moved forward in the second phase of the battle. For its part, the Royal Artillery did not fare particularly well, as 'many shots went over the head of the Prince's army', though Wolfe notes that the British volley had a disordering effect. The shots that hit the front rank damaged morale as well as killing men, not least because trained gun crews firing cannon of consistent calibre well supplied could heavily outfire the Jacobites. But the key development was the command given for two guns to fire at the Royal Standard, which killed at least one groom and which may have been responsible for delaying the order to advance, as at least one and possibly two of the Prince's couriers had the misfortune to be killed by cannonballs on their way to the front line. Andrew Henderson places one of these deaths later, suggesting that it delayed 'orders to the left wing to wheel to the right': this was at any time a complex manoeuvre. The Jacobite centre guns were subsequently silenced, and the Prince and his escort may have taken cover in the small gap between Culwhiniac and the flanking battalions of Lord Lewis Gordon's during the rest of the bombardment. The artillery exchange lasted for about nine minutes or so—just possibly a little longer, though some authorities (such as John Home) suggest incredible times of almost an hour. Some 30–90 rounds were fired from the British Army's front-line cannon, which then at about 1.10 p.m. began to open fire with grape and canister shot: the former might be a bag of scrap iron, the latter a tin or double tin of musket balls (double canister). Based on evidence from the Seven Years War of 1756–63, only about 2 per cent of canister wounds were treatable: it was a murderous weapon. Lying down under this barrage would not have helped: coehorn shells burst in the air, and would have rained down shrapnel. By this stage, although the rain had lifted from the battlefield, the wind was against the Jacobites, and blew the heavy pall of musket smoke towards them.[44]

At this stage, official government accounts (which claimed that the Jacobite Army did not actually make contact with the British right, and that the Jacobite left damaged Barrell's before being driven off by 'Bayonets and Spontoons' only after it had already been flanked) become rather over-optimistic. One of the key areas of such optimism is the *canard* of the new bayonet drill, 'evolved by Barrel's officers' and 'introduced by Cumberland', which recommended each man to bayonet the Jacobite to his right, where the point could not be parried and 'whose upraised sword-arm left his right side temporarily exposed'. Although the new drill seems to have been good for morale when it was practised in Aberdeen, there is no secure evidence that it was of use at Culloden: indeed, Barrell's was one of the few British regiments to break on the field, though one British officer claimed the drill was effective in halting the Jacobite breakthrough at the second line. Most of the evidence of the British second line's effectiveness is with musketry, not the bayonet.[45]

The Jacobite front line was unable to coordinate a simultaneous charge. The order to Lieutenant General Lord George Murray on the right was delayed owing to the decapitation of Charles Edward's messenger, while the order from the Prince by Colonel Ker to the Duke of Perth, lieutenant general on the left wing, to charge the reinforced right over 600 metres of ground, got through; it was intended (as Ker noted subsequently) to be delivered slightly earlier in any case, to correct the slant of the line.[46] Sir John MacDonald was then sent to reinforce Ker's order, while Brigadier Stapleton got through to Lord George to request the right to move. Perth advanced—allegedly with the MacDonalds proving reluctant, because they were not posted on the right (but more likely because they were fearful of flanking by Cumberland's reinforced right or had by now noticed the poor quality of the ground ahead of them)—between 1.11 and 1.15 p.m., but what happened next remains controversial. Government sources claim that the Jacobite left advanced more slowly over boggy ground and, finding rapid advance difficult, began to fire at long range in the hope of breaking the British Army on the right, but without success.

Maxwell suggests that the left were simply slower, and had only got halfway to the British front by the time the right had closed. Henderson suggests a further order to get the left to wheel right, and also suggests that the left lingered, with Lord John Drummond walking across its front to tempt the British hatmen to fire: they were in fact under orders to hold fire to 30 yards (27 metres), though there is no evidence known to me of range markers being planted. It was also possible that canister from the central British battery forced the Jacobites to the right, although the road that ran across the moor (shown in Map 5) may in any case have funnelled troops towards the right in a development which could have been interpreted as 'orders to the left wing to wheel to the right' by Henderson.[47] The *Gentleman's Magazine* account notes that the very reason why Cumberland's army reinforced its right was to counter the threat from the Jacobite left which was recognized as pressing precisely because the ground in front of the British soldiers was no longer boggy; the ground ahead of the Jacobites was around 20 metres lower, however, and rain may well have made it treacherous. Clanranald's and Glengarry's came under heavy fire, while Keppoch's was broken by volleys of grape and canister from the artillery on the government right. Under such fire, it seems that the MacDonald regiments rushed at the British forces and backed off several times: they may have been, as Stuart Reid suggests, wary of advancing and exposing their flanks to the reinforced flanking British dragoons. At 300 metres or less, up to 4–6 rounds of canister could be fired in the remaining ninety seconds to contact, and advancing and retreating before advancing again only compounded this risk. Monaltrie's and Balmoral's Aberdeenshire men in the centre of the front line seem to have got through against the government right, but their numbers were too few to be effective.[48]

On the Jacobite right, the centre had already broken forward by the time that the Atholl Brigade and both battalions of Lochiel's advanced over what was now (since Cumberland's last advance) 400 metres, supported by Ardsheal's. Within half this distance, the force of fire at canister range pushed the crack Cameron troops to veer right under pressure from the Mackintosh and Fraser units trying to avoid the line of fire. Lochiel, the Cameron colonel, was hit by grape in both ankles at 10–50 metres from the British front line, while Lieutenant Colonel Archibald Cameron, his brother and second in command, received a flesh wound from a British musket. By this time, the coehorns were firing into the advancing Jacobites in a hail of artillery and small arms fire that lasted around eight to nine minutes (Wolfe's figure) until 1.20–1.25 p.m. Maxwell notes that a battery on the British left was advanced and was particularly effective with its grapeshot, while the Jacobite volley at 50 metres was inadequate as their right was under so much pressure. As the Jacobites closed, 1,000–1,500 muskets on the British left gave two effective volleys (Land Pattern muskets were 10 per cent effective at 50 metres, though even at 60 metres only 3 per cent of shots caused vital injuries), firing up and down the line as the Jacobite forces halted to fire and charged. At this stage the Jacobites were officially up to 2,000–2,500 strong, but were probably only half that strength given the distortion of the line (and around 200 were casualties to ball, canister, or grape, plus some more in the original bombardment). Despite being slower at loading (a process not helped by having so many guns charged with loose powder not cartridges), the Jacobites were probably better shots, relying on targeting rather than weight of firepower. Munro's and Barrell's—despite both their cannon firing cartridge shot at point-blank range—were broken by Jacobite firepower followed by a frontal attack which breached the line of the British left.[49] Cumberland, 'constantly on the move, and seeing his left hard pressed, sent orders by Yorke to Major-General Huske'. Huske led four battalions of the British second line across to seal the breach in the first, with Bligh's, Sempill's, Ligonier's, and Wolfe's all seeing action, Ligonier's splitting in two to get beyond the Leanach enclosure. Bligh's suffered casualties and Barrell's men continued to die under friendly fire as Sempill's engaged in a desperate firefight at close range; Wolfe's and Ligonier's held the elements of the Jacobite right who broke through. Wolfe's had been moved to cover Barrell's, and this positioning certainly helped prevent a breach in the second line, reinforced at a greater distance by fire from Bligh's guns at the centre. Both front-line cannon were now taken by the Jacobites, as Colonel Rich at the head of Barrell's was cut down, while Lord Robert Kerr fell. At this stage, it seems from the battlefield archaeology that the Jacobites did better than the victors alleged. The flanking volleys of Bligh's and Sempill's from the second line—long a staple of accounts of the battle—were reinforced by the fire of their three coehorns into the melee to prevent the Jacobite Army rolling up the British centre, where the remains of the Munros were attempting to 'refuse its left flank' or indeed retiring behind the front line. In the process, many must have died from 'friendly fire'. For their part, the Jacobite forces returned heavy fire in a firefight at less than 30 metres: the officer commanding the 'grenadier platoon' of Munro's reported six balls through his coat.[50]

The Jacobite right found it hard to push home their advantage. Either the ground or Cholmondeley's and Price's and the four guns in front of them or a complex manoeuvre which did not work, pushed the Jacobite centre, the Mackintosh Regiment and Lovat's 1st in particular, towards their right. This lengthened their distance from the British lines and deflected the advance of the battalions beyond them. The British Army had been heavily drilled by Cumberland, their morale was better, and they were firing by battalion not platoon. The Jacobite breach was narrow and, forming twenty or thirty deep to push through, they could not bring fire to bear over a wide enough front. Attacking in depth had its problems, for as an ostensible eyewitness put it, 'their Lines were formed so thick and deep, that the Grapeshot made open lines quite through them'. In a three-minute struggle, five or six volleys from Sempill's, Ligonier's, and Bligh's sent a huge volume of ball into both the remnants of Barrell's and the Jacobite front. For their part, under orders for 'no body to throw away their guns' and in some cases with fixed bayonets, the Jacobites returned fire and pushed on towards the end of Sempill's bayonets, but they could not break through.[51]

The Jacobite advance was weakened: sustained heavy fire from the rear ranks into the broken front of the British forces was taking its toll. In addition, with the wind behind them, the British Army were better sighted to fire through the clouds of smoke now enveloping the battlefield. Jacobite casualties were now so heavy that the command structure was breaking down: Lochiel was seriously wounded and Murray had had his horse shot from under him, while Colonel Fraser was down; MacLachlan disembowelled or beheaded by cannonball or canister; and the Chisholms, Macleans, Maclachlan's, and Monaltrie's central battalion were all disintegrating. The commander of Mackintosh's, MacGillivray, died later, in a bitter final stand ahead of the Jacobite right at the Well of the Dead.

On the left, Clanranald's and Keppoch's were making a determined effort to open the British right with their two regiments, or what they now had of them. Perhaps 200 Jacobites of these high-quality units tried to cross ground with boggy patches up to 50 centimetres deep to break the reinforced British front line of 2,000 men with six 3-pounders. Keppoch was wounded, fell, and rose again, but was shot mortally just in front of Price's on the centre right of the British front, while Clanranald was hit in the head; nonetheless, MacDonald troops advanced beyond the fallen Keppoch, though they do not seem to have made effective contact with the British right, coming only within some 10–15 metres of the enemy. Nonetheless, 'the *Royals* and *Pulteney*'s hardly took their fire-locks from their shoulders'.[52]

There were now many gaps in the Jacobite left, and their shape was on the point of disintegration. Seeing this, Cobham's dragoon squadron on the British right charged forward at around 1.25 p.m., almost immediately supported by the two squadrons of Kingston's Horse, while Ballimore's men moved in on the enclosures covering the Jacobite right to pin down Lord Lewis Gordon's battalions as the second line advanced to support the first. At roughly the same time, Cobham's and Ker's dragoons on the British left moved to attack the Jacobite rear right while the front rank was engaged. The Jacobite Army did not immediately collapse, however. Keppoch's regiment re-formed and with picquet help held off Kingston's Horse, who bypassed them to cut right across the field of battle and attack the *Royal-Écossais* on the right of the Jacobite second line. Kingston's Horse were looking to undermine any attempt the French regulars might make to shore up Lord Lewis Gordon's men against the harrying from Ballimore's 64th. Ballimore's had set up a desultory fire on the company of Ogilvy's on the Culchunaig ridge, and were now breaking down the last of the Culwhiniac walls to allow freer passage to Cobham's and Ker's, who were still unwilling, however, to break beyond the Jacobite cavalry screen. The *Royal-Écossais* had to move away from Culwhiniac, and were now out of position due to fire from the enclosures; they were possibly in the process of advancing to support the right's breakthrough. They moved to return fire effectively on Ballimore's 64th, who were firing at them under cover of a wall at Culwhiniac, and Ballimore was killed.[53]

But the damage was done, with free passage to almost 500 dragoons. As the right wing fell back from the firefight, the left broke too, under pressure from front and flanks and seeing the units to its right in retreat.[54] The Earl of Kilmarnock, standing ahead of Perth in command of his Foot Guards and taking cover with the *Royal-Écossais* by the Culwhiniac enclosures, sealed his own fate by riding 400 metres to the right up to Cobham's in the mistaken view they were Fitzjames's, and was at once taken prisoner; this does suggest, though, that the Jacobite cavalry screen was holding effectively into the second stage of the battle. Ker's dragoons lost nineteen horses, but they were through. Cobham's and Ker's main dragoon units now divided into ten half-squadrons and moved through the gaps. John Gordon of Avochie's battalion in Lord Lewis Gordon's kept up a steady fire on a squadron of Ker's and two Argyll companies from behind a wall at the north west of the park, diagonally opposite the British point of entry on the south east, until they were driven off by Cobham's. Most of the British squadrons made their way unmolested westward towards the river Nairn and the small settlement of Culchunaig, looking to effect an encirclement.[55]

The British cavalry were now in full cry on both flanks, and Cobham's dragoon picquet on the British right veered across to come up behind the *Royal-Écossais* to complete an encirclement by 1.30 p.m. However, the dragoons found themselves frustrated by the Irish troops in the French service, brought up by Sullivan to cover the Jacobite position and the retreating left. (The position of the picquets on the Jacobite left makes it unlikely that it was the main force of Cobham's on the British left who carried out this manouevre, although accounts differ.) Lord Lewis Drummond, lieutenant colonel of the *Royal-Écossais*, was hit in the leg, but the Franco-Scottish force, attacked on two fronts, did not waver, while the Irish picquets, who drove off Cobham's squadron-strength force, now opened a steady fire to cover the retreating left of the Jacobite front line, screened by Glenbuchat's regiment (the allegation made by some British accounts that the French troops did not fire, 'as remarkable as any Circumstance during the Battel', is a strange one). On the Jacobite right, the *Royal-Écossais*, Lord Lewis Gordon's, and apparently Ogilvy's held firm, and six Jacobite battalions 'gave their fire very well' against the now advancing forces of Ligonier's and Wolfe's and Cobham's and Ker's two dragoon regiments, as well as some of the Argyll troops.[56]

Lord George Murray had meanwhile returned from the right of the front line, who had fallen back. Ardsheal's had heavy casualties, Lochiel's was leaderless and disorganized, and the Atholl Brigade had had almost twenty of its officers killed, so Lord George brought little in the way of reinforcements as the right retreated. Lochiel's men were further damaged by raking fire from remaining Argyll militia behind the Leanach enclosures on the British left, although an advance from there was checked. Murray rallied the Écossais Royale and the remaining battalion of Lord Lewis Gordon's and moved forward and to the left against the now slowly advancing British front infantry line to cover the retreat of the MacDonalds. The picquets continued to hold off the cavalry on the Jacobite left, many of whom had in any case now left the field to join the pursuit, the growing British encirclement having screened out many of the routes of flight except that down the road to Inverness. This was doomed to be a deathtrap for many; several others were also killed down by the river Nairn, far from the battlefield and its grave markers as the dragoon encirclement was nearly completed (it does not seem ever to have been technically fully accomplished, and indeed the British command was criticized for this). Lord George's remaining forces now opened repeated fire—apparently rolling volleys rather than fire-at-will dropping shots—against the now slowly advancing British Army, but they had probably only 500–600 men at best and were outnumbered three to one. The lack of meaningful strength in the second line or reserve meant that once the Jacobite front line had failed to carry the day, victory was impossible and the risk of a rout very real. Nonetheless, the second line did rally to fight, a development alluded to in few accounts of the battle (John Home's was an exception). The British left was too badly damaged to move forward effectively apart from its cavalry and militia on the wing; for its part, the Jacobite second-line right was pinned down by British horse and had dragged itself out of position to rescue what remained of the left, which had bought some time owing to the bad ground slowing the dragoons. A disaster was looming, and was only slightly delayed: the inevitability of defeat was apparent. The Master of Lovat, arriving in view of the battle with Lovat's 2nd, seems speedily to have decided to appear to fall back to 'defend Inverness' (the 'brisk firing' heard by Johnstone may have been a subterfuge of the Master's or he may have mistaken its source) and then to change sides.[57]

Fitzjames's Horse and the Life Guards continued for a short time to delay encirclement by holding some of the dragoons on the Jacobite right, which they did for long enough to allow the retreating and (apart from Lochiel's) largely broken Jacobite right to escape. The picquets kept up their fire from behind the north-east Culloden Park walls to hold the cavalry at bay until they saw the advance of the British infantry, whereupon 'they retreated towards Inverness, carrying with them their wounded commanding officer, Brigadier Stapleton, who died of his injuries a few days later'. While the picquets were still in position, Captain du Saussey's gunners on the Jacobite left opened cannon fire with their 4-pounder, which was effective enough to require four 3-pounders and three coehorns to be moved up from the British front line to destroy it and its crew. Bagot's Hussars collapsed and Colonel Bagot was taken prisoner, while Major General Viscount Strathallan seems to have led his Perthshire Horse squadron and himself to destruction in an attempt to hold the British advance, veering over towards the right as the picquets defended the Jacobite left. Strathallan was mortally wounded (possibly by Colonel Howard, according to the *Gentleman's*

Magazine), receiving the last sacraments in oatmeal and water from the Episcopalian chaplain of Lochiel's (the Cameron regiment had Catholic, Episcopalian, and Presbyterian chaplains), who stayed on the field to minister to the dying.

Meanwhile, the *Royal-Écossais* were now the only Jacobite unit left on the field who were not engaged in the last-ditch defence against encircle- ment. Fitzjames's dragoons retreated under pressure (perhaps at about 1.35 p.m.) and as Lord John Drummond prepared to form them and the *Royal-Écossais* in square to delay any British advance from the front, Sullivan rode up to order Colonel O'Shea of Fitzjames's to rescue the Prince. For his part, the Prince was trying to rally Perth's, Glenbuchat's, and the Edinburgh men at Balvraid, 1 kilometre from Culchunaig and 1,600 metres from the original British front line. Charles Edward was unwilling to retreat until it was clear that the advancing forces of Cobham's and Ker's dragoons threatened his position. Fitzjames's (or just possibly Balmerino's Horse) and a number of other staff officers and confidants took him, protesting, to safety 'towards the ford of Faillie over the Nairn'. Henderson remarks that Charles Edward ordered a 'house behind which he stood to be set on fire, and by means of the smoke he crossed the Nairn'. Lieutenant Colonel Drummond's bat- talion of the *Royal-Écossais* surrendered.[58]

The retreating Jacobite right, covered by Lord George's defensive measures, had left the field, accompanied by at least one more-or-less intact unit of the Jacobite centre, Lovat's 1st, who retreated with their pipes playing, and seem to have been allowed free passage by a small force of dragoons, rather than risk making them desperate. Ogilvy's in retreat covered them as Hawley's men came on, forming square several times, before eventually withdrawing towards Ruthven Barracks, 15 kilometres to the south, across the Nairn, covered by the Écossais Royale in the last stages of their own action and turning repeatedly to volley or fire *en billebaude* at pursuing dragoons.[59] The dragoons pre- ferred pursuing the confused and foolish Jacobite soldiers who had straggled in ones and twos down the road to Inverness, and kept clear of the menace of unbroken and well-armed infantry units, like Ogilvy's

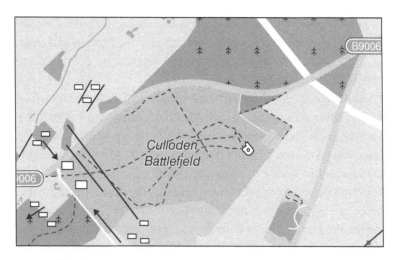

Map 5 The last phase of the battle. British infantry push forward, brushing aside reformed Atholl and Cameron units. Kingston's and Cobham's bypass Glenbuchat's screen for retreating infantry on the left; Glenbuchat retreats. Picquets hold off dragoons but Jacobite horse on the left collapses, and Cobham's bypasses the Irish infantry to sweep across the field. The Jacobite cavalry screen has given way in both directions. Some British dragoons turn right into the last stand of Fitzjames's and the *Royal-Écossais* in square, some pursue Ogilvy's before making for the Jacobite command post.

two battalions, who were thus able both to cover the second stage of the retreat and to get clean away themselves.[60]

Meanwhile, however, the Jacobite left were also in full flight. Government cannon (perhaps those brought up to deal with the irritating Jacobite 4-pounder) now poured their fire into the left as it fled the field, while Kingston's and what remained of the picquet of Cobham's from the British right—about 125 cavalry—were deemed sufficient to pursue the fleeing left on the road to Inverness. This they did—after briefly being delayed by Franco-Irish musketfire from Dillon's, Ruth's, and Lally's picquets—with expedition, cutting down a Mackintosh stand at 'the White Bog' near their 'ancestral burial-ground' and killing women and children who got in their way till the last Jacobite on the road was killed a mile from Inverness. As Elcho puts it, 'Every body that fell into their hands got no quarters'. Cumberland agreed: 'Major-General Bland...made a great slaughter, and gave quarter to none'; Wolfe remarked that 'as few Highlanders were made prisoners as possible'. Three Nottingham butchers, troopers in Kingston's, were 'specially commended by Cumberland'. Kingston's men's zeal has been seen as a result of their suffering at Jacobite hands, with twenty-six casualties at the February fight at Keith. Whatever the truth of that, they were brutal in the pursuit now.[61]

On the field, the systematic advance of the British infantry served as its main purpose the destruction of the Jacobite wounded who lay on the field. Major Wolfe's renowned but only reputed refusal (he himself 'makes no reference' to it) to shoot Fraser of Inverallochy, the injured commander of Lovat's 1st, later became part of the mythology of imperial reconciliation. The involvement of the Frasers in the front rank at the Heights of Abraham in 1759, and Benjamin West's (fictional) portrayal of their commander's presence at the death of Wolfe, drew on this alleged act of mercy. Fraser of Inverallochy died in any case.[62]

Initial estimates were that around 2,000 Jacobites were killed on the field for the loss of only 50 British soldiers: indeed the *Gentleman's Magazine* reported of the Jacobites that, 'according to their own computation, they have lost 2,500 men killed in the field of battle, or in the pursuit'; Wolfe by contrast suggested 1,500 Jacobite dead. In all, the British Army reported 50 men dead and 259 wounded, though Wolfe's impressions were of a somewhat higher figure; most of the wounded do not in any case seem to have survived. In the second line, Ligonier's, Wolfe's, and Sempill's reported 21 casualties between them. Baterau's lost 3 to artillery fire and the Argyll militia claimed 9 casualties. Cobham's and Ker's reported 7 between them.[63]

The figures of 50 and 2,000 are no longer universally believed, though the former is still often quoted. There is good reason to doubt both. Although Jacobite sources are self-interested, Elcho thought there were 250 British dead, and Johnstone that as many British as Jacobites fell. It is likely that there were around 200–250 British dead plus initially surviving wounded (perhaps up to 300–400 dying *in toto* in short order), with the Jacobites losing 1,000 on the field and many more later. The chances of being taken prisoner were low, unless one was a French regular, and the conditions of imprisonment led to death for many. The British Army grave (reputedly on the 'Field of the English', but in reality probably closer to their front line) was 50 metres long and 8–9 metres wide, suggestive of much higher mortality than a few dozen.[64] Twelve Jacobite colours were recorded as captured, together with the baggage train, 30 guns (11 3-pounders, 8 4-pounders, and various others including 1½-pounders), 2,320 muskets, 1,500 cartridges, 1,019 cannon rounds, 22 ammunition carts, and 190 broadswords, guns being more frequently thrown away in flight. Most of the broadswords seem to have been used to manufacture a railing at Twickenham House, Richmond. Government sources recorded 548 prisoners, two-fifths of them French regulars. The Jacobites had not deployed many of their cannon effectively on the field of battle, though it is possible that some of the smaller artillery pieces were in the second line or in the rear, were not recorded, and were overwhelmed before they could be used.[65]

The pursuit was immediate, persistent, and brutal. Bland 'made great slaughter' on the field; Brigadier Mordaunt was sent with two battalions in pursuit of the 3rd Battalion of Lovat's, who had not been at the battle and were still in the field, while Lords Sutherland and Reay pursued and took the rest of Cromartie's. Between 900 and 1,500 Jacobites reached the rallying point at Ruthven on 18 April, only to be greeted by a *sauve qui peut* order from Charles Edward. In truth, as Maxwell notes, he had little option, though his conduct in defeat and disappointment was often wanting. On 19 April, the *Royal-Écossais* and Fitzjames's surrendered at Inverness. After the *Mars* and *Bellona* landed £38,000 in gold at Loch nan Uamh, Lochiel, Glengarry, and Clanranald decided to fight on, but only 600 men rendezvoused on 13–15 May and on the seventeenth the intact Macphersons surrendered, though their commander Cluny spent many years in a concealed wooden cage on the side of Ben Alder. Culloden was over, but its repercussions were just beginning.[66]

4

Aftermath and Occupation

Cumberland, 'moved by hate and fear of the Scots generally', seems to have been determined to ignore counsels of moderation from leading Scottish Hanoverians, from Lord President Duncan Forbes down. Cumberland thought Forbes much too positive about the safety of proceeding mercifully, though in fact Forbes was less clement than is sometimes suggested, and floated the possibility of transportation en masse for some clans, as indeed did Cumberland and Albemarle. The British government had had a bad fright, and the Jacobites would pay for it. Even as late as July, Cumberland noted that 'I tremble for fear that this vile spot may still be the ruin of this island and our family'.[1]

The atrocities began at once, and from the beginning were marked with disinformation and propaganda: early histories could be silent on them altogether. Some 3,000 died on the battlefield or in the immediate aftermath of the battle, probably no more than a third in action. From the beginning, the sources are clear on this. Maxwell notes that 'Exceeding few were made prisoners in the field of battle, which was such a scene of horror and inhumanity, as is rarely to be met with among civilized nations', while Johnstone claims that Cumberland left the wounded to lie on the field before sending out death squads to finish them off where they lay. Indeed, even the British wounded seem to have been left for some time on the field. The historian Bill Speck, who is relatively sympathetic to Cumberland (he is prepared to cast doubt on Jacobite allegations on the authority of the word or memory of a British officer for example), notes:

evidence...demonstrates that there is no necessity to turn to suspect sources in order to document acts committed by the British army, which were outrages even by the standards of contemporaries.

Repeated allegations of horrendous atrocities, not just in the pursuit (which was not untypical of contemporary military practice), but also in cold blood over the following days, surfaced almost immediately. On 17 April, when the Orders of the Day sent a captain and fifty men round all the houses neighbouring the battlefield with a 'licence to kill', the Synod of Moray's minutes advised caution in identifying Jacobites, caution clearly not being shown by the British forces:

> the Synod...hereby do recommend to all the ministers within their bounds to be very careful and cautious in attesting any of those who have been either actually or openly in rebellion or who may have been taken up upon suspicion.

Maxwell took the view that Cumberland's 'greatest barbarities were committed in a manner under his eye, and the principal actors received distinguishing marks of his favour'. Later Chambers notes that seventy wounded were killed the day after by firing squad, that thirty-two men were burnt alive in a building (Ker of Graden recounts this or a similar incident but with a lower figure), and that nineteen officers were shot or clubbed to death together. One of the most famous cases was that of John Fraser, an officer in Lovat's allegedly put on a cart wounded and taken to a place of mass execution where muskets were fired from 2 or 3 metres' range at Jacobite prisoners, before those who required finishing off were clubbed to death with muskets. Fraser lost an eye and had his cheekbone shattered, but survived. A contemporary chronicler thought that far from his case being a 'wild and romantick' story, it was 'a Monument of such a deliberate Massacre, as would make the remotest Savages blush at the Infamy', and called for a 'parliamentary Enquiry' at which it suggested that if only ministers, magistrates, and Hanoverians gave evidence, it would still be enough to convict Cumberland's officers of 'Neronian cruelties'. Lockhart and Scott were named as among the most brutal, and it was alleged once again that between thirty and forty had been burnt alive by British soldiers, including a number of innocent bystanders. The situation in the aftermath of Culloden was much closer to that practised by early modern English forces in Ireland than the standards expected of eighteenth-century British warfare, and was more typical of the Russian and Turkish armies, regarded by many contemporaries as beyond the pale.[2]

A nineteenth-century minister bears witness to a persistent tradition that the wounded were gathered together in heaps and artillery fired into the heaps. Tobias Smollett's description of the barbarities practised by Cumberland's troops led to unavailing efforts by Andrew Henderson to downplay the truth. Henderson claimed that there was only one accidental death, that promises given on surrender were 'always sustained', and that if there was any excess bloodshed, it was the fault of Hawley, not 'the illustrious Son of our King; whose disposition to humanity, and whose real goodness of heart, shine every day with more transcendent lustre'.[3]

For a little while it looked as if this opinion might be generally shared. Cumberland was initially feted for his victory, both in England and Whig Scotland, where the University of Glasgow gave him an honorary degree and Parliament voted him a rise in stipend. Culloden victory medals were issued. In Ascendancy Ireland, Culloden societies were formed to celebrate British Protestant victory. The later societies 'to prosecute Whiteboys' and 1780s 'Orange lodges' may have been descended from the 'True Blue' and 'Loyal Irish Protestant' societies of this era; the Cork True Blue Society was only one founded in direct response to the 'Forty-five.[4] Jacobite areas rushed to show their loyalty: a Cumberland Society was inaugurated at Inverness, and at Preston cockades were worn in the Duke's livery colours on 28 April. On the twenty-ninth the Lords and on the thirtieth the House of Commons thanked Cumberland. In the words of Andrew Henderson:

> The victory at Culloden gave birth to an inexpressible joy through the extensive dominions of the British empire; not only Europe and Africa, but the two Indies joined in the shout, and gave joyful acclamations.

There is indeed some evidence that the Rising was 'perceived as a crisis throughout the British Empire', and that Benjamin Franklin's fears of compulsory conversion to Catholicism if the Jacobites had won were, if laughable, perhaps not untypical. Thomas Prince's sermon at Boston on 14 August 1746 suggested that had Charles Edward won, he would have restored 'Gibraltar and Minorca, if not Jamaica to Spain' and 'no doubt...Cape Breton, Nova Scotia' and part of Newfoundland to France. Indeed, Prince argued, 'it seems highly probable that even all the British America, would either by Gift, Sale, or Conquest, be soon subjected to the power of France' and 'the whole British Empire subservient' to the Bourbons.[5]

Cumberland acquired, in Geoffrey Plank's words, a 'nearly godlike status' in the American colonies as the guarantor of Protestant liberties, while he was described as a 'Hero-God' in London panegyric. The guns sounded from the Tower and from ships at harbour in the British capital, small arms were fired and 'Judas Maccabeus' and 'Britons Strike Home' were played. Cumberland was voted an extra £25,000 a year, to more than double his allowance. Children in some parts of Scotland were even baptized 'Cumberland William'. York Corporation 'sent its congratulations on "the late glorious success over rebellious savages"', Ludlow termed them 'barbarians, enemies to all civil society', and elsewhere they were called 'mountain savages' and 'wild beasts'. Yet for all the dehumanizing rhetoric visited on the defeated Jacobites, Cumberland's popularity was not to last.[6]

On 1 May, a question 'was asked at a masquerade if the Duke had ordered his men to give no quarter to the rebels', and questions began to appear in the press as to why Jacobite prisoners were so seldom suffering from wounds. Before 'the end of May', it was reported 'that when the duke came back to the capital he was to be made a freeman of the Butchers' company'. The name stuck. The mischievous little pamphlet Mercy the Truest Heroism, dedicated to Cumberland, noted multiple examples of noble clemency from the ancient world, with a clearly implied message for the Duke (Figure 11).

Figure 11 *The Butcher* (19 December 1746). How Cumberland was being viewed by the end of the year of his greatest triumph.

Although he became chancellor of Trinity College Dublin in 1751 and continued to be celebrated as victor of Culloden for many years, in the end the growing negative press and Cumberland's lack of subsequent success combined to poison the well of his reputation.[7]

After the 'first official reports of the battle…reached London on 23 April', alleged orders from Lord George Murray to give the British forces no quarter were circulated extensively both in England and the colonies (for example, appearing in the *Virginia Gazette of Williamsburg*). The original orders are in the Cumberland Papers, so were known to the government. They were reprinted a number of times in early accounts, such as James Ray's *Compleat History* and Michael Hughes's *Plain Narrative*. It was alleged that they were left behind by a Jacobite during the night attack, and as early as 17 April, the day after the battle, Cumberland issued orders to his company commanders that 'officer & men will take notice that the publick orders of the Rebels yesterday were to give us no quarter', which suggests that the tampered orders were already in circulation. They seem to have had a strong effect. James Ray remarked that 'if we had known that they had strict Orders before the Battle to give the Duke's Troops no Quarter, we should not have troubled ourselves with making so many Prisoners'. Black propaganda of this kind, together with lurid and sensationalist tales of the Jacobites as cannibals or savages, allegations about their raiding on campaign, and accusations that they had killed British wounded at Prestonpans and Falkirk, combined with the provocation the British troops had suffered by 'their former disgraces' and the sense of being an occupying force in enemy country to create the perfect breeding ground for what would today be called war crimes. Speck thinks Cumberland 'must be given the benefit of the doubt' over forging these orders, and that revised orders involving no quarter may have been issued for the night attack. If this were so, then Jacobites claiming excuse, disillusionment, or subsequent opposition to the cause might have acknowledged them; and the order, with its inserted sentence, looks clearly doctored, by whom being admittedly quite another matter. Maxwell's summary, that it was an 'impudent forgery' seems very likely; that Cumberland was personally responsible is more doubtful.[8]

It was claimed that it was difficult to tell which Scots might be in arms and which not, and alleged atrocities carried out by Jacobites over the last thirty years began to be circulated. Deep suspicions (often justified) of the Scottish population in general fed the spirit of atrocity, as in later colonial wars: the bloody display of mastery assuaged the anxiety of the British forces that, although 'every one thought themselves obliged to put on the Appearance of being pleased', they were in reality mourning 'the Total Defeat of their Friends'. Those who had been involved in the 'Forty-five had to inform the authorities, who in their turn were obliged to make a careful search after the Jacobites in their area. Given the conduct of the British administration and local sympathies, under-reporting was an obvious problem, as was lukewarm pursuit; as we have seen from the Synod of Moray minutes, even hard-core Presbyterians were much less gung-ho than the British command, and much less likely to proceed on suspicion or accusation. This Scottish outlook in its turn could only serve to feed suspicion among the occupying forces.

Recaptured Edinburgh, where on 30 January James Ray had noted the widespread wearing of 'Breast-knots and Ribbons' as favours for the Prince even in the presence of the British Army, saw pro-Jacobite disturbances in the Town Guard continuing into February 1746, while on 27 March, James Pringle wrote that 'were an Englishman to come here it would Confirm him in the Notion they have, that the Scots are all Jacobites'. On 23 April, Cumberland told Newcastle that Edinburgh 'has been so very ill affected', and after the outcome of Culloden became known, houses in Edinburgh which did not display candles 'or whose houses were only inhabited by Stewarts had their windows broke and were robb'd'. The grant of the Freedom of the City to Cumberland on 1 April 1747 can only have assuaged such suspicions at best. In East Lothian, the allies of the British forces likewise found little fellow feeling among the population, from whom they could not 'buy horses for Govt. use save at an extravagant price', a third more than normal.[9] On 29 June, Cumberland let Newcastle know that 'I have nothing to say new from this country [Scotland] but that to my great astonishment I find them a more stubborn and villainous set of wretches than I imagined could

exist'. On 1 August, following significant provocation from the occupying force of Fleming's 36th, 'the windows and inhabitants of Aberdeen
were stoned by occupying British troops for refusing to show lights in
honour of the Hanoverian succession', despite the—disingenuous if thoroughly Aberdonian—plea from the city magistrates of the 'Considerable
expence' of lighted windows.[10]

In Angus and Mearns, opposition was even stronger: Johnshaven
was seen as 'totally Jacobite' by Cumberland, who could identify only
a 'Small Number of the well Affected' in Brechin, who required troops
to guarantee their safety; the Town Council Minutes were destroyed.
In Forfar, there was Jacobite recruitment up to the day before the
British Army entered the town; Arbroath claimed that the council had
not taken the Oaths because they were 'overawd' by the Jacobite
forces, to which they nonetheless contributed in no small degree. At
Montrose, there was an open Jacobite procession on King James's
birthday in 1746. Matters were not dissimilar in Aberdeenshire and
Banffshire, while Inverness and Nairn were hardly a hotbed of
Hanoverian loyalism either. This was little surprise given that, as the
Provost of Inverness wrote to Lord President Forbes, 'we are all
accounted Rebells, we have no persons to complain to, nor do we
expect redress'. Provost Hossack of Inverness was himself 'kicked and
imprisoned'. Further unrest continued in Edinburgh and other towns
and cities for at least two more years. The 1743 edition of Bland's *Treatise
on Military Discipline* had recommended a respectful attitude by occupying military forces towards the civilian population: in Scotland
three years later its author sought to kill rather than to take prisoner
and on 22 May ordered Loudoun to 'destroy' as many as he could. It
was little wonder that British troops treated Scottish towns and their
inhabitants with contempt: as late as 16 April 1750, British soldiers in
Inverness celebrated the fourth anniversary of Culloden by breaking
the town's windows, possibly in response to their being unlit, possibly
for no reason at all.[11]

To add to the sense of initial unease felt by the British forces, significant units of armed Jacobites continued to appear in the field even after

around 1,000 men mustering at Ruthven in Badenoch had received orders from Charles Edward to *sauve qui peut*. The MacGregors had marched home unmolested, 'with colours flying and pipes playing'. On 26 April, it was rumoured that there were 120 in arms at Balquhidder; in the same month four British battalions had to be deployed against Jacobite units. In May, one battalion of Lochiel's regiment was still operational, as were 500 under Clanranald; 'in July, significant numbers of Stewart of Ardsheal's Foot had yet to surrender arms, and Ardsheal was still dealing with arrears of pay'. Orkney remained under Jacobite control until late May, despite British attacks, and four of the local Jacobite lairds remained successfully hidden. Jacobite expresses were sent until August; troops were reported in Strathdee in September, and in the same month there were insurgents in Angus. A British regiment was deployed across Banffshire in the summer. In November, Jacobite units were reported still in the field and still being paid; in March 1747, two officers of Lord Cromartie's regiment carried out a raid on Dingwall. In December 1747, Colonel Watson noted that 'Attainted Rebels...continue to appear publickly, in the Shires of Aberdeen, Banff and Angus, where they hold Traiterous Caballs'. Arms surrenders in the Mearns continued almost into the summer of 1748. British atrocities may have been carried out against helpless victims, but there were plenty of continuing Jacobite threats.[12]

Cumberland sent out search parties to 'pursue and hunt these vermin amongst their lurking hills'. Brigadier Mordaunt was sent into Fraser country with two battalions 'to destroy all the rebels he found there'; Loudoun was ordered 'to seize or destroy all persons you can find who have been in the rebellion or their abettors'. Lord George Sackville took 500 men across country from Fort Augustus to Glenelg, with Cornwallis taking '300 along Loch Lochy and up Loch Arkaig' for an eventual rendezvous with Sackville. Major General John Campbell was let loose on Sunart and Morven, laying it waste even though arms were surrendered, while Captain Fergusson's *The Furnace* scoured the Western Isles and Captain Caroline Scott took control of the country 'from Fort William around Loch Eil'. Those who surrendered—like the Grants of

Glen Moriston and Glen Urquhart—were rarely well treated in the initial stages after the battle, with three men who surrendered on 2 June at Fort William being drowned. 'Equivocal surrenders of old rusty weapons' led to a vicious reaction. Certain British officers stood out in their cruelty, and this was recognized from an early stage. Chambers notes:

> General Hawley was one of the most remorseless…The names of Lieutenant-colonel Howard, Captain Caroline Scott, and Major Lockhart are also to be handed down as worthy of everlasting execration.

It remained the case, however, that on balance 'Scottish officers tended to treat their countrymen more leniently than did the English'. Cumberland made his base at Inverness; other British commanders were based in Fort William and Skye. The Campbell militia were set loose to burn in Atholl. These were the 'soft admonitions' spoken of by the *Scots Magazine*, where British forces were 'carrying fire and destruction as they passed, shooting the vagrant Highlanders that they meet…and driving off their cattle'. This kind of brutal approach was perhaps exacerbated by the refusal of Cumberland's secret offer of an amnesty to Lochiel.[13]

Cumberland moved his main force to Fort Augustus on 22–3 May to begin the pacification of the West Highlands. The islands and sea loch coast had already come under attack from Captain John Fergusson and the Royal Navy, Fergusson's men capturing Lord Lovat in Morar 'on the night of 4/5 June'; on 19 June, Major General Campbell's command even landed on St Kilda, determined to chase all Jacobites down to their lairs. By 18 July, matters were sufficiently settled for Cumberland to depart for England, leaving the Duke of Albemarle in charge. Despite Linda Colley's contention that the Jacobites enjoyed 'negligible civilian support', especially in the towns, by the end of August 1746 the British Army found it requisite to have deployments in place at Berwick, Kelso, Haddington, Dalkeith, Dumfries, Ayr, Stranraer, Cupar, Inverness, Nairn, Forres, Elgin, Banff, Newburgh, Aberdeen, Stonehaven, Inverbervie, Johnshaven, Montrose, Arbroath, Dundee, Perth, Stirling, Linlithgow, Glasgow,

Edinburgh, and Dunfermline: between 12,000 and 13,000 troops, 75 per cent regulars. This was not a Highland pacification but a national occupation. And they were needed: over 400 men were requested for disarming Cameron forces in October; as late as 1748–9, five companies were deployed against raiding in the north-east. By summer 1749, there were still ten regiments in Scotland with many patrols: these were not a regular establishment but an occupying force. As late as December 1756, there were still sixty British Army patrols in Scotland. Historian Bob Harris is right in noting 'that *force majeure* was the ultimate basis for Hanoverian rule'. The historian Chris Whatley is even more forthright:

> Scotland was not settled until the 1750s, and then only through the impos-
> ition of 'systematic state terrorism' was…Jacobitism finally defeated.[14]

Some 3,000–3,500 Jacobite soldiers or supporters were imprisoned following the failure of the Rising. Around 120 officers and men were executed and almost 1,000 transported from 3,400 prisoners, while around 750 were 'pardoned on enlistment', joining the British Army in such dangerous and disease-ridden spots as Antigua or Jamaica. Between 500 and 1,000 of those who escaped joined one of the three Scottish regiments (Royal Scots, Albanie, or Ogilvy) in the French service; Lochiel, Elcho, and Ogilvy were all offered French colonelcies, as was the Master of Lovat, who refused his and joined the British Army.[15]

Charles Edward, after many famous and well-rehearsed episodes, escaped from Loch nan Uamh with Lochiel on 20 September. By the end of the year Elcho, Forbes of Pitsligo, Glenbuchat, John Hay, Chevalier de Johnstone, Macpherson, Ogilvy, and Charles Stewart of Ardsheal were all among those who had either escaped abroad or gone successfully to ground (sometimes for a long time: Pitsligo was on the run for sixteen years, despite being in his late sixties when Culloden was fought). The jails of Lancaster, Lincoln, and York were full of the less fortunate, as were transport ships at Tilbury, on which 70 per cent of those held died, the survivors being 'transported to slavery in Barbados'. Catholic priests were held in these conditions also and their books and vestments burnt, while Fr Alexander Cameron SJ was so brutalized by Captain Fergusson that he died. The Scottish courts were not trusted to carry out trials, and not only trials but also executions were carried out in England. Among those transported, the most fortunate were the 149 on *The Veteran*, liberated off Antigua on 28 June 1747 by a French privateer and landed on Martinique, who included George Keith, a 35-year-old Aberdeen shoemaker in Glengarry's, William Bell, a Berwickshire bookseller, and Mary MacDonald. Women also were transported; some, like the 25-year-old Isabel Chalmers, were given a regimental attachment—in her case, Glengarry's. Cameron and MacDonald prisoners may have been more likely to have been transported to the West Indies than the American colonies—and in Jamaica in particular, pro-Union and anti-Jacobite Campbell interest was strong, which meant these men were going into the care of their hereditary enemies.[16]

Deserters were hanged out of hand in the earlier stages, and shot later, while the greatest theatre attended the execution of the 'rebel lords', the cavalry officers Kilmarnock and Balmerino, and Lord Lovat, whose beheading on 9 April 1747 on Tower Green was the last in British history. Those lacking titles recognized in the British peerage were hanged, drawn, and quartered, which technically involved being disembowelled while semiconscious after a half-hanging; some were spared this and were dead or almost dead when cut down, some were not. Theatrical scaffold appearances—probably deliberately heightened for dramatic purposes—helped to create what Daniel Szechi has called a 'Jacobite Theatre of Death', while songs and relics of the martyred victims of the Rising served to create an intense and quasi-sacral memorialization, which anticipated the creation of the cult of celebrity by nineteenth-century memorabilia and public commemoration.[17]

Songs and dances and the mute public display of tartan or playing of seditious airs all composed a language of cultural resistance. On the one hand, Jacobite 'martyrs' were portrayed (and portrayed themselves) as patriots, as Lord Balmerino died with his tartan cap on the scaffold, or Lovat with his 'Dulce et decorum est pro patria mori' (It is a sweet and fitting thing to die for one's country [in this case Scotland]).[18] The idea of the Jacobites as imaginative and sensitive, attuned to the emerging discourse of sensibility, emerged in poems such as that on Jemmy Dawson's fiancée, who allegedly expired on seeing her beloved drawn and quartered: 'Upon a young lady, who died on seeing her lover, Mr. Dawson, executed on the 30th of July 1746'. In the end, this presentation of the brutal and heroic under the patina of contemporary sensibility reached its apogee in James Macpherson's adaptation of primary Gaelic source materials into the Ossian poems in the 1760s, creating a displaced world of primary epic long on emotion but short on violence, and encapsulating the dream of the triumph of Gaelic culture. Macpherson was helped in his translations by his cousin Lachlan, lieutenant in Cluny's regiment in 1745, and the poet used some of his wealth to restore the Macpherson estates.[19]

Jacobite units remained active in the field, engaging in either war or banditry, depending how one chooses to define it. Assassinations took place of unpopular government officers or sympathizers, such as Munro of Culcairn in Lochaber and Colin Campbell of Glenure near Ballachulish. Campbell was killed on 14 May 1752, on the eve of evictions from Ardsheal, and the trial of James Stewart of the Glens for this 'Appin Murder' was widely held to be a miscarriage of justice, as the majority of jurors were Campbells. Meanwhile recruitment continued to the Irish Brigades and to Scottish forces in the service of France: at Edinburgh on 13 August 1754, Ronald MacDonald was banished for seven years for enlisting in the French service. Throughout northern Scotland in the aftermath of the Rising, 'communities were devastated, impoverished and angry'.[20]

In engaging with plans of settlement in the Highlands, Cumberland had initially considered transporting the entire population of 'Lochaber and surrounding districts', and in the event there were limited 'clearances of the disaffected' there and in Morvern. In this sense, Culloden and the Clearances are indeed historically linked, and the fact that Argyll had recently introduced 'competitive bidding to secure leases' on traditional Campbell lands foreshadowed the economic dispossession of Jacobite—though not only Jacobite—Highlanders which laid its shadow over the next century and more of Scottish history.

The clearances of 1746 anticipated the Acadian deportations from Nova Scotia in 1755, when Cumberland looked forward to the French inhabitants being 'drove out'. Similar police actions against native or francophone peoples in Canada in this period both demonstrate the influence on colonial policy of Cumberland and his senior officers and the rising status of the British Army, a status cemented by the triumph at Quebec in the *annus mirabilis* of 1759. More immediately, the Earl of Albemarle and Lieutenant Colonel Cornwallis, as well as notorious officers such as Lockhart and Scott, were to the forefront of what Allan Macinnes has described as a policy of 'genocide' against Gaelic Scotland. Certainly, as in Ireland in 1798, the element among the insurgents which was most different—most the 'other'—became the scapegoat for the whole Rising. Secular and Presbyterian United Irishmen, despite their importance to the 1798 Rising, became marginal as both Unionist and Catholic nationalist sources sought to portray '98 as an outbreak of Gaelic nationalism. A similar process occurred in the characterization of the 'Forty-five as a 'Highland' Rising: Gaelic speakers in north-west Scotland received more of the blame and the suffering to a great extent because they were more 'other' and thus more easily demonized than the equally if not more fervent Jacobites of the small towns of Angus and Banff. The charge of 'genocide' could be seen by some as inflammatory and presentist given the word's more recent terrible connotations, though what might now be termed 'ethnic cleansing' was certainly considered in the aftermath of Culloden and to a limited and unsystematic degree took place.[21]

There were moderating voices in government policy, not least the Earl of Loudoun. A 'legislative offensive' followed the immediate military 'pacifications' of 1746, directed against feudal power, the Episcopalian Church, and the status of tartan as a patriot garb. Newcastle proposed six developments to Cumberland, including the destruction of superiorities and private jurisdictions, the suppression of clan names, the suppression of Episcopal chapels, and the annexation of forfeited estates to the Crown. As the victor of Culloden, with enormous immediate credit (despite some growing murmurings), Cumberland's hard-line outlook was influential on Parliament. An Act of Attainder 'was passed in June 1746', followed by a Disarming Act and in 1748 'the use of Highland dress was forbidden' (Cumberland thought tartan to be 'what makes their uniform'). 'Wardholding [by which a vassal might render military service to a superior] as a system of tenure was abolished', as were heritable jurisdictions, which could give holders of baronies and regalities rights of life or death over their tenants in criminal cases. Regalities were ended and baronial courts circumscribed. Military tenure—already in decline—was ended, and the Secretaryship of State for Scotland abolished, not to be fully reinstated until 1936 (although a non-Cabinet Secretaryship was restored in the era of the Napier Commission in the 1880s). Extensive compensation was given to Argyll and, through him, to the Hanoverian holders of heritable jurisdictions. Legislation was used to break the feudal power of the Scots magnates that continued to show such capability in putting substantial military forces in the field. The legislative attacks on tartan (which for so long had been a mute sign of oppositional politics in both town and countryside, yet one which was invulnerable to prosecution) and in particular the Episcopal Church of Scotland were effective in disrupting cultural networks. Not only were Episcopalian meeting houses burnt, but it became effectively illegitimate for any priest not ordained by English or Irish Anglican bishops to minister in Scotland. The 'suppression of nonjurant meetings' was significantly stronger than any attack on the numerically much weaker Catholics, and a number of Episcopalians appear to have switched to hearing Mass, especially in the stronger Catholic areas.[22]

Attempts to annex the estates of Jacobite magnates ran into problems, not least the overstatement of debt burdens on the estates by those greedy for themselves or sympathetic to the politics of the Jacobite nobility. The British government sought estate factors who would have no connection 'with the forfeiting persons or under the influence of neighbouring families', but in a close-knit community like Scotland, this was easier said than done, although 'any official who had unauthorised dealings with relatives of the attainted was liable to instant dismissal'. In 1752, it was decided that fourteen of the forfeited Jacobite estates (including Perth's,

Strowan's, Cluny's, Cromartie's, and Lochiel's) would be 'annexed inalienably to the Crown' by a commission which 'became operational' over the following decade, and whose purpose was 'to civilise...diversify the Highland economy and promote Presbyterianism'. Many of these estates (such as Perth's) had already seen improvement: there was no real link between agricultural modernity and politics. The Annexed Estates Commission had less than the desired effect in these areas, but nonetheless actively broke up traditional communities in favour of 'single-tenant farms' and 'planned villages'. Meanwhile, tenants with a less than loyal record who fell into debt were singled out for pursuit; in some cases their indebtedness may have been the result of continuing to pay rent to the former landlord in exile.[23]

The castle strongholds were often either left to rot, their owners exiled and dispossessed (as at Glenbuchat, Glengarry, and elsewhere), or converted into barracks (as Corgarff had already been), or replaced with buildings constructed in tribute to victory (as at Inveraray). Scotland was under extensive military occupation, the most visible legacy of which was the construction of the vast white elephant at Fort George, completed in 1769, which cost more than the annual GNP of Scotland to build. This monstrous fort by William and John Adam, 'one of the most outstanding fortifications in Europe' with a potential garrison of almost 2,000 able to be accommodated on its 17-hectare site, was itself a more than eloquent witness to the reality of the Jacobite threat in the minds of eighteenth-century policymakers. Fort George's complex landward defences were the priority, and these were built in 1748–53, with a 300-metre ditch, 50 metres wide: on three sides the fort was protected by the Moray Firth, so only outright defeat for the Royal Navy and a French fleet in the Firth could threaten it from there. The outworks, classically designed in the 'high masonry walls with projecting towers' manner, were designed to stop 'the enemy from bringing heavy guns close enough to bear': 'I look upon that fort to be impregnable', Lord Ligonier said in 1759, ten years before building was complete. With seventy guns, including 32-pounders which could sink a ship outright and a bomb-proof storage depot (in tribute to the direct hit on the magazine at Fort

Augustus from Jacobite artillery), Fort George was a formidable and expensive instrument of occupation, not a sensitively built defence: the Scottish arms over the main gate (1756) were inaccurate.[24]

Even as Fort George was being begun, it was clear why the British government thought that it was needed. There was unrest and resistance throughout Scotland, and not merely in the Gaelic-speaking north and west. On 9 January 1748, General Bland wrote to Secretary Newcastle of the army's difficulties with the civil authorities in the process of suppressing Jacobites in Edinburgh, where there was marching in Jacobite uniform as late as the autumn of that year.[25] There were reports of attempts to intrude Jacobites into positions of legal authority, and the Court of Session ruled that it was unlawful to seize the goods of Jacobites or apprehend them without a warrant. Civil authorities were seen as obstructive in part because they upheld the rule of law, which no occupying force appreciates: on 18 July 1750, Lieutenant Colonel James Wolfe complained to the Provost of Perth regarding the legality of the sentence passed by an artilleryman who had 'been charged by Convenor Buchan of insulting him in the public street', noting that 'the Colonel farther desires the Provost to consider whether defamation, or scandal can properly be called Criminal, or indeed whether a Soldier can be guilty of such a Fault'. 'Forced enlistment and quartering of soldiers' had been used by the British Army in Perth for many years, and there was a clear unwillingness to respond to civilian complaints or to concede the rights of 'civil magistrates having jurisdiction over soldiers': as the Provost and magistrates had remarked as long ago as 1718 in the aftermath of a previous Rising, 'even the greatest Criminals amongst the military are suffered to escape without punishment'. In Stirling, British soldiers were abused and called 'English Bougers' before being attacked. Irish brigade recruitment for the French service on the east coast continued for several years.[26]

Popular feeling, initially extremely hostile to the Jacobites in London and elsewhere, softened relatively quickly, if popular contempt did not.[27] However, the Jacobite analysis of the actions of the British government discerned a much longer-term policy of weakening Scotland and breaking its cultural divergence from the wider British polity. This was given voice by Chevalier de Johnstone, who, on returning from Canada to France after the victory of British forces in North America, noted

> The almost total extermination of the race of Highlanders which has since [Culloden] taken place, either from the policy of the English government, the emigration of their families to the colonies, or from the numerous Highland regiments which have been raised, and which have been often cut to pieces during the last war.

More recent scholarship has endorsed the extremely high casualty rates among infantry from ex-Jacobite areas in the Canadian war. The recruitment of Scots from 'Highland' areas to the Canadian front in particular from the mid–late 1750s was a classic case of 'set a thief to catch a thief' in the context of the increasingly fierce colonial policy against non-British inhabitants being practised in Canada, and the fact that the Scots would be fighting their historic allies, the French, who themselves had many Scottish soldiers in their ranks. In this sense, the Seven Years War of 1756–63, with its policy of internal clearance of native peoples and francophones and use of ex-Jacobites as expendable soldiery in Canada, was the culmination of the aftermath of Culloden. In this context, 1759 was the victory and the year that changed everything, and laid the foundations of British imperial modernity's teleological reading of itself just as much as the battle which occurred thirteen years before. Fittingly, the last Jacobite attempt was defeated by Admiral Hawke's victory at Quiberon Bay in the same year. This narrative was summed up in two paintings by David Morier and Benjamin West, which are discussed in Chapter 5.[28]

5

The Battle That Made Britain?

Historiography and Evidence in the Case of Culloden

Seldom has the adage that history is written by the victors been more accurate or appropriate than in the case of Culloden. British historians have long framed the battle as a crucial event, not just militarily, nationally, or dynastically, but also as a moment of transition—almost an epiphanic moment in some accounts—between the old and new, the modern and traditional, the Scottish and British. This is a process which was emplaced by two developments: first, the modelling of history as stadial (that is, moving forwards progressively in distinct stages of increasing refinement, civility, and modernity) in the hands of the writers of the Scottish Enlightenment from the 1750s onwards, which in its turn gave rise to much of what came to be described as Whig history; and secondly, the propaganda value placed by the British government, press, and society on the victory, and its reflection in the way in which the 'Highlands' were read as an entity. As we saw in Chapter 4, Andrew Henderson claimed that the whole of the British Empire had rejoiced over the victory at Culloden. There was a definite attempt—as we shall see—to make the battle an epic encounter of global significance, a defeat of savagery (as reflected not only in propaganda, but in loyal addresses from the provincial towns) by civilization, a token or avatar of future global triumph over both indigenous peoples and over France and its allies.

There were thus both strong intellectual and political imperatives in presenting the victory as a crucial staging post in social and imperial development. Progress was itself a fairly new concept (the literary and ideological battle between the ancients and moderns was only half a century old) and the cultural memory of Culloden in British history was framed as the hour that made the *Pax Britannica* and the worldwide triumph of its civility and commerce possible: even as late as 2006, *The Battle That Made Britain* was the title of a BBC programme on Culloden. The framing of the battle in these terms remains intense, determining, and obtrusive. It is the key reason for the inadequacy of much of the scholarship on the conflict of 1745 up until recent times: the need to reiterate belief outweighs the search for evidence, a situation that arises more often than historians perhaps always admit. It is only since the British Empire came to an end and the contemporary nature of 'Great Britain' as a state began to be questioned that Jacobitism and the 'Fortyfive have received more strongly evidence-led attention, while Scottish nationalists like Irish nationalists before them have both used and been characterized in the inherited discourses of Jacobitism. The frame of cultural memory of Culloden as a bloody, and to that extent alone regrettable, victory of progress over backwardness, the modern over the traditional, and the systematic and technologically advanced army over the bravery of the individual warrior, nonetheless remains very strong in our wider culture.

History and historians have a tendency to set themselves apart from memory studies. As Wulf Kansteiner puts it, 'memory studies have not done enough to establish a clear conceptual and methodological basis for collective memory processes', while Geoffrey Cubitt notes that 'the notion of a collective memory...masks what are often radical discontinuities in social consciousness'.[1] Lacking clarity, conceptual process, and with an ever-present risk of masking and its accompaniment, the 'masquerade', memory studies are seen by some scholars as an approach which occludes the delineation of the past in favour of its representation.

Ironically, this kind of critique has received indirect support from the core of memory studies itself, as both Maurice Halbwachs and later Pierre Nora in *Les Lieux de mémoire* (the published English translation as 'realm', so close to *royaume,* itself carries an implication of obsolescence and finitude) drew a strong distinction between memory and history. As Michael Rossington and Anne Whitehead put it, Nora's 'elegiac tone and too easy an opposition between memory and history…implicitly positions memory as an anti-historical discourse'.[2]

Yet memory can have a direct influence on the subject matter, practice, and operational categories of history. First, there is the ability of memory to make history directly and to be the key agent in its manufacture. The Russian occupation of eastern Ukraine in the Ruin of 1657–86 (then the Cossack Hetmanate, called 'Little Russia' in Russian diplomatic correspondence, and not followed up by occupation of the non-Austrian west of Ukraine until 1793) was followed not only by the move of church authority from Constantinople to Moscow in 1686, but also by failed attacks on Crimea in 1687 and 1689, before victory at Azov in 1696. Access to the Black Sea, Constantinople, and Balkan protectorates were as much a part of Russian policy in 1854 and 1914, and their echoes are with us yet. Because the age of Marlborough or Saxe, Culloden, or Charles XII seems so remote to us, it does not follow that this is a universally applicable category. Memory time creates disjunctions invisible to chronology, and this is itself what can create the ideological framework of the history that appears merely to record what happened. Useful as concepts such as 'decline', 'rise', 'inevitability', 'progress', and 'modernization' may sometimes be, their Enlightenment teleology, the sinews of their intellectual power, muscles aside the particularity of the locus and circumstance of memory, which, if allied to power, can change or make history. Quite simply, Putin—and many Russians—see the situation in Ukraine in terms we have historicized but which they *remember.*

Secondly, historiography itself responds to memory, particularly as communicative memory (indicative of memory of an event occurring within the lifetime of its communication, and itself a primary source with the provisos attendant on oral history) gives way to cultural memory (memory existing beyond the lifetimes of those who originally communicated it). The social longing to celebrate the last great victory of the British Empire provides the market fed by the history of the Second World War, and therefore the economic base on which the study of the Third Reich rests. History is the main agent for making memory: archival footage, primary evidence, is presented in heavily editorialized form on television; baroque enquiries into Nazi byways combine with celebratory anaphora in the historiographical market for the Second World War. In the recent centenary of the outbreak of the First World War, can we really separate historiographical enquiry from the manufacture of cultural memory? The symbiosis between what Roland Quinault called 'the cult of the centenary' and historiographical enquiry is not a new thing. In the age of Thomas Carlyle, Auguste Comte, and Frederic Harrison it led to *On Heroes and Hero-Worship*, the *Positivist Calendar*, and the *New Calendar of Great Men*, as well as explosions in artistic portrayals of historical moments which in turn fed the illustrated histories of the early twentieth century. Indeed, the modern broad-based discipline of history itself (and indeed the literary canon) was probably engendered by the 'ritual...and melo-drama' of the age of public celebration which ran from Garrick's 1769 Shakespeare Jubilee to the millennium of Alfred the Great in September 1901 (Alfred of course died in 899) and beyond.[3]

Thirdly, history operationalizes itself in terms infused by memory, and the stronger the impetus to remember things in a certain way, the stronger is the infusion. The frame places the episode it presents, gives it a locus, within a framework of the national past, itself in its banal nationalism representative of a combination of memory and history. Historiography has for centuries framed the Jacobite era, both in its culture and its military threat, in a markedly directive way. In doing so, it has itself responded to the terms of the memorialization of the episode presented by the British response to it. History here is often found far from the documents, infused by memory.

The framing of the Jacobite period began with the political cartoon. From the early eighteenth century on, in a typology strongly reinforced in 1745 and revisited in the Bute and Wilkes era of the 1760s, the Scot was seen as often potentially if not actually disloyal, and was associated with aggression, hairiness, infestation, lust, the kilt, and starvation (although paradoxically Scots were also presented as physically large).[4] Irrespective of origin or ability to speak Gaelic, such figures were often characterized as 'Highlanders': for example, Wolfe describes both Lord Kilmarnock and the Franco-Irish Brigadier Stapleton as 'Highlanders' in the aftermath of Culloden. David Morier's *An Incident in the Rebellion of 1745* remains one of the most famous images from the immediate aftermath of the battle, which characterizes this point of view and provides a crossover between the political cartoon and 'high' art (Figure 12). Morier, who was largely a military painter, enjoyed Cumberland's patronage from 1743 onwards and may have been present at the battle: certainly it is likely that the painting used captured Jacobites as models. *An Incident* may have been one of a group of four done for Cumberland portraying military prowess in different nations. It portrays advancing Jacobite troops making contact with Barrell's grenadier company on the British front line. Among all the swords, targes, or Lochaber axes, there is not a gun to be seen on the Jacobite side, which is composed of large and virile men: two of the three chins we can see are unshaven, while a fallen Highlander has his right leg artistically raised at the knee so that his naked and muscular thigh is visible. It is not quite apparent, but strongly suggested, that he wears nothing under his kilt.

Morier's *Incident in the Rebellion of 1745* collates the elements of the anti-Jacobite political cartoon in its presentation of the large, hirsute, virile, and primitively armed Scottish force ('all the offscourings of the earth', as Dougal Graham called them) at Culloden, presented as using Lochaber axes and swords, innocent of firearms, although Thomas Sandby's contemporary picture clearly shows Jacobite guns in use by the forward ranks. Morier's image was of a piece with contemporary propaganda pictures of the Jacobite Army, which stressed the ungovernable sexuality and appetites of its soldiery ('A Pack of Vagabons') and the unnaturalness of the *Female Rebels* (the title of a 1747 tract)— women who supported the Jacobite army, sometimes with arms in their hands or even in positions of military command. Cross-dressing was a repeated theme: in March 1746, the London *Evening Post* reported

Figure 12 David Morier, *An Incident in the Rebellion of 1745.*

that over 100 Jacobite soldiers had been seized in Aberdeen wearing women's clothing; such reports helped support the British Army attacks on women which occurred in the aftermath of the Rising. Up to 2,000 women may have accompanied the army into England, and 'there are repeated references in contemporary reports to Jacobite "Amazons"; one garbled French account apparently (wrongly) suggesting that a whole regiment entirely consisting of women had been raised'. Figures such as the half-mythical Jenny Cameron, 'Colonel' Anne Mackintosh who raised the Mackintosh regiment and Lady Ogilvy who drew her sword to proclaim James at Cupar, were all examples of the challenge not only of Jacobite 'savages' but also of 'wild women': one pro-government print, *Tandem Triumphans*, even shows 'women being attacked by British army soldiers with drawn swords at Culloden, apparently in a spirit of self-congratulation'. Such attitudes persisted for some time, despite the apparently chivalrous release of Flora MacDonald (1722–90), who had been central in helping Prince Charles Edward to escape.

Dougal Graham's 1752 edition of his *Full Particular and True Account of the Rebellion* observed of 'Colonel' Anne Mackintosh at Culloden, 'Great Pity it was she fell not there'. The anti-Jacobite trope of unnatural women was so widespread that Peg Woffington's ballad 'The Female Volunteer: or, an attempt to make our men Stand' drew on the propaganda imagery of Scots Jacobite virility (as for example in the print *The Scotch Broomstick & the Female Besom*) to draw satirical attention to the detumescent conduct of the British forces at Falkirk.[5]

Jenny Cameron was mocked in Thomas Arne's *Harlequin Incendiary, or Columbine Cameron* (1746), which depicts the 1745 Rising as the Pope in alliance with the Devil to destroy 'old England'. There is no doubt that the Rising is perceived in national terms. The Devil is Harlequin, and the harlequin portraits of Charles Edward became increasingly popular in this period (Figure 13).

In 1759, another potential Jacobite attempt was portrayed in *Harlequin's Invasion*. While Harlequin was a staple of the 'comic or "grotesque" sections' of eighteenth-century pantomime, the dismissive

Figure 13 John Worsdale, *Charles as Harlequin* (c.1746). One of the 'Harlequin' portraits of the era, depicting Charles Edward as a comic grotesque.

humour in which it characterized political threat had an unmistakable undertone of fear and contempt: in 1781, *Harlequin Teague* moved focus to a new object of satirical loathing. The strong link between the stage and the visual cartoon can be seen not only in the Harlequin representations of Charles Edward, but also in terms of title: *Highland Fair* is both a ballad opera of 1731 and an anti-Jacobite political cartoon of 1745.[6]

But it is the framing of Morier's, an iconic painting based on the political caricature of the era, which remains core to the visualization as to the history of the Rising of 1745, the fluidity of the moment and its possibilities forever imprinted on the wall in a single shape. The presentation of the Jacobite Army in Victorian genre painting, in Peter Watkins's 1964 *Culloden*, in the BBC's 1996 *Rebellion!*, and in the National Trust for Scotland's audiovisual displays of 1984 and 2007, where to this day hirsute and dirty men jostle in a parody of military order prior to their futile charge, are all indebted to Morier's initial conception. Morier's painting defined the image of the Scots rebel, just as Benjamin West's *Death of General Wolfe*, which I will turn to shortly, provided closure and an enfolding into British history for the 'loyal Highlander' by its image of that rebel (both Scots and Native American) tamed by incorporation into Britain's empire.

Morier's picture has major agency in the manufacture of cultural memory, but it also became key to historiographical presentation. It is paralleled in James Ray's note (though it may possibly be only attributed to Ray) of 30 April 1746 that 'the Broad Sword and Target, is unequal to ... Musket and Bayonet', though Ray was with the British Army and must have been well aware, as Sandby was, that guns were the normal arm of the Jacobites. Other hostile contemporary commentators noted that it was the British cavalry that were the key arm, for 'in the Heat of the Foot Engagement, both the Right and Left Wings of our Cavalry flank our Enemies ... disperse their second Line, and get behind their First'. This was, as Chapter 3 has shown, much closer to the facts of the battle than its presentation as a conflict between sword and musket, but it was the latter view that was to prevail.[7]

In their way, early Jacobite memoirs such as that of Chevalier de Johnstone from the 1760s also drew on the idea of the Jacobite Army as heroic and primitive swordsmen, because this characterization emphasized their loyalty to the Scottish martial tradition, just as terming the Jacobite Army 'Highland' reinscribed the traditional link between Scottish patriotism and the valour of the Scottish north. Gaelic celebration of the sword as the weapon of a heroic officer class also had its part to play, as in Iain Ruadh Stiùbhart's own writing, where 'bullets round our faces…spoiled swordfighting, more's the pity'. Alasdair MacMhaighstir Alasdair, leading Gaelic poet of the century and captain in the Prince's army, also portrayed his own side in antique, traditional, and heroic terms, which overstressed (for example) swords and virility, not drill, the firefight, and the fact that the average height of the army was under 5 foot 6 inches. Alasdair's long masterpiece of the 1750s, *Birlinn Chlann Raghnaill*, presents the fate of Gaelic-speaking MacDonald culture in the post-Culloden era in antique and traditional terms, alien from the lifestyle of its eighteenth-century leaders. Similarly, James Macpherson's memorialization of Culloden and the significance of it as a defeat through his Ossian poetry, translations, and adaptations in the 1760s, reinforced the idea of Scottish authenticity as deriving from the immemorially antique, not from an alternative modernity. In such ways did the Jacobite world play into the hands of its opponents' desire to marginalize and primitivize it. Swords continued to play a significant part in stories about the battle and heroic last stands. Thus two politically contested collective memories mutually reinforced each other to serve a single narrative. To take only one example of this, when John Leyden toured Scotland in the late summer of 1800, his discussion linked the Battle of Culloden directly to the fact that 'Mr Fraser informed me that he had heard a Captain MacDonald of Breakish in Sky repeat *Temora*…Near Culloden we saw a fine Druidical circle'. The battle is seen as a last survivor into modern times of an Ossianic Scotland of deep antiquity. Not untypically for the age, Leyden had the Highlanders described to him as 'The Indians of Scotland', and his tour is marked with an almost relentless search for the authentic roots of Ossian and Ossianic values.[8]

It was through characterizations such as this that the image of the reconciliation of Scottish martial valour to the British state presented by Benjamin West in *The Death of General Wolfe* (1770) was in harmony with the historiography of the era. In the picture (available online), a Native American contemplates the fallen hero. Wolfe in his ultimate vulnerability is yet the master of such indigenous peoples, just as he had been at Culloden in 1746 over Lieutenant Colonel Simon Fraser, who is in the picture but did not fight in the engagement. Fraser, Lovat's son, was of course a battalion commander at Culloden, but did not reach the field in time. The picture states a simple tale: even in death, Wolfe is ascendant over the untamed natives of North America, who contemplate him with awe. They will become integrated into the British Empire by his victory, just as he has barely thirteen years earlier incorporated the natives of Scotland by an earlier triumph. His alleged mercy to the commander of Lovat's 1st Battalion on the field of Culloden is referred to in the continuing loyalty of the (in reality absent) Fraser of Lovat to Great Britain.

If the images of the Jacobites as savages to be tamed dominated early reaction and representation of the 1745 Rising and its final battle, historiography soon integrated this strong binary framework into its own more sophisticated approaches. The Jacobite cause was a key subject of one of the greatest historiographical innovations of all produced by those who wished to distance themselves from any odour of national disloyalty. The creation of effective stadialist historical models by the Scottish Enlightenment writers served a narrative of progress in which Jacobitism could appear to be an anachronistic final stage in feudal barbarity. The suggestive theorization of stadial development by Giambattista Vico and others earlier in the century was taken up by Turgot in France and Thomas Blackwell in Scotland, whose notion of increasing social refinement through time may have influenced both Adam Smith's *Theory of Moral Sentiments* (1759) and James Macpherson's rather muted and displaced sense of violence in *Fingal* (1761). Notably, *Moral Sentiments* uses the imagery of violence to suggest ideas of sympathy, understanding, and reconciliation: a motif which modern writers have seen as having particular application to Scotland in the 1746–60 era.

Adam Smith's four-stage theory of development in his 1762 lectures in jurisprudence suggested that a warlike society 'should give way to a society pursuing personal betterment in a commercial environment'. Meanwhile William Robertson's *History of Scotland* (1759) stated that the past of countries like Scotland was better forgotten rather than celebrated, and that the country was much better off for emerging—with the British legislation of 1746–7—from its feudal past. A limited space of sentiment was allowed to the unfortunate Stuarts (principally Mary) in Robertson's model (though not in Hume's in his *History of England* (1754–61)), but the degree of such sentiment was inversely proportional to the dynasty's political relevance. In its way, the homage being paid by the primary sources of communicative memory, such as Bishop Robert Forbes's *Lyon in Mourning* on the Jacobite side, was itself accommodated to this language of sentiment, as all too soon the terminology of militancy and political change, rendered impossible by circumstance, began to transmute into a cultural memorialization built on relics and souvenirs, and indeed may have initiated the genre of history painting itself. Gavin Hamilton's *Mary Queen of Scots Resigning Her Crown* (1765–8) (Figure 14), painted for Boswell and passed on to him in Scotland by Andrew Lumisden, secretary to the Jacobite court (who later supported Runciman in his Ossianic painting), became the first in a long line of depictions which framed Scottish history as patriotic if defeated at a time when the dominant voices of Enlightenment historiography were consigning it to outmoded irrelevance. Hume of course regarded anyone who thought Mary innocent a Jacobite fanatic. In this way a space was preserved for Jacobite and Jacobite-related discourse, but one which could not contest its political repression by stadial historical modelling, and indeed depended, as time went on, on the stadial model itself to generate continuing nostalgia for the Jacobite era and the Scottish martial past. Political nostalgia was a control mechanism for the idea of progress: a sense of loss could be accommodated without ever proving to be disruptive.[9]

The Jacobite period has been strongly and almost certainly systematically misremembered within ensuing historiography in order to emphasize a secure framework for the development of a British habitus. A history which threatened the very existence of the state has been

Figure 14 Gavin Hamilton, *Mary Queen of Scots Resigning Her Crown* (1765–8). An early example of sentimental history painting relating to the fall of the Stuart dynasty through several generations. Hamilton wrote to Boswell of his 'compassion' for the Queen.

presented in terms which are designed to foreground it as a foundational part of the success of that state, technologically, financially, culturally, and militarily. Michel Foucault identified as the *loi de rareté*, the principle of scarcity, the point where a diverse set of data and possible memories or histories are condensed through 'the selectivity of recall, the convergence of memories, the recursivity in remembrance, the recycling of models of remembrance and memory transfers'. Anaphoric historiography, which feeds on itself and repeats its own secondariness rather than identifying fresh primary sources, has been a feature of the treatment of the Jacobites in British history, whose modelling up to recent times has been brutally binary. Just as Horace Walpole represented the feudal past haunting the usurpation of the present in *The Castle of Otranto* (1764), so British history modelled its own Gothic chiaroscuro on to the complex realities of Culloden battlefield and the forces engaged on it.[10]

The key oppositions used in Jacobite history were in place from an early date as shown in Table 1.

Table 1

Jacobite political values	British government values
Absolutist and anachronistic	Constitutionalist and progressive
Catholic	Protestant
Divisive and local	Stable and universal
Foreign/French/Celtic and Gaelic	British
Oral and antiquarian	Documentary and professional

It is worth noting with respect to Table 1 that the supposition that Jacobitism was oral and antiquarian may be linked to long-standing omissions by many to consult a wide range of readily available primary sources on (for example) Jacobite regimental and military organization. In a related vein, the idea that the Jacobite Army or militant Jacobite support was largely Catholic disappears when the context alters: for example, in respect of Highland regiments in the Seven Years War of 1756–63 and subsequently, alleged Catholicism mysteriously vanishes, though no mass conversion is ever recorded. The need to brand them as 'other' has simply disappeared.

A similar schema can be seen operating in analysis of the Jacobite Army in Table 2.

Table 2

Jacobite Army	British Army
Clannish and tribal	State and patriotic
Swordsmen and individual warriors	Muskets and collective drill
Savage amateurs	Civilized professionals
Hillmen and troglodytes	Bourgeois and propertied interest
Rural and barbaric	Urban and civilized

Until quite recently, historians have been content to frame the Rising in these strong and oppositional primary colours. In the nineteenth century this was linked to a division of Scotland into two quasi-separate ethnic and cultural (and at times political) entities: the 'Highlands' and the 'Lowlands'. This division is still in frequent and popular use today, even though, as the leading historical geographer Charles Withers reminds us,

> a separateness between Highlands and Lowlands did not exist. In eco-
> nomic relations, in tenurial practices, in marriage patterns, and in the rou-
> tines of seasonal migration, the Highlands and Lowlands were closely
> connected…In explaining the geography…we should not suppose the
> Highlands and the Lowlands separate regions.

As with Culloden itself, the actual evidence of Highland–Lowland economic and social integration presents a much more complex and integrated picture than the stark binary oppositionalism promoted in
cultural memory, and until recently by much historiography.[11]

From the 1740s, historians often took their cue from the language of
anti-Jacobite propaganda. There were some unsurprising exceptions:
for example James Macpherson, a Jacobite sympathizer from a Jacobite
family, asserted 'the racial and ethnic superiority of the Celts to the
English', and made it clear that Jacobitism had a clear political goal, as
'The Scottish Jacobites were resolved to risk every thing to prevent the
union'. There were also some unusually fair-minded writers like Henry
Hallam.[12] However, the general framework of Culloden as the victory of
progress over backwardness was clearly visible from the loyal addresses
of the 1740s to the historians of the nineteenth century. Even the not

unsympathetic Robert Chambers, writing in 1827, saw the Jacobites as deriving from 'the rudest and least civilized part of the nation', addicted to a 'patriarchal form of society', and thus primitive in stadial terms. These 'children of the mountains' were in their 'vigour' (a term which bears out the language of Morier and the cartoon tradition) 'willing and ready as ever to commence a civil war'. Though some historians, such as Catherine Macaulay, were sufficiently radical to be relatively positive on Jacobitism in the face of Whig corruption, the general Whig inter-pretation held. It has recently been stated that the term Whig history 'lacks specificity and historians should no longer utilize this prejudicial title', but the application of stadialism to historical study, the assump-tion of teleological progress towards the condition of modernity, and above all the conflation of victory and chauvinistic pride with moral categories can be characterized by no other term so well.[13]

In the middle of the nineteenth century, Henry Buckle saw the 1745 Rising as 'the last struggle of barbarism against civilisation', while Macfarlane and Thomson in 1861 sneered at the very notion of a Jacobite chain of command, and Justin McCarthy in 1890 noted that the 'clansmen' were 'as savage and desperately courageous as Sioux or Pawnees'. In 1899, Sir John Fortescue's magisterial history of the British Army noted (perhaps with more recent conflicts on the North West Frontier in mind) that 'the campaign ended, as victorious campaigns against mountaineers must always end, in the hunting of fugitives, the burning of villages, and the destruction of crops'. For Fortescue, Culloden meant that 'Jacobitism...the curse of the kingdom for three quarters of a century, was finally slain, and the Highlanders, who had been a plague...were finally subjugated', being 'little else' than 'half-savage mountaineers'. Here the history of the conclusion of the Rising is presented in a way which barely veils the subtext of Jacobitism as an avatar of the challenges faced by British imperialism.[14]

In 1939, Basil Williams took a slightly different tack, personalizing the Rising as a misadventure which resulted from the 'winning charm' of Charles Edward, 'which appealed to the romantic Scots', despite the Prince's lack of 'character or strategy'. The 'romantic attachment' which led to the unfortunate Rising was itself a character flaw of course, one of fey individualism and the triumph of sentiment over rationality. No evidence of course was adduced for these sweeping ethnocultural judgements and personality assessments; and Williams's point was simply repeated in 1974 by John Owen, who noted that 'the romantic appeal and personal charm of Charles Edward had proved no substitution for judgement and leadership'. Cumberland put down the Rising with a firm hand, it was true, but 'scarcely...savagery'.[15]

At the same time, the imperialist metaphors of the Jacobites as 'backward colonials' continued to be reiterated. The image of Morier's picture, drawn as its gaze was from the expectations of political cartoon propaganda, presented the Jacobites as virile and sexually charged (the upraised leg and naked thigh), savage and violent. If their attachment to their 'Bonnie' prince was a sign of the sentimental over-emotionalism that made them in darker contexts irrationally and animalistically sexual, so their violence and savagery aligned them with Britain's global struggles against tribal societies, built—like the victory at Culloden as depicted by Morier—on technological and moral superiority. As the empire decayed, these tropes lingered. In 1952, G. M. Trevelyan identified the Rising as 'a fantasia of misrule...in defiance of Parliament and its laws...an Afghanistan...within fifty miles of the "modern Athens"'. The 'immemorial zest for plunder' of the 'hill tribesmen' was Churchill's view in 1956, while in 1973 Charles Chevenix Trench proclaimed the Jacobite army to be 'a savage Highland horde, as alien...as a war party of Iroquois'. J. H. Plumb's approach in 1950 was somewhat different: in *England in the Eighteenth Century*, Jacobitism is apparently irrelevant enough not even to appear in the index—this is *loi de rareté* at its most acute, scarcity translated into absence. John Prebble's very popular study *Culloden*, first published in 1961, presented Jacobitism as a backward ideology of 'a race of tribesmen' whose chiefs were 'civilised savages' defending a society 'as obsolescent' as the Jacobite cause itself. In 1981, J. A. Houlding noted that 'not only were many of the clansmen Catholic...but they were a primitive people whose tribal social organization was utterly archaic'. Paul Langford noted 'the preservation of

England against a Highland rabble' in 1989, while Rex Whitworth in 1992 characterized the army and its leader as 'the upstart and his rabble [of] ferocious Highlanders'. In the same year, Linda Colley utilized the motive of bankruptcy rather than that of charisma to explain away Jacobite support—economic rather than rational incompetence—when noting (incorrectly) that 'only the poorer Highland clans' supported Charles. While more balanced accounts begin to increase as we near the present day (although American historiography remains more resolutely Whiggish and still often reacts in a hostile way to the very mention of Jacobitism), the fundamental account we inherit is based on this narrow and highly binarized version of the victory—and indeed the teleology—of civility over barbarism. It may have begun to pass from academic to popular history, but its power remains. It was just as well in the terms of this construction that what it identifies as Charles Edward's band of deluded and sexually incontinent savages were 'cut to pieces by withering artillery' on Culloden battlefield.[16]

The same kind of strongly framed accounts have traditionally prevailed with regard to specific issues relating to the Rising and Culloden. To take only one example, Charles Edward's conduct in the battle has long been characterized by Lord Elcho's reputed words on his unavoidable flight after defeat, terming him 'an Italian coward and a scoundrel' sometimes popularized as 'There you go, you cowardly Italian'. This account has long seemed to carry more weight than the alternative, where a cornet in the Horse Guards noted that the Prince wanted to charge forward and save the day, while Sullivan ordered Colonel O'Shea of Fitzjames's to take Charles Edward to safety. 'They won't take me alive!' he screamed, minutes before being led off the field, guarded by Glenbuchat's men and the soldiers of the Edinburgh Regiment. Still he tried to return to the fray, before a Scottish officer, Major Kennedy, 'seized the bridle and led the prince firmly away from the scenes of carnage'. As Charles Edward later noted, 'he was forced off the field by the people about him'.[17] This is especially interesting as the sources for the latter account are Sullivan, Elcho, the Stuart Papers, and the Historical Manuscripts Commission (HMC) papers: there is strong corroboration.

And yet the source for the former account is not Elcho himself (though he loathed Charles Edward and had little motive to conceal it), but an article by Sir Walter Scott. Scott's account was comprehensively rebutted by A. C. Ewald in 1875, who noted that it was not in Elcho's Manuscript Journal and was inconsistent with other accounts. It is not the only piece of Scottish history for which Scott is the uncorroborated source. Yet, despite the comprehensive documentation available elsewhere, this characterization of Charles's cowardice is frequently alluded to, even if its original source is forgotten. It is a powerful denominating line in Peter Watkins's influential film of 1964, even though modern historians are careful to describe it as a 'tradition'.[18]

This episode typifies the persistence of unevidenced allegation and imprecision in describing Culloden; to take one other example, the National Trust for Scotland (NTS) at the Visitor Centre still describe Elcho's and Balmerino's Life Guards, Bagot's Hussars, and Strathallan's Perthshire Horse as 'Highland Horse', though there was nothing 'Highland' about any of them. Morier's depiction, reinforced by Gaelic romanticism, continues to frame events strongly in such repetitive and limited ways, just as it is telling how many of the more serious historians quoted above virtually repeat each other word for word in their rein-scriptions of the permitted, defined, and authorized portrait of Culloden.

The outer parts of this frame were the first to get damaged. History from below and the reassessment of the degree of urban and rural unrest in an age of stability seemed to have little to do with Jacobitism, but began to open up the possibility of considering it in a similar light: it was no coincidence that E. P. Thompson recognized the unacknowledged social strength of Jacobitism, for example. From a different perspective altogether, the view that the Scottish Enlightenment was a product of the benefits brought by Union and the defeat of Stuart 'absolutism' was under sustained challenge by the late 1980s. Bruce Lenman's verdict in *The Jacobite Clans of the Great Glen* (1984) that Lovat's abiding passion was Scottish nationalism, and John Gibson's use of a contemporary SNP slogan in his history of the '08, *Playing the Scottish Card* (1988), both sig-nalled the abundant presence of evidence which historiography had in general chosen to ignore but which of course was very much alive in nineteenth-century cultural memory, which saw the 'Forty-five as a Scottish rising against the Union: since the Union was a good thing, that was nothing to worry about. Bruce Lenman's clear distaste for the personal and political qualities of the Jacobite leadership made his assessment of the significance of the movement all the more credible, while Frank McLynn's work on the military side of the Rising sticks close to the documents in *France and the Jacobite Rising of 1745* (1981), *The Jacobite Army in England* (1983), and the magisterial and intensely archive-driven *Charles Edward Stuart* (1988). McLynn's position on the political left set him apart from Catholic romanticists like Sir Charles Petrie, and his arguments— as those of Daniel Szechi and Jeremy Black, whose study of *Culloden* first appeared in 1990—could be contested, but were not overturned. A generation of historians who no longer romanticized Jacobitism but reframed it (though others had done extraordinarily good work before, this was seldom conceptual) proved difficult to combat because dismissiveness had replaced fresh research in so much of the work of their adversaries. Paul Monod's *Jacobitism and the English People* (1989) made large claims, but these have gone effectively unanswered, as have those of Allan Macinnes in *Clanship, Commerce and the House of Stuart* (1996) and Eamonn Ó Ciardha's *Ireland and the Jacobite Cause* (2002). Moreover, far from being ignored, Macinnes's and Monod's books in particular are heavily cited. Daniel Szechi's *The Jacobites* (1994) and *1715* (2006) sometimes make strong claims, but have effectively been acknowledged as advancing an unanswered case, while the present writer's *Myth of the Jacobite Clans*, first issued in 1995 and last updated in 2009, has to a greater or lesser extent been accepted in its case that the Jacobite Army was a conventional, popular, and substantially non-Gaelic force. Its archive-based argument has been supported by those, such as Tony Pollard and Stuart Reid, who approach the Battle of Culloden from very different perspectives. Essentially, archaeological, historical, and other evidence approached directly and freshly is presenting a new picture of Culloden, and a new frame in which to place the battle.

6

Culloden in British Memory

Objects, Artefacts, and Representations of the Conflict

As the beginnings of large-scale travel and tourism through Scotland began within fifteen or twenty years of the Battle of Culloden, it might have been expected that the conflict would become an early memory site. Culloden would surely begin to appear as a place in which the confirmatory victory of Great Britain and British values could be implanted as part of the collective memorialization of the internal Grand Tour and its recording of a diversity now reduced from threat to theatre by the securing of the Union through British arms.

Many exiled Jacobites became commemorated abroad as heroic leaders, not least Field Marshal James Keith, the hero—following his death at Hochkirk in 1758—of Prussian song and, as 'Der Earl Marischal', 'an authentic Prussian folk hero'.[1] If the battlefield was not to become a *lieu de mémoire* before 1840, the portable relics of Jacobitism most definitely were. Robert Forbes's *Lyon in Mourning* itself incorporated relics such as 'the prince's blue velvet garter and tartan waistcoat, various souvenirs of the women's clothes he has used to escape from South Uist to Skye...and a piece of wood from the boat he had used to reach Benbecula'. Garters, flags, and other relics of ordinary officers and units were regularly preserved, while an increasingly emotional and sentimental language began to surround the Prince himself, not least in the context of the Flora MacDonald story: the West Highland Folk Museum has a 'handkerchief reputedly stained with the tears of his daughter Charlotte'.

Eventually this language of sentiment became transferred to George III and some of his successors.[2]

The Rising was also present in a wider range of cultural representation, including china Highlanders modelled on the models made of the 1743 mutineers of the Black Watch Mutiny, and 'battle gardens', which first appeared in the middle of the eighteenth century, though these commemorated a wider variety of conflict: the Earl of Stair's garden at Culhorn in Wigtownshire 'represented the armies at the battle of Dettingen (1743)' but perhaps this was itself an oblique reference to Culloden. Gothic architecture, starting with the new Inveraray Castle, begun in 1747 for the Dukes of Argyll, presented the heroic past as both incorporated and repressed; the same was true of the trophy of arms placed over the fireplace in Blair Castle in Perthshire in 1750. In general, Jacobite landscapes were overdramatized: for example, post-1747 depictions of Strathtay by Thomas and Paul Sandby (Cumberland's draughtsman and the official draughtsman to the military survey in Scotland respectively) were 'made more dramatic, with loftier peaks and crags'. Arguably, these exaggerations helped to underpin what the cultural historian Corinne Harol has identified as an ideology of Whig superiority to the 'symbolic practices' of Jacobitism, whereby the Whig view was defined by its 'superior relationship to reality' in contrast to the mummery and 'pageantry' of Jacobite symbolism. Presenting the Jacobites as caricatures in a caricature landscape was an important part of this. It is, however, also the case that the eighteenth-century British military tended to describe the obstacle presented by upland landscape in terms later periods would find exaggerated. The threat of the Scottish landscape was inflected by the eighteenth-century gaze, just as its inhabitants were.[3]

Culloden battlefield itself was far from being a tourist venue in these years, despite the somewhat optimistic view expressed in the contemporary interpretation that a 1752 coin found on the battlefield was 'possibly dropped by a soldier visiting these war graves in the years after the battle'. Discussion of the battle seems to have begun by being largely oblique, and was often omitted altogether. The *Inverness Courier* carried only one reference to it at all prior to 1822 and only four between 1825 and 1841. This was at a time when souvenirs and relics of the Jacobite movement were being assiduously collected and preserved, making their unobtrusive journey from treacherous objects to Romantic relics, no longer the tools of political futurity but the depoliticized nostalgia of cultural memory, one which was increasingly collectivized as Jacobite memorabilia became more and more conflated with the insignia of success associated with Highland regiments in the British Army. And yet, perhaps because the incorporation of Scottish troops into the army was so much part of the language of British reconciliation in the post-Jacobite era, the details of British Army success at Culloden tended to be downplayed in the records of those who travelled round northern Scotland. When it was mentioned, the battle was often presented at a distance, as if a vast gulf of time instead of a few years separated the visitor from the conflict. Culloden was seen as a battle of under an hour that had changed British history forever, but its significance in time and its displacement from time were both far greater than the chronology would indicate. Memory both expanded temporal distance and compressed temporal significance into the single story of British modernity. In the most successful era of Britishness, Britain remembered the battle as out of time, while Scotland preferred not to remember it at all: it was a source of shame and defeat for a way of life better shamed and defeated, but why dwell on that?[4]

In his tour of 1758, Sir William Burrell took 'a view of Culloden Moor, famous in the annals of the country for the defeat of the rebel forces in 1745', but for him already a remote event recorded in 'the histories of the time'. Terms like 'annals' and 'histories' strongly suggest the scale of Burrell's chronological displacement of the battle from the immediate past. Even at a time before stadial history had established itself, Culloden was being presented in terms of a disjunct chronology. Twelve years after the battle there were still British Army patrols in large parts of Scotland; if not live politics, there was still an aftermath in operation. Culloden was very much within the sphere of communicative memory, yet Burrell presents it as if it were out of range of recollection, best not remembered save when veiled under the remote eye of history. And yet the battle was not remote at all.[5]

Richard Pococke, Bishop of Meath, who toured Scotland between 1747 and 1760, notes that 'the Pretender' had situated himself in a cowardly position 'beyond the summit of the hill entirely out of sight', and that the Jacobite clans 'advanced with great fury in a highland trot…in an unsoldierlike manner firing without order' (note the reference to musketry). He has nothing to say about atrocities or the conduct of the British Army, referring only to the 'immortal Laurels' of the Duke of Cumberland. Pococke thus deals with the battle as a display of both the moral and military inadequacy of the Jacobite forces through their poor drill and the cowardice of their commander, with the strong implication that they have been rightfully overcome. For Thomas Pennant in 1769, matters were even more stark: Culloden was 'the place that North Britain owes its present prosperity to, by the victory of April 16, 1746', and as a consequence, while he admits the atrocities of the British Army, he does so obliquely and in the manner of a felix culpa: 'But let a veil be flung over a few excesses consequential of a day productive of so much benefit to the united kingdoms'. The purpose of a visit to Culloden is not to remember, but to forget. For Pococke, what is worth recollecting is the moral and military inadequacy of the Jacobites (and as we saw in Chapter 5, many who claim to be objective historians have since engaged in similar rhetoric); for Pennant, the memory of Culloden is one of a magic moment, an immediate and historic transition to modernity. The battle itself and its aftermath embarrass with their suffering the point of the outcome for British civilization. They are best forgotten; what is worth remembering is the frame for British modernity provided by British victory that day.[6]

From the 1770s until well into the nineteenth century, the battlefield was—perhaps as a consequence of this approach—often forgotten by outside commentators. It was what happened there and its effects that were important, not how it happened: it was the birthplace of Britain, but the labour pains and the unprepossessing place of nativity were alike best left unvisited or at least unrecounted. In 1773 Boswell and

Johnson went to see the ancient stones of Clava, barely 1 kilometre away from the battlefield as it is now presented and still closer to the British lines as they stood in 1746, but they did not visit the site of the conflict itself. Nor apparently did John Leyden in 1800, though he went both to Clava and to the (new) Culloden House, which lay just beyond the Jacobite left, noting only that 'To the south-west...lies the bleak heath on which the fatal battle of 1746 was fought which decided the fate of the ancient Stuart line'. Burns made a point of visiting Scottish battlefields, but although he visited Culloden he was deeply reticent about it, possibly for political reasons: 'Come over Culloden Muir reflections on the field of battle' was all he wrote of it on 5 September 1787. Elsewhere he notes of his family that 'what they could they did, and what they had they lost...they shook hands with Ruin for what they esteemed the cause of their King and their Country'. Even Sir Walter Scott, who so definitively took the Jacobites as one of the major themes of his novels, omitted direct discussion of Culloden from his groundbreaking *Waverley* in 1814, while the generations of novelists who have succeeded him have again and again returned to the Jacobite topos while somehow omitting discussion of the battle that both sealed the defeat of the 'Forty-five and ensured its symbolic importance in denominating the transition to British imperial modernity. Jacobitism remained a topic for fiction in R. L. Stevenson's *Kidnapped* (1886), John Buchan's *Midwinter* (1923), Naomi Mitchison's *The Bull Calves* (1947), and many other places, but Culloden is normally absent. Buchan's *A Lost Lady of Old Years* (1899) is an exception to this, but one which confirms the inevitability of defeat at Culloden and aligns it with the 'auld sang' of Scottish nationality, and the end of hopes for Scottish independence; its theme prefigures the haunting alignment of Jacobitism with sexuality in Barrie's *Farewell Miss Julie Logan* (1931). For Neil Gunn in *Butcher's Broom* (1934) the battle is only as a catalyst to the Clearances, an avatar of the suffering of Gaelic Scotland. Creative writing (with the exception of songs which sound the elegiac note) does not tend to remember Culloden directly.[7]

Yet official British memorialization did remember the battle, and remembered it as a key triumph. Although it does not appear on the battle honours of the British Army, the Royal Navy—whose seapower and ability to blockade supplies formed such a major feature of the British victory, as well as arguably delaying the onset of the night march by the Jacobite Army, which might well have been successful otherwise—repeatedly returned to the battle. On 9 September 1747, a seventy-four-gunner HMS *Culloden* was launched, and by the time a 1776 third rate bearing the same name ran aground in pursuit of the French near New York and gave its name to Culloden Point, two more ships had borne the name. The last and most famous HMS *Culloden*, launched in June 1783, was also a seventy-four-gun third rate which played a significant role in Nelson's actions in the Napoleonic Wars. It is possible that the navy had no need to be as sensitive as the army, where the incorporation of Scottish regiments was a key part of military development and success from the 1750s on. The Royal Family also perpetuated the memory of the British victory of 1746 by creating the title Baron Culloden, initially for a son of George III in 1801, then recreated in 1928.

As has been argued by Colin McArthur and John and Margaret Gold, the creation of Culloden as 'sacred space' was a phenomenon of the nineteenth century, and one which postdated the rise of public memorials to history and historical figures. It was not until after the restoration of some of the Jacobite titles (1824) and Catholic Emancipation (1829) that it was fully possible to revisit Culloden as a memory site. By that time of course, the historiographical framing discussed in Chapter 5 had delimited—in collaboration with the political cartoon and depictions such as Morier's—what exactly could be remembered of the battlefield's significance, if not of the battlefield itself. Culloden now definitively formed (as was earlier hinted by Burrell) what the cultural theorist Joep Leerssen has described as an 'allochronic periphery': a region, a site, 'imagined as belonging to an earlier era'. In this context, the celebration of the battle could begin more easily, for its disassociation from any continuing historical or political significance enabled it to serve in 'establishing a sentimental and affective bond to the new order'. There was a quid pro quo in that affective bond, though: Cumberland's equestrian statue in Cavendish Square was removed from public view in 1868, while Queen Victoria may have had 'Culloden' obliterated from his memorial obelisk in Windsor Great Park. Cumberland's brutality came more and more to be seen as an obstacle to the premiss of modernization and unity which his victory at Culloden had come to symbolize. If the battlefield was to be remembered, the brutality of the British commander could not be forgotten. Queen Victoria's 1842 visit to Scotland (when she became the first reigning Hanoverian to request a Jacobite song) was met at Atholl by the Duke's retainers carrying Lochaber axes in a tribute to the military past of the family in the Jacobite era, while the 1844 royal visit concluded with the presentation in 1845 of 'the Queen's Colours, giving the right to bear arms' to the Atholl Highlanders, thus restoring a picturesque 'fighting tail' of four companies and a band to the Dukes of Atholl. These were acts of reconciliation with the past, played out in a consciously anachronistic fashion. At the same time, the deerstalking and field sports enjoyed by Albert and practised at Balmoral symbolized both love for Scotland and control over its resources within a relationship heavily influenced by Ossianic rhetoric. Hunting deer became an integral part of this, not least perhaps because of the Stuart dynasty's long association with the animal: the symbol of the king as hunted deer dates back to John Denham's *Cooper's Hill* in the seventeenth century, if not beyond, while Gaelic poetry of the 'Forty-Five had also placed the Jacobites in the same light. The deer hunt could thus be seen as symbolically reinscribing Stuart defeat even while nostalgia for the Jacobite era grew. As Balmoral itself was redecorated in the 1850s, with a strong royal commitment to Scottish culture and Highland Games, and as even Queen Victoria professed herself a Jacobite, it became progressively easier to incorporate Culloden more inclusively into a cultural memory of misplaced loyalism, now properly directed to the Hanoverian dynasty. Such a discourse had arguably been initiated in the 1822 visit of George IV to Scotland; it was brought to completion by the middle of the century. Victoria's Scotland was her 'dear Paradise', but like any paradise after the first, it was only possible after death: Culloden was that death, but was now becoming a kind of 'holy dying'. It was a sign of the worthiness of Scotland to experience political defeat and displacement in the cause of becoming an aristocratic pleasure garden, full of Queen's Views, where the royal example of the deer hunt helped to lead to 10 per cent of Scottish land being under deer by 1884, and contributed to developments in land use which remain politically sensitive in the twenty-first century. From Jacobite warrior to British soldier (usually depicted as huge and hairy, like his predecessors) or loyal ghillie, the Scottish Highlander lived out a new role in empire and sentiment on the proceeds of death and defeat. The virility of the kilted soldier and his aggression was a Victorian leit-motif: Morier's image lived, but beyond the graves of Culloden and Scotland. In later generations, Culloden was to become a place of pil-grimage for many who identified themselves as part of the Scottish dias-pora, because part of its memory became associated with the Clearances and the dissolution of Highland life into colonial emigration.[8]

In the later Victorian period, the narrative re-enactment of episodes from the Jacobite era permeated society, up to and including the *tableaux vivants* at Balmoral itself. These were part of the fashion of the era, which developed in one strand into the living theatricals of Celtic cultural nationalism, which were much in evidence in Scotland and elsewhere at the turn of the twentieth century, not least in the extraordinary cos-tumery of the Celtic Congress at Caernarfon in 1904.[9] Early Scottish nationalists such as Theodore Napier focused on 'Culloden Day' cele-brations as a means of commemorating the defeat of the Scottish nation and its way of life, and analogies were drawn between British conduct in Transvaal in the Boer War and in Scotland (Napier also may have insti-tuted the modern form of the Bannockburn Rally in 1901, possibly as a counterweight to the millennium celebration of Alfred the Great). Both commemorations continue to this day: in 1996, almost 5,000 came to Culloden for the 250th anniversary of the Rising and to listen to the prayers instituted by the Gaelic Society of Inverness in 1925, which still continue. The laments and wreath-laying make clear their elegiac format, which has been carried forward into the era of the National Trust for Scotland (NTS). In 1963, the Military History Society of Ireland set up a commemorative marker for the Irish Brigade picquets (interest-ingly, Peter Watkins's film, made the next year, is one of the very few which acknowledges the presence of Irish troops), while in 1994 a marker was set up for the *Royal-Écossais*.[10]

The model of Culloden as a war grave was thus the one inherited and developed by the new NTS. The battlefield itself long remained obscured by tree plantations from the later nineteenth century, which may have helped make the soil more acidic and obscured the extent to which the conflict took place on farmland.[11] These plantations were followed by telegraph poles, a bungalow, and a tea shop. From 1937 onwards, the NTS gradually acquired the southern part of the battlefield, with what became a developing mission 'to preserve the integrity, atmosphere, graves and memorials of the battlefield; to restore it to its 1746 appearance; and to interpret it to the visitor'. In pursuit of this,

> the 1937 bungalow and the wooden cafés could be removed, the telephone lines placed underground, and the B9006 Inverness–Nairn road, which ran across the site, rerouted. The tree plantations too, could be cleared.[12]

This all took until the 1980s, with the bungalow and tea shop going in 1972. Telephone lines were placed underground in the 1960s, the road was moved in the 1970s, and over 40 hectares of Forestry Commission land were bought in the early 1980s. An initial visitor centre was set up in Old Leanach Cottage in 1959 (of the cottage and its authenticity or otherwise, more later), followed by a car park, the first-generation Visitor Centre in 1970, a second (when most of the site improvements had been carried out) in 1984 and the present centre in 2007. From the 1990s, the NTS site was increasingly landscaped back into a semblance of authenticity, with (for example) prisoners used for battlefield clearance and sheep kept on the field to keep down the persistent return of saplings on the Forestry Commission land. Visitor numbers reached 83,000 a year in 1966; by the 1990s, they were estimated at 250,000, with half of these paying to enter the centre. Paying visitor numbers were around 130,000 in the first year of the new centre in 2007–8. Culloden remains a key site for visitors, not least from overseas, who respond to its interpretative theme of Highland diaspora.[13]

The cairn, the graves, and the memorial service had all set the tone which the NTS continued (and in which it was strongly supported by its governance) in its attempt to replicate the contemporary battle site. In preventing or indeed removing development, and by not supporting revenue earners such as battlefield re-enactment, the NTS continued the presentation of the battle as a gravesite (the Gaelic Society of Inverness had itself suggested diverting the road). In 2009, signs were erected stating that 'Culloden Battlefield is a War Grave', an unusual development for an early modern battlefield.

While the Victorian associations of Culloden with a patriotic Scottish struggle were present in early NTS interpretations, by the time of the second-generation Visitor Centre (1984–2007) there was a strong emphasis on the battle as 'a civil war' fired by the reckless dream of Charles Edward Stuart, and the battle 'the graveyard of the dream for which men died'. There was also a secondary narrative, clearest in the audiovisual presentation, of the conflict as a 'last battle between the Highlanders and the strangers', a final and noble resistance by an out-moded way of life, itself an approach eminently compatible with the Whig historiography which dominated the discussion of the Rising. The suggested number of government dead increased markedly, to 400, which helped position the 'Highland' resistance as more heroic.[14] When the 2007 centre opened in the year of the first Scottish National Party government in Edinburgh, the civil war version of events was stressed strongly to the media. In an era of British unity, the Scottish national dimension of the 'Forty-five could be stressed with impunity; in the age of Scottish nationalism, it was seen as necessary to remember Culloden as a civil war in order to neutralize its force. The interpretation of the battle at the 2007 centre was far more alert to historical scholarship than its predecessor had been; nonetheless the audiovisual experience remained highly conservative and largely loyal to the inherited framing narrative of a primitive and disorganized Highland army.

Since the 1950s and particularly since the 1984 centre development, Culloden has been a site of what the cultural theorist Alison Landsberg terms 'prosthetic memory', the acquisition of the memory of others by the visitor through the agency of experiential sites.[15] The slight danger of the idea of prosthetic memory, however, is that it suggests the visitor is a victim, with an absence waiting to be filled by the framing (cadres), narrative, sights, and sounds of the visitor experience. In the case of a battle like Culloden, however, as the cultural theorists John and Margaret Gold point out, many visitors bring their own memories and expectations. These in turn are often the legacy of the strong historical framing which has taken place around the battle for centuries, with the powerful rhetoricization of binary opposites above, modified by Victorian sentimentality. The 1984 displays and particularly the audio-visual presentation catered to that cultural memory; the 2007 revamp does more to challenge it, beginning to give the sense that it was 'part of a much larger global war'.[16]

The elegiac and graveyard quality of the battle in public and collective memory proved to be inescapable in the broader culture. Even those Scottish nationalists who made use of it frequently did so in such terms, which arguably undermined the futurity of their cause. Pittendrigh Macgillavray's address to the '45 Club in 1911 is a typical example, with its references to 'The Gael...in quest of a dream...spoilt children of the mist...were they not indeed Romance personified!' Romance, of course, is a discourse with which politics has nothing to do: so it was that the battle continued to be marginalized both by those who were content with the result and those who might have wished to see it reversed. Thus the defeated side of the binary framing of British historiography accepted the characterization of the primitive, heroic, and anachronistic Highlander offered them by Whig historiography, merely sugaring it a little with sentiment. Thus was 'The Myth of the Jacobite Clans' born. The very survival of the commemoration of final defeat seemed curiously to offer the possibility of another discourse. In 1945, Hugh MacDiarmid somewhat eccentrically declared in favour of Jacobitism's 'unexhausted evolutionary momentum', while his readoption of the white rose as a symbol for Scotland, not just the Stuart cause, led to its being worn by the nationalist members at the opening of the Scots Parliament in 1999. Slightly eccentric patriots even dabbled with the idea that there was a current Jacobite claimant in the shape of Michael Stewart, whose book claimed this for himself, *The Forgotten Monarchy of Scotland*, reached no. 5 in the Scottish bestseller charts in 1998.[17]

The representation of the conflict in Scottish national terms was more comfortable to an era before the rise of modern Scottish nationalism. In Alexander Korda's *Bonnie Prince Charlie* (1948), starring David Niven, Charles Edward and Scotland are alike victims, and Culloden the 'doom' that Scotland faces. In the aftermath of the battle, an unmistakably Ossianic harper sits lamenting ('They've gone to their doom') among a group of women and old men in a setting of moral chiaroscuro in a bleak landscape. Charles Edward himself, 'a beast of burden for the will of Scotland to rule', parts with the dying Keppoch against the background of a burning saltire, Scotland being consumed by the destructive power of the victors. The aged commander commends his Prince to 'keep...alight' 'the one speck of liberty left in our hearts'. Unashamedly nationalistic language of this sort was clearly safe in the context of post-war Labour Britain, but was to become much less so by the 1970s, 1980s, and 1990s. In these years the conflict increasingly came to be portrayed as the bloody culmination of an unnecessary civil war. This was an interpretation which coexisted in sometimes unacknowledged tension with the historiographical account and cultural memory of Culloden as 'the battle that made Britain': the final reckoning with political Scotland and a victory that converted the country into an imperial partner externally and internally to a rural playground with a delightful frisson of the magical, uncanny, or supernatural—a 'dear Paradise'.

If, as has been argued, the films of the 1950s and early 1960s focused on Charles Edward's defeat and escape as a personal and faintly romantic travelogue, Peter Watkins's *Culloden* of 1964 represented a major departure. Although it kept the formulation of the government army as 'English', its primary function was to present the victory of modernity over a native people led by incompetent aristocratic and feudal overlords, responsible for 'one of the most mishandled and brutal battles' in history. Charles Edward is presented as an idiot obsessed with the Divine

Right of Kings and an embezzler, and Sullivan is shown as a complete fool. Despite Sullivan choosing a 'flat' battlefield despite all military sense, Watkins cannot resist intensifying this photomontage of folly by showing the British Army advancing from the high ground which does not exist in flat battlefields. Although we are informed that Lord George Murray has twice led this 'Highland surge of nationalism' to victory, it is hard to see the Jacobite force portrayed by Watkins as capable of any victory, not least since these representatives of an 'ancient and ruthless society' carry no firearms that work, have no battlefield tactics, and are pitted fruitlessly against the 'musket and cannon' of modernity. 'Charles pitted these men against modern musketry', drones the portentous received pronunciation of the voice-over; the opportunity to undercut the onlooking Andrew Henderson, who appears as a character observing the battle from behind a dyke, is not taken.[18] The documentary formula gave Watkins's film a compelling immediacy and the appearance of verity which was intended to undermine the romantic and national version of Jacobite history, as 'Charles Edward's war is a civil war'; yet the film itself—closely linked to John Prebble's *Culloden* (1961)—reinforced the Whiggish dimension of these very stereotypes.

Watkins's portrayal—itself derived from a framing of the battle as the conflict of unwashed savages with modernity, found all the way back to Morier—was influential and compelling by its contemporary framing, influencing later presentations such as Culloden's opening cameo in *Kidnapped* (1973), *Chasing the Deer* (1994) (which clearly recognizes the connection between the deer hunt and the Jacobites as victims), and BBC1's 1996 *Rebellion!*, and indeed (despite the scholarship and battlefield archaeology which the NTS had engaged with on the site), the 2007 Visitor Centre video,[19] which shows a shapeless attack by primitive swordsmen. Watkins's film was in its own way, however, as well as being a more subtle form of atmospheric chiaroscuro, a romanticized portrayal, presenting a heady mix of Whig historiography and Marxisant social analysis in terms of the battlefield journalism of the Vietnam War era. Culloden as a site of memory in Watkins is a place where tribalism meets modernity and the poor of both dispensations are the losers. The officers are seen as perpetuating ideological positions to act as collective frames for the dictates of personal vengeance for injuries received by friends or family. This sense of the personal was continued by the NTS interpretations in the 1990s, which presented the British Army in terms of regiments and the Jacobite Army as clans or families: a classic example of the binary framing discussed in Chapter 5, and now largely abandoned in NTS interpretation.

The 1984 NTS audiovisual presentation showed Culloden as an ethnocultural fight for a way of life, 'the last battle of the Highlanders and the strangers', a point of view as preposterously remote from the issues at stake as to suggest that Richard III was a Yorkshire nationalist. It did, however, perpetuate the notion that the Ossianic way of life had been finally sacrificed in vain for a foreign princeling on this remote and windswept moor, a point of view which, as we have seen, dates back to the eighteenth century. We might expect to turn to the BBC for a more balanced and contemporary perspective. However, the 1996 programme *Rebellion!* portrayed the Jacobite Army as swordsmen who never took a bath and presented them in a frame not only with musketeers, but also with Harrier jumpjets, to emphasize the (false) disparity between the weapons of this primitive group of deluded individuals and the military and technological ascendancy of the Hanoverian state. More recently, the BBC[20] notes that

> Culloden is an evocative place for many people. Not only is it the site of the last full-scale battle to take place on British soil, and the last stand of an ancient royal dynasty which traced its ancestry back to the Dark Age Gaelic Kingdom of Dal Riata and beyond, but it is also the place where the Highland clan culture of Scotland sang its last song.

Once again the idea of the battle as a conflict which extinguished an almost immemorial civilization and its leaders holds sway, while the 'last song' metaphor conflates the Earl of Seafield on the Union ('There's ane end of ane auld sang') and the idea of Gaelic culture as an elegiac and ineffective location, clearly framed in English culture from Wordsworth's 'Solitary Reaper' onwards.

Education Scotland gives the same sense of ineffectiveness, inadequacy, and primitivism:

> Charles Edward Stuart's choice of rough, marshy ground was catastrophic, and the Jacobite swords and daggers were no match for the Hanoverian cannon and guns...One of the many myths of this event is that it was a Scottish versus English affair. In fact, far more Scots supported and fought on the Hanoverian side than on the Jacobite.

The website for Education Scotland[21] performs a familiar rhetorical strategy, which presents a largely inaccurate version of the battle militarily in order to provoke a sentimental reaction, which is then displaced from any possibility of national sentiment by the audience being informed that such sentiment is a 'myth'. Yet even Robert Chambers in 1827 describes the British forces as 'English', while in 1867 Peter Anderson criticizes the atrocities of the 'English soldiery', and, as we have seen, the partial truth that the Jacobite Rising was an Anglo-Scottish conflict was widely understood in times when the Union was not seen as under threat or problematic. This is then followed by an assertion which is often repeated with no attention to detail whatsoever: that more Scots fought against Charles Edward at Culloden than for him. In presenting two unsubstantiated statements as 'facts' and disparaging any other views as 'myths' this web resource for school students is a particularly bad example of the creation of a prosthetic political memory since the 1960s by those uneasy with the patriotic aims of Scottish Jacobitism (similar uneasiness can be seen in the glosses of Culloden provided in the 2014 Highland tattoo, which exaggerates Scottish involvement in the British Army and caricatures the political goals of the Jacobites[22]). The primitive arms the Jacobites are alleged to have carried are of course a *canard* of much longer duration, though one which also has a nation-building purpose: to endorse the rise of British modernity by presenting its chief political opponent as backward, tribal, and savage. Pictures of Jacobites with swords accompany the text (though there are some unexplained muskets on show). The elegiac quality of such popular representation renders all the more relevant Colin McArthur's reservations from the 1990s about the role the memory of Culloden plays in Scottish culture as an opportunity for 'an orgy of lachrymose breast-beating'.[23]

The website for Undiscovered Scotland focuses on presenting the current NTS Visitor Centre and battle site.[24] Interestingly enough, while it presents the Victorian memorial stone 'Mixed Clans' in all seriousness as 'A Grave for Mixed Clans', it shows the 'Field of the English' stone as 'a misleading name which reflects the Victorian view of the battle', though why the stoutly Unionist Victorians should have wanted to present the battle falsely in terms of Anglo-Scottish conflict is of course not stated. The view of the battle as a gravesite predominates: a *lieu de mémoire* for Scots and those of Scottish descent visiting from abroad who believe their ancestors fought there. The most recent memorial stone on the site is also shown; the fact that it records donations neatly links the presentation of the battle as a cemetery and its intended appeal to a contemporary audience who are invited to perpetuate its memory by paying for its upkeep. Such a presentation is of course entirely consistent with the memory of Culloden as the end of an immemorially ancient way of life; indeed, it rather encourages it. This elegiac note persists in the meteorological chiaroscuro on the NTS's Culloden Facebook page, which on its 10 December 2014 posting noted that '#funfact latest research shows that on the day of the battle, Culloden Battlefield was the only place in the UK which wasn't experiencing nice sunny weather'. Even the weather knew that this site of memory would become a *locus horribilis*.

Sources which might be thought to be sympathetic to the Jacobite side often continue to remember it in similar terms, as the tone confirms both the gravity of the cause and the seriousness of what was lost. So the Scottish Tartans Authority notes that

> The '45 rising of the clans which culminated in the Battle of Culloden—the last major battle to ever be fought on British soil—was probably the most disastrous event ever to overtake Scotland...What of the aftermath? Existing schisms were widened even more...clan set against clan...church against church...community against community...country against country...senior figures in Scottish clan society killed in battle, executed

or transported...the carrying of weapons, the wearing of tartan and Highland dress, the playing of bagpipes...all banned...whole communities pillaged and sent into the hills for no crime other than an inability to speak English...the total extinction of the ties between clan chief and clan...18th century ethnic cleansing with a vengeance![25]

The memory here is equally of Culloden as a battle fought by 'clan society' against those who threaten it externally, as is the historiographical framing which reaches back to the 1740s. Bagpipes are presented as being banned (they weren't) and the post-Culloden picture is not of a brutal police action against a major military challenge, but of an attack on an ethnic or racial group, thus conflating the British response to the military threat posed by the leaders of the West Highlands with a genocidal campaign. While there is undoubtedly plenty of evidence of quasi-racial prejudice against Jacobites (the primitivist thesis is itself an example of this), the memory of Culloden and its aftermath as an assault against a people and their way of life divorces it almost entirely from its political and military context, just as much as the traditional historiographical framing of Cumberland's victory as a sign and precondition of modernity.

Culloden continues to inspire many songs which are very popular. Déanta's 'Culloden's Harvest', posted and popular on social media since 2007, again personalizes the battle within the context of the fate of primitive Gaeldom ('musket and cannon' face 'honour and courage'): the YouTube covering picture is (rather intriguingly) Edward Burne-Jones's *The Prince Entering the Briar Wood*, an image which evokes the enduring context of Victorian sentimentality in which Culloden is remembered. Isla Grant's 'The Ghosts of Culloden' (almost 600,000 views on YouTube in its various guises by early 2015) conjures up the same image of the defeated past and its culture ('through the mist you hear, the lonely piper play'), but one with a more explicitly nationalist tinge, as her soldiers died with 'such pride and dignity | Their lives were not in vain, we still remember them | They fought to to save their land and died for liberty'. Clann an Drumma's 'Culloden' (pipes and drums), posted with a video of the bleak moorland of Culloden traversed by cars, has been viewed over 500,000 times.[26] Its theme is the destruction of the clan system, Culloden as ethnocultural genocide, and the music veers between militancy and sentiment.

Songs of the 'Forty-five in general are almost equally popular. 'Hey Johnnie Cope' had in the region of 150,000 views by the beginning of 2015, while the related sentimental Victorian song 'Glencoe' (construed as an earlier assault on the Gaelic-speaking way of life) has almost 700,000 views in The Corries' version. 'Wha Wadna Fecht for Charlie' and others approach the 100,000 mark.

Despite the increasingly evident desire to frame the battle as the culmination of a civil war in order to undermine its potential utility as a shibboleth of political nationalism, the commemoration of Culloden continues to arouse strong feelings. An innocent battlefield re-enactor from Carlisle who came to the 250th anniversary and dressed as a redcoat was spat at on the battlefield, while a proposed soap statue of the Duke of Cumberland in Cavendish Square in 2012, 'as part of a City of Sculpture art project' in London, roused tempers. A local councillor described it as 'an affront … not the kind of thing that will improve relations between the Highlands and England'. The deputy leader of Westminster City Council probably did not help matters by suggesting that Scots would not find it offensive as English people were not provoked 'by statues of William Wallace or Robert the Bruce'. These two figures had not, however, been nominated as one of the ten 'worst villains' of British history, as Cumberland had in 2005.[27]

The rise of contemporary Scottish nationalism has seen a return to the frame of the eighteenth-century political cartoon. Richard Willson's *Highland Revolt* cartoon, first published in The Times on 28 August 1998, shows Alex Salmond at the head of a Jacobite charge, with Tony Blair and Donald Dewar commanding the opposing British Army: to Blair's accusation that 'I'Faith Mr Dewar Y've been somewhat lackadaisical in the defence of the realm', Dewar responds 'By God, Sir, We've thrown in everything we have, but they still keep coming'. Another shows Alex Salmond as Charles Edward Stuart and his then deputy, Nicola Sturgeon, as Flora MacDonald.[28] During the Scottish Referendum campaign, the blogsite 'Lallands Peat Worrier' jokingly affirmed:

> Study reveals average SNP member is 'stunted Jacobite bogle'
> Ecclefechan Mackay (MA), Political Correspondent
>
> He is four foot three inches tall, is devoted to the House of Stuart, and whenever anyone invites him to remove his bobble hat during Scotland's only warm summer day, he takes it as a personal insult—say hello to the Scottish National Party's everyman. The comprehensive dissection of the SNP's membership in a new academic study reveals for the first time the political, ideological, and personal make-up of the thousands of low-slung atavistic hobgoblins who have helped the party to power at Holyrood.
>
> The study, conducted by Dr William Augustus of Cumberland University, involved distracting SNP members with a 'shiny groat' while persecuting them with a series of increasingly personal questions, from their attitudes towards a range of aberrant sexual practises [sic] to the precise length of their inseams...
>
> Controversially, the study also found that only 19.7% agree with an independent Scotland retaining the Hanoverian succession.[29]

On the other hand, the 'Scottish Jacobite Party' (which has received up to 400 votes in constituencies where it has stood) is highly critical of the SNP.[30] The SJP website had 'Culloden' as its leading entry on the left-hand column of its homepage. Posted the day after the anniversary of the battle in 2014, the text concluded:

> In 2014, The Scottish Jacobite Party stands on a platform of Freedom. Free from the restraining hand of Europe and free from the financial bonds of London Bankers. A country where hard work is rewarded in a proportional tax system. A country of small government where markets are free of government interference. Where Scotland is a proud member of the family of nations. A land of confident citizens using their talents and the country's natural resources for the benefit of all.
>
> In the memory of all those who died on an April morning 268 years ago, can we have an open, informed debate on the issues that really matter? The issues that matter to the men, women and children of Scotland?

The death of northern Scotland's way of life is here a sacrifice not for crofting and common ownership, nor for Union and stability, but for a small republic run on right- wing market-led lines outwith the EU. Culloden remains different things to different people.

And this will continue to be the case. The NTS, whose interpretation has been so influenced by the footprint of the site it owns, has recently been exploring ways to extend that site, or at least to extend the commemoration of that site, towards the Jacobite left and the British right. The exact boundaries of Culloden Parks are being explored, while interpretation on the site itself is improving and changing all the time. Anndra Grannd MacCoinnich, who became property manager in 2014, is open-minded and positive in pursuing new interpretations and developments, not least those associated with the dragoon envelopment, still not acknowledged properly in NTS interpretation. Culloden today at the NTS site is a different battle from how it was presented twenty years ago. History and archaeology have broken through the carapace of heritage, and new interpretations are reaching a wider and wider audience.

Whatever the interpretation of the Battle of Culloden, however it is framed in memory, it is always an end out of which a new beginning can come: the British Empire, Balmorality, the Crofting Acts, Scottish Renaissance, even the Scottish Jacobite Party or the 2015 general election result, as depicted in Jon Snow's 27 April 2015 report for Channel 4, which framed SNP success as a reversal of the result of Culloden. It is that ability to compel the construction of memory towards elegy, while finding a grain of contrasting hope and continuing relevance for the future in the irreversibility of the loss suffered on that day, that continues to make Culloden a great battle in the memory of the English-speaking world and the descendants of its Gaelic-speaking allies and enemies. Culloden has long been seen as key to both the breaking and making of Britain, and with it its empire, to which so many Jacobite prisoners and fugitives, and those who believe their ancestors to be Jacobite prisoners and fugitives, emigrated. Culloden will continue to frame the possibility of remembering the last phase of an independent Scottish culture in the early modern period, what has been termed 'an elegiac quality' which marks the defeat of the "real" Scotland'.[31] This is a

Figure 15 Calum Colvin, *Vestiarum Scoticum I–III* (2005).

quality which renews itself, being revisited in different forms from generation to generation. The distinguished Dundee artist Calum Colvin's *Vestiarum Scoticum I–III* sums this up (Figure 15). Behind the bright tartan portrayal of Scotland in the first image lies the shadows of butchery; in the second, the genealogy of tartan in the hands of the Sobieski Stuart pretenders in the nineteenth century (*Vestiarium Scoticum*) blends into the warp and woof of Scotland's heathery landscape itself, till none can tell what is fact and what is fiction; in the third, the identity of Scotland is circumscribed by the emotional netherworld of Jacobite military imagery that has been created as a means of perpetuating the memory while betraying the politics of the Jacobite cause. In every image, there are the signs of death and the trophies of the hunt, chiefly the deer, symbol of the Stuarts, and the beast for which the land was cleared and so many of the people of Scotland suffered. The same themes—of suffering and violence—can be found in the controversial *Highland Rape* designs of Alexander McQueen (Autumn/Winter 1995), themes he revisited in *Widows of Culloden* (Autumn/Winter 2006), the soundtrack of which suggested an analogy between Culloden and the Holocaust.[32]

The politics of Jacobitism has been strongly framed as primitive because of the threat it posed, and the function the defeat of that threat has in a national narrative of foundational reconciliation. However regular were the Jacobite armies, however well armed and decently led, however welcome their officers in the courts of Europe, the framing power for both British state teleology and Scottish patriot nostalgia relies on an image, ultimately Morier's image and that of the cartoonists of his era. This is the framing story of dirty badly armed primitives sacrificing themselves with pointless nobility to the orders of an Italian princeling, but in the end not contemptibly as they were in reality defending an ancient way of life. Arguably no battle out of living memory is remembered so powerfully and so falsely. On Culloden Moor on 16 April 1746, what was in some ways the last Scottish army—constructed so, paid so, and drilled so—with its Franco-Irish and Scoto-French allies, sought to restore Charles Edward's father to a multi-kingdom monarchy more aligned to European politics than colonial struggle. They were in many essentials a regular army; if they had not been, they would not have had to fight, nor would the Prince willingly have led them. Outnumbered but not outgunned, cavalry proved their downfall. Ironically, it can be argued that it was not British ball that brought down kilted swordsmen as much as British dragoon blades that cut down Jacobite musketeers. The effect of flanking cavalry on an overextended infantry formation with little effective reserve was a constant in warfare for centuries, and it is the key to Culloden. The traditional qualities of the battle are as much British as Jacobite. Culloden as it happened is in fact much more interesting than Culloden as it is remembered. It was neither a sacrificial hecatomb of Highland history nor a catalyst for the triumph of British modernity. It was the last battle fought on British soil and ended the last armed conflict in which the nature of Britain—and indeed its existence—were at stake. But it no more ended Scotland and Scottish identity than it encapsulated it.

NOTES

Chapter 1

1. Somhairle MacGill-Eain, 'Tha na beanntan gun bhruidhinn'/'The mountains are speechless', in MacGill-Eain, *An Cuilithionn 1939: The Cuillin 1939 & Unpublished Poems*, ed. Christopher Whyte (Glasgow: Association for Scottish Literary Studies, 2011), 284–5.

2. 'The British Grenadier', quoted by Owen Dudley Edwards, 'Margo', *The Drouth* 48 (2014), 19–31 (21). The early substitution of 'Tow-row-row' for the name of the Duke of Cumberland was indicative of the separation of the significance of the Battle of Culloden from the acknowledged excesses of its victor in British collective memory.

3. Christopher A. Whatley, 'Reformed Religion, Regime Change, Scottish Whigs and the struggle for the "Soul" of Scotland', *c.*1688–*c.*1788', *Scottish Historical Review* 92 (2013), 66–99 (68).

4. Steven Pincus, *1688: The First Modern Revolution* (New Haven: Yale University Press, 2009). For the effective autocracy thesis (albeit presented sceptically), see Jeremy Black, *Eighteenth-Century Europe* (1990; 2nd edn, Basingstoke: Macmillan, 1999), esp. ch. 10.

5. See Murray Pittock, *The Myth of the Jacobite Clans: The Jacobite Army in 1745* (1995; Edinburgh: Edinburgh University Press, 2009).

6. Konstanze Glaser, *Minority Languages and Cultural Diversity in Europe* (Clevedon: Multililingual Matters, 2007), 83.

7. See Murray Pittock, 'Historiography', in Alexander Broadie (ed.), *The Cambridge Companion to the Scottish Enlightenment* (Cambridge: Cambridge University Press, 2003), 258–79.

8. Marianne Hirsch, 'Connective Histories in Vulnerable Times', *PMLA* 129/3 (2014), 330–48 (339). Hirsch introduced this concept to memory studies in 1997.

9. Thomas Pennant, *A Tour in Scotland, 1769* (Chester, 1771),), ed. Brian D. Osborne (Edinburgh: Birlinn, 2000), 144.

10. See e.g. Michael A. Penman, 'Robert Bruce's Bones: Reputations, Politics and Identities in Nineteenth-Century Scotland', *International Review of Scottish Studies* 34 (2009), 7–73. Scottish memorialization preceded the French Revolution's secular festivals: Hume (1777–8) was the first, and Burns (1798) and

Wallace (1814) followed (Penman, 'Robert Bruce's Bones', 40–2). See John R. and Margaret M. Gold, '"The Graves of the Gallant Highlanders"', *History & Memory* 19/1 (2007), 5–38 (22) for the developing visitor outlook.

11. Christine MacLeod, *Heroes of Invention: Technology, Liberalism and British Identity 1750–1914* (Cambridge: Cambridge University Press, 2007), 18.
12. John and Margaret Gold, '"Graves of the Gallant Highlanders"', 22; Judith Pascoe, *The Hummingbird Cabinet* (Ithaca, NY and London: Cornell University Press, 2006), 3.
13. John and Margaret Gold, '"Graves of the Gallant Highlanders"', 22–4.
14. Elspeth Masson and Jill Harden, 'Drumossie Muir: Memorialization, Development and Restoration with Evolving Historical Landscape', in Tony Pollard (ed.), *Culloden: The History and Archaeology of the Last Clan Battle* (2009; Barnsley: Pen and Sword, 2011), 203–17 (205–8); John and Margaret Gold, '"Graves of the Gallant Highlanders"', 22–4.
15. Clifford Geertz, *The Interpretation of Cultures* (1973; London: Fontana, 1993), 242–3.
16. Daniel Woolf, *The Social Circulation of the Past* (Oxford: Oxford University Press, 2003), 272, 274, 294–5, 298, 376, 393; Alexandra Walsham, *The Reformation of the Landscape* (2011; Oxford: Oxford University Press, 2012); Masson and Harden, 'Drumossie Muir', 203.

Chapter 2

1. Eveline Cruickshanks, *Political Untouchables: The Tories and the '45* (New York: Holmes & Meier, 1979), 3–4; Daniel Szechi, *Jacobitism and Tory Politics 1710–1714* (Edinburgh: John Donald, 1984).
2. Jonathan Clark, *From Restoration to Reform: The British Isles 1660–1832* (London: Vintage, 2014), 208–9.
3. Padre Giulio Cesare Cordara, 'Commentary on the Expedition to Scotland Made by Charles Edward Stuart, Prince of Wales', *Miscellany of the Scottish History Society* 4, ed. Sir Bruce Seton Bart (Scottish History Society, 3rd ser., 9; Edinburgh: Constable, 1926), 1–174 (56). For the evidence to support these numbers, see Daniel Szechi, *1715* (New Haven: Yale University Press, 2006); Murray Pittock, *The Myth of the Jacobite Clans: The Jacobite Army in 1745* (1995; Edinburgh: Edinburgh University Press, 2009), 65–81 and elsewhere.
4. Jeremy Black, *Eighteenth-Century Europe* (1990; 2nd edn, Basingstoke: Macmillan, 1999), 358; Cruickshanks, *Political Untouchables*, 17, 35.
5. Frank McLynn, *Charles Edward Stuart* (London: Routledge, 1988), 77.
6. Cruickshanks, *Political Untouchables*, 54; Christopher Duffy, *The '45* (2003; London: Phoenix, 2007), 43.
7. Andrew McKillop, 'Local Battle and Global War: Culloden and the International Balance of Power', in *Cùil Lodair/Culloden* (Edinburgh: National Trust for Scotland, 2007), 13–15 (14).
8. Murray Pittock, *Jacobitism* (Basingstoke: Macmillan, 1998), 88.

9. Frank McLynn, in *France and the Jacobite Rising of 1745* (Edinburgh: Edinburgh University Press, 1981), made a strong case for the reality of French intentions. McLynn's case has been challenged, but it has changed the parameters of the debate.

10. About £36,500 following the 1726 currency stabilization: see David Weir, 'Tontines, Public Finance and Revolution in France and England, 1688–1789', *Journal of Economic History* 49/1 (1989), 95–124 (99 n.); Pittock, *Jacobitism*, 85.

11. Edward Corp, *The Stuarts in Italy, 1719–1766* (Cambridge: Cambridge University Press, 2011), 229.

12. Pittock, *Jacobitism*, 86, 88, 97–8; Duffy, *The '45*, 45; Stuart Reid, *The Scottish Jacobite Army 1745–1746* (Oxford: Osprey, 2006), 4.

13. Katherine Tomasson and Francis Buist, *Battles of the '45* (London: Batsford, 1962), 31; Duffy, *The '45*, 173, 212; Pittock, *Jacobitism*, 97–8.

14. Pittock, *Jacobitism*, 99.

15. Tomasson and Buist, *Battles of the '45*, 51; Stuart Reid, *Culloden 1746* (2005; 2nd edn, Barnsley: Pen and Sword, 2011), 19; Duffy, *The '45*, 14.

16. Stuart Reid, *Highland Clansman 1689–1746* (1997; Oxford: Osprey, 1999), 24; Christopher Duffy, 'The '45 Campaign', in Tony Pollard (ed.), *Culloden: The History and Archaeology of the Last Clan Battle* (2009; Barnsley: Pen & Sword, 2011), 17–37 (22–3); Duffy, *The '45*, 17–18.

17. Peter Simpson, *The Independent Highland Companies 1603–1760* (Edinburgh: John Donald, 1996), 29; Reid, *Highland Clansman*; Reid, *Scottish Jacobite Army*, 12–13; Tomasson and Buist, *Battles of the '45*, 64: J. A. Houlding, *Fit for Service: The Training of the British Army, 1715–1795* (Oxford: Clarendon Press, 1981; repr. Sandpiper, 2000), 354–5; Duffy, *The '45*, 20; Geoffrey Plank, *Rebellion and Savagery: The Jacobite Rising of 1745 and the British Empire* (Philadelphia: University of Pennsylvania Press, 2006), 33.

18. Pittock, *Jacobitism*, 98–9.

19. Pittock, *Jacobitism*, 100; Cruickshanks, *Political Untouchables*, 80.

20. Reid, *Culloden*, 124.

21. Chevalier de Johnstone, *A Memoir of the 'Forty-Five*, ed. Brian Rawson (London: Folio Society, 1958), 122.

22. Pittock, *Jacobitism*, 100–1 for a discussion of Charles Edward's Edinburgh declarations of 9 and 10 October; see also Andrew Henderson, *The Life of William Augustus, Duke of Cumberland* (1766), ed. Roderick Macpherson (London: Pickering & Chatto, 2010), 104.

23. Johnstone, *Memoir*, 45.

24. Pittock, *Jacobitism*, 100; A. W. Secord (ed.), *Defoe's Review Reproduced from the Original Editions* (New York, 1938), vi. 486 (cited from F. Bastian, *Defoe's Early Life* (London and Basingstoke: Macmillan, 1981), 152).

25. M. Hook and W. Ross, *The 'Forty-Five* (Edinburgh: HMSO, 1995), 62.

26. For the assessment of Charles Edward's army, see Sir John Fortescue, *History of the British Army*, 13 vols (London: Macmillan, 1899–1930), ii. 131–2; Donald

Nicholas (ed.), *Intercepted Post* (London: Bodley Head, 1956), 118; Reid, *Scottish Jacobite Army*, 41–3.

27. James Maxwell of Kirkconnell, *Narrative of Charles Prince of Wales' Expedition to Scotland in the Year 1745* (Edinburgh: Maitland Club, 1841), 72.

28. Frank McLynn, *The Jacobite Army in England: The Last Campaign* (Edinburgh: John Donald, 1983), 125–31; Rupert C. Jarvis (ed.), *Collected Papers on the Jacobite Risings*, 2 vols (Manchester: Manchester University Press, 1972), vol. ii, pp. ix–x; Nicholas (ed.), *Intercepted Post*, 145; Duffy, *The '45*, 301; Johnstone, *Memoir*, 58–61, 65; Maxwell, *Narrative*, 73–5.

29. Duffy, *The '45*, 302 for a discussion of the possibilities of an engagement at Northampton.

30. Cruickshanks, *Political Untouchables*, 92–3.

31. McLynn, *France and the Jacobite Rising of 1745*, 108, 115, and *passim*. Eveline Cruickshanks places the figure for French troops at 12,000; see *Political Untouchables*, 95.

32. Robert Forbes, *The Lyon in Mourning*, ed. Henry Paton, 3 vols (Edinburgh: Edinburgh University Press/Scottish History Society, 1895), ii. 197; Reid, *Culloden*, 22 puts Hawley's force at 6,200.

33. Pollard, 'Capturing the Moment: The Archaeology of Culloden Battlefield', in Pollard (ed.), *Culloden*, 130–62 (151); Duffy, *The '45*, 206–7, 436. See Bruce Lenman, *The Jacobite Clans of the Great Glen* (London: Methuen, 1984) for Lovat's Scottish nationalism.

34. Henderson, *Life of William Augustus*, 129; Pittock, *Jacobitism*, 106–7; Reid, *Culloden*, 32–4; Reid, *Scottish Jacobite Army*, 4–5; Reid, *Highland Clansman*, 58; Johnstone, *Memoir*, 116; Duffy, *The '45*, 461–6, 525.

35. James Allardyce (ed.), *Historical Papers Relating to the Jacobite Period 1699–1750*, 2 vols (Aberdeen: New Spalding Club, 1895), i. 310–11; Reid, *Culloden*, 34–7; Duffy, 'The '45 Campaign', 34; Duffy, *The '45*, 487, 498–500.

36. Reid, *Culloden*, 38–40.

37. Alan J. Guy, 'King George's Army, 1714–1750', in Robert C. Woosnam-Savage (ed.), *1745: Charles Edward Stuart and the Jacobites* (Edinburgh: HMSO, 1995), 41–56 (51).

38. Pollard, 'The Battle of Culloden—More than a Difference of Opinion', in Pollard (ed.), *Culloden*, 1–16 (9).

39. 'Firings' are discussed at the end of the chapter. Reid, 'The Jacobite Army at Culloden', in Pollard (ed.), *Culloden*, 38–61 (43, 45, 59–60); Duffy, *The '45*, 116–17.

40. Pittock, *Myth*, 190–4 and *passim* gives more details.

41. Roger Turner, *Manchester in 1745* (Royal Stuart Society Paper 49; London, 1997), 12, 17.

42. Allan Carswell, '"The Most Despicable Enemy That Are": The Jacobite Army of the '45', in Woosnam-Savage (ed.), *1745*, 29–40 (38); Katherine Tomasson, *The Jacobite General* (Edinburgh: Blackwood, 1958), 35; Thomas B. Lindsay,

'Highland Dress', in *Scottish Weapons, Scottish Art Review Special Number* 9/1 (1963), 6–10, 33 (6); Duffy, *The '45*, 88–9.

43. Martin Kelvin, *The Scottish Pistol: Its History, Manufacture and Design* (London: Cygnus Arts, 1996), 197; Reid, *Highland Clansman*, 18, 43 (pl. K); Reid, *Scottish Jacobite Army*, 16–17.

44. Reid, *Highland Clansman*, 14; Reid, *Scottish Jacobite Army*, 3.

45. Corp, *Stuarts in Italy*, 252.

46. Kelvin, *Scottish Pistol*, 3, 23, 24, 128, 180, 186; Daniel Defoe, *A Tour through the Whole Island of Great Britain* (1724–6), ed. Pat Rogers (Harmondsworth: Penguin, 1971), 664.

47. Tomasson and Buist, *Battles of the '45*, 43.

48. Reid, *Highland Clansman*, 4, 15, 18; Reid, *Scottish Jacobite Army*, 49; Pollard, 'Capturing the Moment', 143, 150.

49. Kelvin, *Scottish Pistol*, 55, 81, 95, 97, 110, 127, 162; Hamish Sloane and James B. McKay, 'Scottish Pistols-4', *Dispatch* (1983).

50. William Reid, 'Walter Allan, Armourer in Stirling', in *Scottish Weapons, Scottish Art Review* 9/1 (1963), 16–21; Kelvin, *Scottish Pistol*, 39, 42; Stuart Reid, *Scottish Jacobite Army*, 46.

51. NLS Adv. MS 82.4.1 (Gask Papers), fo. 135; Reid, *Scottish Jacobite Army*, 48.

52. Stuart Maxwell, 'The Highland Targe', in *Scottish Weapons, Scottish Art Review* 9/1 (1963), 2–5, 33 (2–3); Reid, *Highland Clansman*, 31.

53. TNA, SP 54/26/240.

54. Stuart Reid, 'The Battle of Culloden', 126.

55. Tomasson and Buist, *Battles of the '45*, 69.

56. Carswell, 'Despicable Enemy', 36; Nicholas (ed.), *Intercepted Post*, 36; Reid, *Scottish Jacobite Army*, 53–4; Pittock, *Myth*, 35, 96; W. A. Speck, *The Butcher* (Oxford: Basil Blackwell, 1981), 149. For British Army drill, see Humphrey Bland, *A Treatise of Military Discipline* (London: Buckley, 1727).

57. MS Order of General Hawley, repr. in David, Lord Elcho, *A Short Account of the Affairs of Scotland in the Years 1744, 1745, 1746*, with a Memoir and Annotations by the Hon. Evan Charteris (Edinburgh: David Douglas, 1907), 459–60; David Stevenson, *Highland Warrior: Alasdair MacColla and the Civil Wars* (Edinburgh: John Donald, 2003).

58. Elcho, *Short Account*, 39; Reid, *Highland Clansman*, 15–16; Pittock, *Myth*, 98.

59. Tomasson and Buist, *Battles of the '45*, 67.

60. Tomasson and Buist, *Battles of the '45*, 37; Reid, *Highland Clansman*, 9.

61. Xenophon, *The Persian Expedition*, trans. Rex Warner with an introduction by George Cawkwell (1949; Harmondsworth: Penguin, 1977), 213–14.

62. 'March of the Highland Army, in the Years 1745–1746, Being the Day Book of Captain James Stuart, of Lord Ogilvy's Regiment', in *Miscellany of the Spalding Club*, i (Edinburgh, 1841), 275–344 (277–9, 281, 284–5, 290–1); Reid, *Scottish Jacobite Army*, 48; Christopher Duffy, *The Military Experience in the Age of Reason* (London and New York: Routledge & Kegan Paul, 1987), 222–3. For the

battlefield archaeological evidence, I am indebted (as are all scholars) to the outstanding work of Tony Pollard, whose finds matched the archival evidence I first adduced in 1995 and corroborate the heavy firepower of Charles Edward's army and the stiff resistance put up by his troops: see Pollard, 'Capturing the Moment', 144–5.

63. Pittock, *Myth*, 177; McLynn, *Jacobite Army*, 24, 28, 95; Duffy, *Military Experience in the Age of Reason*, 233.

64. TNA SP 54/26/550; Reid, *Scottish Jacobite Army*, 42; Reid, *Culloden*, 130.

65. Simpson, *Independent Highland Companies*, 197–8; McLynn, *Jacobite Army*, 29; NLS Adv. MS 82.4.1 (Gask Papers), fos. 41, 101, 102; NLS MS 3787 (Order Book of Appin's Regiment); Pittock, *Myth*, 95.

66. Angus Archives, F 1/1/4 (Forfar Minutes, 1737–58).

67. NLS Adv. MS 82.4.1, fo. 156. For riot, see Perth and Kinross Archives, PKC B59/30/70: 'Skirmish here betwixt the Loyal Inhabitants & the Rebels on the 30th of October 1745'.

68. Angus Archives, B1/1/2: Brechin Town Council Minutes 1713–59; F 1/1/4: Forfar Town Council Minutes 1737–58; David Dobson, *The Jacobites of Angus, 1689–1746*, 2 vols (St Andrews, 1995), ii. 35, 42.

69. NLS MS 17514, fo. 58 ('Intelligence Report on the Rebellion').

70. McLynn, *Jacobite Army*, 97, 105.

71. NLS Adv. MS 82.4.1, fo. 156; NLS Adv. MS 82.4.2 (Gask Papers); NLS MS 3787.

72. Houlding, *Fit for Service*, 9–11, 28, 118. For the size of regimental units, see Pittock, *Myth*.

73. Houlding, *Fit for Service*, p. vii (from Public Archives of Canada M.G.18 L5 III/2: 390–1), 100, 104; Stuart Reid, 'The British Army at Culloden', in Pollard (ed.), *Culloden*, 62–86 (76).

74. See Reid, *Culloden*, 115; Houlding, *Fit for Service*, 63, 67, 68, 70–2.

75. Houlding, *Fit for Service*, 51, 92–5, 318–22; Bland, *Treatise*, 2–4, 67. For a comparison of Covenanter, British Army, and Jacobite unit sizes, see Pittock, *Myth*, 65–9 and *passim*.

76. Duffy, *Military Experience in the Age of Reason*, 207, 209, 210.

77. Houlding, *Fit for Service*, 137–9, 145–7; Pollard, 'Capturing the Moment', 155–6; Duffy, *Military Experience in the Age of Reason*, 211; Alan Guy, *Oeconomy and Discipline*, (Manchester: Manchester University Press, 1985), 146.

78. Houlding, *Fit for Service*, 137, 140, 145–8, 194, 281, 284; Elcho, *Short Account*, 460; Duffy, *The '45*, 140–1; Duffy, *Military Experience in the Age of Reason*, 210, 211; Pittock, *Myth*, 98.

79. Houlding, *Fit for Service*, 143, 149–51; Duffy, *The '45*, 215, 222–3.

80. Houlding, *Fit for Service*, 159, 162, 179–82, 195–6, 369–70, esp. 181 n.; Duffy, *The '45*, 142, 144–5.

81. Pollard, 'Capturing the Moment', 146.

82. Bland, *Treatise*, 15; Pollard (ed.), *Culloden*, 260–1 n.; Johnstone, *Memoir*, 67. For the importance of pipes after Falkirk, see Duffy, *The '45*, 422.

83. Daniel Szechi, 'Jamie the Soldier and the Jacobite Military Threat, 1706–1727', in Allan Macinnes and Douglas Hamilton (eds), *Jacobitism, Enlightenment and Empire* (London: Pickering & Chatto, 2014), 13–28 (21).
84. Henderson, *Life of William Augustus*, 81.

Chapter 3

1. References to maps in this chapter are from http://wiki.openstreetmap.org/wiki/WikiProject_Scotland. OS numbers are references to Ordnance Survey.
2. *A Particular Account of the Battle of CULLODEN. April 16, 1746* (London: T. Warner, 1749), 4; David, Lord Elcho, *A Short Account of the Affairs of Scotland in the Years 1744, 1745, 1746*, with a Memoir and Annotations by the Hon. Evan Charteris (Edinburgh: David Douglas, 1907), 423–6, 430; Stuart Reid, 'The Battle of Culloden: A Narrative Account', in Tony Pollard (ed.), *Culloden: The History and Archaeology of the Last Clan Battle* (2009; Barnsley: Pen & Sword, 2011), 103–29 (103); Stuart Reid, *Culloden 1746* (2005; 2nd edn, Barnsley: Pen & Sword, 2011), 41, 55–6.
3. Robert Forbes, *The Lyon in Mourning*, ed. Henry Paton, 3 vols (Edinburgh: Edinburgh University Press/Scottish History Society, 1895), i. 254, 257; Reid, *Culloden*, 41, 57; Christopher Duffy, 'The '45 Campaign', in Pollard (ed.), *Culloden*, 17–37 (35); Christopher Duffy, *The '45* (2003; London: Phoenix, 2007), 502–4; *A Particular Account*, 4.
4. *A Particular Account*, 4.
5. *A Particular Account*, 4.
6. James Maxwell of Kirkconnell, *Narrative of Charles Prince of Wales' Expedition to Scotland in the Year 1745* (Edinburgh: Maitland Club, 1841), 155.
7. Katherine Tomasson and Francis Buist, *Battles of the '45* (London: Batsford, 1962), 134.
8. Stephen Bull, 'Battles of the '45', in Robert Woosnam-Savage (ed.), *1745: Charles Edward Stuart and the Jacobites* (Edinburgh: HMSO, 1995), 57–71 (64).
9. Duffy, *The '45*, 41, 143.
10. Maxwell, *Narrative*, 158.
11. Forbes, *Lyon in Mourning*, i. 266–7; John Prebble, *Culloden* (1961; London: Pimlico, 2002), 14; Reid, *Culloden*, 41.
12. Forbes, *Lyon in Mourning*, i. 362 (Colonel Ker's account); Tomasson and Buist, *Battles*, 169; Christopher Duffy, *The Military Experience in the Age of Reason* (London and New York: Routledge & Kegan Paul, 1987), 211.
13. Jeffrey Stephen, 'Irish Intrigues and Scottish Councils: Post-Culloden Narratives and Their Recriminations', in Pollard (ed.), *Culloden*, 187–202 (197).
14. Elcho, *Short Account*, 426; Forbes, *Lyon in Mourning*, ii. 275.
15. Forbes, *Lyon in Mourning*, i. 255; *A Particular Account*, 11.
16. Tomasson and Buist, *Battles*, 134–41 (137); Reid, *Culloden*, 41–8; Duffy, 'The '45 Campaign', 36; Duffy, *The '45*, 505–10; Frank McLynn, *Charles Edward Stuart* (London: Routledge, 1988), 245–6.

17. Tomasson and Buist, *Battles*, 142–3.
18. Tomasson and Buist, *Battles*, 143–6 (144); *A Particular Account*, 16.
19. Reid, 'Battle of Culloden', 103; Reid, *Culloden*, 49.
20. Tomasson and Buist, *Battles*, 146–7; Forbes, *Lyon in Mourning*, i. 261; Stephen, 'Irish Intrigues and Scottish Councils', 195; also see Pollard, 'Capturing the Moment: The Archaeology of Culloden Battlefield', in Pollard (ed.), *Culloden*, 130–62 (150).
21. Tony Pollard, 'The Archaeology of Scottish Battlefields', in Edward Spiers et al. (eds), *A Military History of Scotland* (Edinburgh: Edinburgh University Press, 2012), 728–47 (735–6); Pollard, 'Capturing the Moment', 150.
22. Reid, 'Battle of Culloden', 104; Reid, *Culloden*, 56; Pollard, 'Capturing the Moment', 131.
23. Tomasson and Buist, *Battles*, 134–41; Stephen, 'Irish Intrigues and Scottish Councils', 180–1; Duffy, 'Battle of Culloden', 35; Pollard, 'Capturing the Moment', 132 139, 141, 142; for discussion of NTS claim, see David McCrone, Angela Morris, and Richard Kiely, *Scotland the Brand* (Edinburgh: Edinburgh University Press, 1995), 192.
24. Reid, *Culloden*, 57–9; Pollard, 'Archaeology', 736; Pollard, 'The Battle of Culloden—More than a Difference of Opinion', in Pollard (ed.), *Culloden*, 1–16 (3–4); Pollard, 'Capturing the Moment', 133; Duffy, *The '45*, 512–15; Tomasson and Buist, *Battles*, 147.
25. Forbes, *Lyon in Mourning*, i. 255; Tomasson and Buist, *Battles*, 161.
26. Forbes, *Lyon in Mourning*, i. 190. A company had allegedly stopped off for entertainment locally, and missed the battle (Tomasson and Buist, *Battles*, 161).
27. J. T. Findlay, *Wolfe in Scotland in the '45 and from 1749 to 1753* (London, New York, and Toronto: Longmans, 1928), 107; Reid, *Culloden*, 60–1, 70; Reid, 'The Jacobite Army at Culloden', in Pollard (ed.), *Culloden*, 38–61 (41–2); Robert C. Woosnam-Savage, '"To Gather an Image Whole": Some Early Maps and Plans of the Battle of Culloden', in Pollard (ed.), *Culloden*, 163–86 (172, 179); Elcho, *Short Account*, 424; Maxwell, *Narrative*, 150; Tomasson and Buist, *Battles*, 145–6.
28. Duffy, *The '45*, 224.
29. Forbes, *Lyon in Mourning*, ii. 277; John Home, *The History of the Rebellion in Scotland in 1745* (Edinburgh: Peter Brown, 1822), 163; Stuart Reid, *The Scottish Jacobite Army 1745–1746* (Oxford: Osprey, 2006), 31; Reid, *Culloden*, 61; Reid, 'Jacobite Army', 41, 54.
30. See Johnstone, *Memoirs* (1958), 126; Elcho, *Short Account*, 432–3; Maxwell, *Narrative*, 149; Woosnam-Savage, '"To Gather an Image Whole"', 183.
31. Tomasson and Buist, *Battles*, 163–4, 170; Reid, *Culloden*, 61.
32. *Gentleman's Magazine* 16 (1746), 209–10; James Ray (attrib.), *A Journey Through Part of England and Scotland Along with the Army Under the Command of His Royal Highness the Duke of Cumberland* (London: Osborne, 1747), 158.

33. Forbes, *Lyon in Mourning*, i. 361–2 (Colonel Ker's account); Home, *History of the Rebellion*, 165; W. A. Speck, *The Butcher* (Oxford: Basil Blackwell, 1981), 135–6, 140; Tomasson and Buist, *Battles*, 146, 150, 152, 155, 161, 162; Prebble, *Culloden*, 20; Duffy, *The '45*, 516.

34. Reid, *Scottish Jacobite Army*, 42; Reid, 'Jacobite Army', 38–9, 62–3; Tomasson and Buist, *Battles*, 160–2; Woosnam-Savage, '"To Gather an Image Whole"', 179; Speck, *The Butcher*, 139.

35. Maxwell, *Narrative*, 153.

36. Reid, *Scottish Jabobite Army*, 55.

37. Tomasson and Buist, *Battles*, 163.

38. *Culloden/Cuil Lodair*, 49, 55; *Gentleman's Magazine* (1746), 210; Forbes, *Lyon in Mourning* ii. 278. For the firing of mortar bombs, see Reid, 'Jacobite Army', 59 and Reid, 'The British Army at Culloden', in Pollard (ed.), *Culloden*, 62–86 (68–74); also Reid, *Culloden*, 17, 65–7; Pollard, 'Capturing the Moment', 148.

39. *A Particular Account*, 11; Tomasson and Buist, *Battles*, 156.

40. Bull, 'Battles of the '45', 63–4; Woosnam-Savage, '"To Gather an Image Whole"', 180. For the French appraisal of the British Army at Dettingen, see Louis Ducros, *French Society in the Eighteenth Century*, trans. W. De Gryer with a foreword by J. A. Haggs-Walker (London: G. Bell and Sons, 1926), 310.

41. *Gentleman's Magazine* (1746), 210; Tomasson and Buist, *Battles*, 158.

42. Tomasson and Buist, *Battles*, 155, 167; Reid, *Culloden*, 67–72; Duffy, *The '45*, 514–16; Forbes, *Lyon in Mourning*, i. 86 (John Cameron's account), 262, 361; ii. 278; Johnstone, *Memoirs*, 126; Elcho, *Short Account*, 432; Reid, 'Battle of Culloden', 108–11; Maxwell, *Narrative*, 151.

43. Forbes, *Lyon in Mourning*, ii. 278; Speck, *The Butcher*, 141; Tomasson and Buist, *Battles*, 165, 167; Reid, *Culloden*, 73.

44. Home, *Rebellion*, 166; Findlay, *Wolfe in Scotland*, 106; Tomasson and Buist, *Battles*, 166–7, 169; Murray Pittock, *Jacobitism* (Basingstoke: Macmillan, 1998), 109; Forbes, *Lyon in Mourning* ii. 278; Reid, *Culloden*, 76, 78, 142, 150; Reid, 'Battle of Culloden', 111–12; Duffy, *Military Experience*, 265; Andrew Henderson, *The Life of William Augustus, Duke of Cumberland*, ed. Roderick Macpherson (1766; London: Pickering & Chatto, 2010), 182. I am grateful to Daniel Szechi for the point about the effect of coehorn airburst shells.

45. Tomasson and Buist, *Battles*, 162, 179.

46. Forbes, *Lyon in Mourning* i. 363 (Ker's account); Tomasson and Buist, *Battles*, 174; Reid, *Culloden* 76–7; Reid, 'Battle of Culloden', 112.

47. Maxwell, *Narrative*, 153; Henderson, *Life of William Augustus*, 181–2; Reid, *Scottish Jacobite Army*, 51; Reid, *Culloden*, 69; Tomasson and Buist, *Battles*, 174.

48. *A Particular* Account, 11; Reid, *Highland Clansman 1689–1746* (1997; Oxford: Osprey, 1999), 27; Reid, 'Battle of Culloden', 103, 114; Tomasson and Buist, *Battles*, 185.

49. Maxwell, *Narrative*, 152; Forbes, *Lyon in Mourning* ii. 279; Tomasson and Buist, *Battles*, 175, 178, 180; Duffy, *Military Experience*, 207; David Blackmore, 'Cavalry in the '45', in Pollard (ed.), *Culloden*, 87–102 (91); Reid, 'Battle of Culloden', 114–16.

50. Home, *Rebellion*, 168; Findlay, *Wolfe in Scotland*, 107; Bull, 'Battles of the '45', 68; Reid, *Highland Clansman*, 27; Reid, *Culloden*, 78; Reid, 'Battle of Culloden', 119; Tomasson and Buist, *Battles*, 176–8.

51. Michael Hughes, *A Plain Narrative and Authentic Journal of the Late Rebellion* (London: Henry Whitridge, 1747), 39; Home, *Rebellion*, 168; Reid, 'Battle of Culloden', 119–20; Pollard, 'Archaeology of Scottish Battlefields', 737–8.

52. *Gentleman's Magazine* 16 (1946), 210; Johnstone, *Memoirs*, 128; Reid, 'Battle of Culloden', 120–1.

53. Maxwell, *Narrative*, 154.

54. Johnstone, *Memoirs*, 128.

55. Kilmarnock's account in James Allardyce (ed.), *Historical Papers Relating to the Jacobite Period 1699–1750*, 2 vols (Aberdeen: New Spalding Club, 1895), i. 322–3; Bull, 'Battles of the '45', 66–8; Reid, *Highland Clansman*, 29; Tomasson and Buist, *Battles*, 169, 175–6, 179, 187–8; Blackmore, 'Cavalry in the '45', 100–1; Reid, *Culloden*, 82, 83, 87, 98, 99, 102; Reid, 'Battle of Culloden', 117, 123–6; Pollard, 'Archaeology of Scottish Battlefields', 736.

56. John Lawrie, *The History of the Wars in Scotland from the Battle of the Grampian Hills in the Year 85 to the Battle of Culloden in the Year 1746* (Edinburgh: W. Darling, 1783), 312; Forbes, *Lyon in Mourning* i. 262; Hughes, *Plain Narrative*, 40; Reid, *Highland Clansman*, 27; Tomasson and Buist, *Battles*, 187–8; Pollard (ed.), *Culloden*, 263 n.

57. Home, *History of the Rebellion*, 169; Johnstone, *Memoirs*, 142; Henderson, *Life of William Augustus*, 182; Tomasson and Buist, *Battles*, 188–90, 198; Reid, *Culloden*, 106–7; Reid, 'Battle of Culloden', 125–6, 128.

58. *Gentleman's Magazine* 16 (1946), 210; Henderson, *Life of William Augustus*, 182; Tomasson and Buist, *Battles*, 188–95; Prebble, *Culloden*, 107, 114; Reid, 'Battle of Culloden', 126–8; Daniel Szechi, 'The Significance of Culloden', in Pollard (ed.), *Culloden*, 218–38.

59. Maxwell, *Narrative*, 154.

60. Tomasson and Buist, *Battles*, 195–6; Johnstone, *Memoirs*, 129.

61. Findlay, *Wolfe in Scotland*, 108; Tomasson and Buist, *Battles*, 196–7; Elcho, *Short Account*, 434; Prebble, *Culloden*, 112.

62. Findlay, *Wolfe in Scotland*, 110–11; Tomasson and Buist, *Battles*, 198.

63. *Gentleman's Magazine* 16 (1946), 212; Findlay, *Wolfe in Scotland*, 106, 107, 108; Reid, 'The British Army at Culloden', 64–72, 85.

64. Reid, *Culloden*, 107; Elcho, *Short Account*, 435; Johnstone, *Memoirs*; Duffy, *The '45*, 524.

65. *Gentleman's Magazine* 16 (1946), 210–11; Henderson, *Life of William Augustus*, 182.

66. *Gentleman's Magazine* 16 (1946), 210; Maxwell, *Narrative*, 158; Reid, *Culloden*, 112–13; Duffy, *The '45*, 525–6.

Chapter 4

1. Andrew Henderson, *The Life of William Augustus, Duke of Cumberland*, ed. Roderick Macpherson (London: Pickering & Chatto, 2010), p. xxv; Duncan Warrand (ed.), *More Culloden Papers*, 5 vols (Inverness: Carruthers & Sons, 1930), v. 100; Annette M. Smith, *Jacobite Estates of the Forty-Five* (Edinburgh: John Donald, 1982), 1; W. A. Speck, *The Butcher* (Oxford: Basil Blackwell, 1981), 168; Roger Emerson, *An Enlightened Duke: The Life of Archibald Campbell (1682– 1761) Earl of Ilay 3rd Duke of Argyll* (Kilkerran: humming earth, 2013), 305.

2. *A Copy of a LETTER From a GENTLEMAN in London To His FRIEND at Bath* (Bath, 1750), 1–2, 4, 7; John Home, *The History of the Rebellion in Scotland in 1745* (Edinburgh: Peter Brown, 1822) ignores them altogether. For Irish comparators, see David Edwards, Pádraig Lenihan, and Clodagh Tait (eds), *Age of Atrocity: Violence and Political Conflict in Early Modern Ireland* (2007; Dublin: Four Courts, 2010).

3. James Maxwell of Kirkconnell, *Narrative of Charles Prince of Wales' Expedition to Scotland in the Year 1745* (Edinburgh: Maitland Club, 1841), 154, 169; Chevalier de Johnstone, *A Memoir of the 'Forty-Five*, ed. Brian Rawson (London: Folio Society, 1958), 129; James Allardyce (ed.), *Historical Papers Relating to the Jacobite Period 1699–1750*, 2 vols (Aberdeen: New Spalding Club, 1895), i. 320; Robert Chambers, *History of the Rebellion of 1745–1746* (1827; London: W. & R. Chambers, 1929), 307–8; Henderson, *Life of William Augustus*, 185, 186, 188, 189; Speck, *The Butcher*, 141, 148, 159–61.

4. Padre Giulio Cesare Cordara, 'Commentary on the Expedition to Scotland Made by Charles Edward Stuart, Prince of Wales', *Miscellany of the Scottish History Society 4*, ed. Sir Bruce Seton Bart (Scottish History Society, 3rd ser. 9; Edinburgh: Constable, 1926), 1–174 (121); John Prebble, *Culloden* (1961; London: Pimlico, 2002), 236; Jacqueline Hall, 'Loyal Societies in Ireland, 1690–1790', in James Kelly and Martyn J. Powell (eds), *Clubs and Societies in Eighteenth-Century Ireland* (Dublin: Four Courts, 2000), 181–202 (182, 183, 186, 195, 200).

5. Thomas Prince, *A Sermon Deliver'd at the SOUTH-CHURCH in Boston* (Boston, 1746; repr. Edinburg: R. Fleming, 1747), 14–15; Henderson, *Life of William Augustus*, pp. xxv, 195–6; *A Panegyric; INTITLED, The POOR MAN's honest Praises and Thanksgiving To His ROYAL HIGHNESS WILLIAM DUKE OF CUMBERLAND* (London: Cooper, 1746), 3; Geoffrey Plank, *Rebellion and Savagery: The Jacobite Rising of 1745 and the British Empire* (Philadelphia: University of Pennsylvania Press, 2006), 4, 87.

6. Plank, *Rebellion and Savagery*, 93; Speck, *The Butcher*, 147, 158–9.

7. *Mercy the Truest Heroism*…(London: M. Cooper, 1746); Speck, *The Butcher*, 159–61.

8. James Ray, *A Compleat History of the Rebellion* (Bristol: Farley, 1750), 342, 348–9: Michael Hughes, *A Plain Narrative and Authentic Journal of the Late Rebellion* (London: Henry Whitridge, 1747), 57; John Lawrie, *The History of the Wars in*

Scotland from the Battle of the Grampian Hills in the Year 85 to the Battle of Culloden in the Year 1746 (Edinburgh: W. Darling, 1783), 313; Allan Macinnes, 'The Aftermath of the '45', in Robert Woosnam-Savage (ed.), *1745: Charles Edward Stuart and the Jacobites* (Edinburgh: HMSO, 1995), 103–13 (104, 106, 109); Maxwell, *Narrative*, 169; David, Lord Elcho, *A Short Account of the Affairs of Scotland in the Years 1744, 1745, 1746*, with a Memoir and Annotations by the Hon. Evan Charteris (Edinburgh: David Douglas, 1907), 461–2; Speck, *The Butcher*, 147, 153, 155; Plank, *Rebellion and Savagery*, 57 for raids.

9. NLS MS 17514, fo. 55; NLS Adv. MSS 23.3.28, fos. 203, 204, 277; *Memorials of John Murray of Broughton*, ed. Robert Fitzroy Bell (Scottish History Society; Edinburgh: Constable, 1898), 210 n.; James Ray (attrib.), *A Journey Through Part of England and Scotland Along with the Army Under the Command of His Royal Highness the Duke of Cumberland* (London: Osborne, 1747), 97; W. Forbes Gray et al., *The Book of the Old Edinburgh Club XXVII* (Edinburgh: T. & A. Constable, 1949), 10–11; W. Forbes Gray and John H. Jamieson, *A Short History of Haddington* (Edinburgh: Neill & Co., 1944), 56; Mary Ingram, *A Jacobite Stronghold of the Church* (Edinburgh: Grant & Son, 1907), 33; Macinnes, 'Aftermath', 107–10; Cordara, 'Commentary', 119.

10. Warrand (ed.), *More Culloden Papers*, v. 79; Murray Pittock, *The Myth of the Jacobite Clans: The Jacobite Army in 1745* (1995; Edinburgh: Edinburgh University Press, 2009), 112–13; Aberdeen City Archives L/L/2: 11, 16; Christopher Duffy, *The '45* (2003; London: Phoenix, 2007), 530.

11. Pittock, *Myth*, 118–19; Plank, *Rebellion and Savagery*, 45–6, 55, 118; Warrand (ed.), *More Culloden Papers*, v. 123, 134; NLS MS 17514, fos. 87, 90; MS 17522, fos. 35 ff., 66, 83, 85, 87; MS 17523, fos. 197–8; NLS Adv. MSS 23.3.28, fo. 96; TNA SP 54/37/36; Angus Archives A 1/1/2; F 1/1/4; M 1/1/7.

12. Pittock, *Myth*, 125–6; NLS Adv. MSS 23.3.28, fo. 273; NLS MS 17514, fos. 26, 268, 271, 274–5; MS 17527, fos. 76, 105; NLS ACC 5039; NRS GD 14/98; GD 26/9.498; TNA SP 54/35/53; Allardyce (ed.), *Historical Papers*, i. 308; Duffy, *The '45*, 532, 533–4.

13. Chambers, *History*, 328; Duffy, *The '45*, 527–30; Speck, *The Butcher*, 164, 165, 168, 169; James Hunter, *On the Other Side of Sorrow: Nature and People in the Scottish Highlands* (Edinburgh: Mainstream, 1995), 29–30.

14. NRS GD 26/9/490; NLS ACC 5039; NLS MS 3142, fo. 154; MS 17505, fos. 65 ff., 78; MS 17525, fo. 97; Linda Colley, *Britons* (New Haven and London: Yale University Press, 1992), 83, 85; Bob Harris, *Politics and the Nation* (Oxford: Oxford University Press, 2002), 170, 179, 182; Christopher A. Whatley, 'Order and Disorder', in Elizabeth Foyster and Christopher Whatley (eds), *A History of Everyday Life in Scotland 1600–1800* (Edinburgh: Edinburgh University Press, 2010), 191–216 (191); Pittock, *Myth*, 130; Duffy, *The '45*, 530–3.

15. Stuart Reid, *The Scottish Jacobite Army 1745–1746* (Oxford: Osprey, 2006), 57; Speck, *The Butcher*, 181; Francisque Michel, *Les Écossais en France / Les Francais en Écosse*, 2 vols (London: Paternoster Row, 1862), ii. 448.

16. Alexander Geddes, *Some Account of the State of the Catholick Religion in Scotland during the Years 1745. 1746. & 1747*, ed. Fr Michael Briody (Moodiesburn, n.d.), 7, 9; David Dobson, *Directory of Scots Banished to the American Plantations 1650–1775* (Baltimore: Genealogical Publishing, 1994), 10, 19, 20, 28, 85, 109; Duffy, *The '45*, 534–9.

17. Daniel Szechi, 'The Jacobite Theatre of Death', in Eveline Cruickshanks and Jeremy Black (eds), *The Jacobite Challenge* (Edinburgh: John Donald, 1988), 57–73.

18. Horace, *Odes*, 3. 2. 13.

19. Robert Forbes, *The Lyon in Mourning*, ed. Henry Paton, 3 vols (Edinburgh: Edinburgh University Press/Scottish History Society, 1895), i. 241; Henderson, *Life of William Augustus*, 207; see Murray Pittock, *The Invention of Scotland* (1991; London: Routledge, 2014).

20. Dobson, *Directory*, 109; Plank, *Rebellion and Savagery*, 104, 108; Emerson, *Enlightened Duke*, 195–7 for a more benign view of judicial process following the Appin murder.

21. Plank, *Rebellion and Savagery*, 5, 6, 164–9; Macinnes, 'Aftermath', 107, 109–10.

22. NRS GD 95/11/11/2; NRS RH 15/201/17–29, correspondence between Clotilde Prunier and the author, 24 September 1999; J. T. Findlay, *Wolfe in Scotland in the '45 and from 1749 to 1753* (London, New York, and Toronto: Longmans, 1928), 137; Speck, *The Butcher*, 171, 173, 175; Smith, *Jacobite Estates*, 2.

23. Smith, *Jacobite Estates*, 7, 12, 13, 24, 58.

24. Iain MacIvor [Revd Doreen Grove], *Fort George Ardesier* (1988; Edinburgh: Historic Scotland, 2009), 1, 6–7, 9, 10–11, 16, 29, 30, 32.

25. TNA, SP 54/38; *The Albemarle Papers*, ed. Charles Sanford Terry, 2 vols (Aberdeen: New Spalding Club, 1902), i. 350–1; Forbes, *Lyon in Mourning*, ii. 221–2, iii. 305 ff.

26. Pittock, *Myth*, 126–7, 129; Harris, *Politics and the Nation*, 175; NLS MS 17514, fos. 271, 274; MS 17527, fos. 76, 105; TNA SP 54/35/1; 54/35/8B; 54/35/23A; 54/35/31C; 54/37/36; 54/38/1A; 54/38/5; Perth and Kinross Archives, PKC B59/32: 22, 23, 25 (1–2), 31, 32, 37, 41.

27. Hall, 'Loyal Societies in Ireland, 1690–1790', 181–3, 186, 200.

28. Johnstone, *Memoir*, 133; James Michael Hill, *Celtic Warfare* (Edinburgh: John Donald, 1986).

Chapter 5

1. Wulf Kansteiner, 'A Methodological Critique of Collective Memory Studies', *History and Theory* 41 (2002), 179–97; Geoffrey Cubitt, *History and Memory* (Manchester: Manchester University Press, 2007), 17.

2. Pierre Nora et al., *Realms of Memory: The Construction of the French Past*, ed. Lawrence D. Kritzmann, trans. Arthur Goldhammer, 3 vols (New York: Columbia University Press, 1991); Michael Rossington and Anne Whitehead,

'Introduction', in Rossington and Whitehead (eds), *Theories of Memory: A Reader* (Edinburgh: Edinburgh University Press, 2007), 5.

3. Roland Quinault, 'The Cult of the Centenary', *Historical Research* 71 (1998), 303–23 (304, 306–8, 318, 321–2).

4. See Murray Pittock, '"To See Ourselves as Others See Us": The Scot in English Eyes Since 1707', *European Journal of English Studies* 13/3 (2009), 293–304.

5. Murray Pittock, *Jacobitism* (Basingstoke: Macmillan, 1998), 80–1; Dougal Graham, *A Full Particular and True Account of the Rebellion in the Years 1745–1746* (2nd edn, Glasgow: Dougal Graham, 1752); Geoffrey Plank, *Rebellion and Savagery: The Jacobite Rising of 1745 and the British Empire* (Philadelphia: University of Pennsylvania Press, 2006), 67–9, 74.

6. Roger Fiske, *English Theatre Music in the Eighteenth Century* (London: Oxford University Press, 1973), 112, 169, 475; John O'Brien, *Harlequin Britain* (Baltimore: Johns Hopkins University Press, 2004), pp. xxiv, 40; Murray Pittock, *Celtic Identity and the British Image* (Manchester: Manchester University Press, 1999), 53.

7. James Ray (attrib.), *A Journey Through Part of England and Scotland Along with the Army Under the Command of His Royal Highness the Duke of Cumberland* (London: Osborne, 1747), 163; Thomas Prince, *A Sermon Deliver'd at the SOUTH-CHURCH in Boston* (Boston, 1746; repr. Edinburgh: R. Fleming, 1747), 28.

8. Ronald Black (ed.), *An Lasair* (Edinburgh: Birlinn, 2001), 129; John Leyden, *Journal of a Tour in the Highlands and Western Islands of Scotland in 1800*, ed. James Sinton (Edinburgh and London: William Blackwood and Sons, 1903), 86, 88, 109, 137, 216, 252.

9. For a detailed discussion, see Murray Pittock, 'Historiography', in Alexander Broadie (ed.), *The Cambridge Companion to the Scottish Enlightenment* (Cambridge: Cambridge University Press, 2003), 258–79 (esp. 262, 270); See also Anthony Brundage and Richard A. Cosgrove, *British Historians and National Identity* (London: Pickering & Chatto, 2014), 14.

10. Murray Pittock, 'What is a National Gothic?', in Mary-Ann Constantine and Dafydd Johnston (eds), *Footsteps of Liberty and Revolt: Essays on Wales and the French Revolution* (Cardiff: University of Wales Press, 2013), 231–45.

11. Charles W. J. Withers, *Urban Highlanders: Highland–Lowland Migration and Urban Gaelic Culture, 1700–1900* (East Linton: Tuckwell Press, 1998), 23, 233.

12. James Macpherson, *Original Papers: Containing the Secret History of Great Britain*, 2 vols (London: Strahan and Cadell, 1775), ii. 1; Henry Hallam, *The Constitutional History of England*, 3 vols (1827; London: John Murray, 1867), iii. 251, 336–7; John Kenyon, *The History Men* (London: Weidenfeld & Nicholson, 1983), 65–8.

13. Robert Chambers, *History of the Rebellion of 1745–1746* (1827; London: W. & R. Chambers, 1929), 30, 32, 33; Brundage and Cosgrove, *British Historians*, 57.

14. Neil Davidson, *Discovering the Scottish Revolution 1692–1746* (London: Pluto Press, 2003), 174; Charles Macfarlane and Thomas Thomson, *The Comprehensive*

History of England, 4 vols (Oxford: Blackie, 1861), iii. 275, 284, 289; Justin McCarthy, *A History of the Four Georges*, 4 vols (London: Chatto and Windus, 1890), ii. 294; Sir John Fortescue, *History of the British Army*, 13 vols (London: Macmillan, 1899–1930), ii. 146–7.

15. Basil Williams, *The Whig Supremacy 1714–1760* (Oxford: Clarendon Press, 1939), 244; John B. Owen, *The Eighteenth Century 1714–1815* (London: Nelson, 1974), 65.

16. G. M. Trevelyan, *History of England* (3rd edn, London: Longmans, 1952), 536, 538; Sir Winston Churchill, *A History of the English-Speaking Peoples*, 4 vols (New York: Dodd, Mead, 1956), iii. 109; John Prebble, *Culloden* (1961; London: Pimlico, 2002), 36, 38, 54; Charles Chevenix Trench, *George II* (London: Allen Lane, 1973), 234, 236; J. A. Houlding, *Fit for Service: The Training of the British Army, 1715–1795* (Oxford: Clarendon Press, 1981; repr. Sandpiper, 2000), 64; Paul Langford, *A Polite and Commercial People* (Oxford: Clarendon Press, 1989), 197; Rex Whitworth, *William Augustus, Duke of Cumberland* (London: Les Cooper, 1992), 56, 57, 58; Linda Colley, *Britons* (New Haven and London: Yale University Press, 1992), 77; W. A. Speck, *Stability and Strife: England 1714–1760* (London: Arnold, 1977), 251.

17. A. C. Ewald, *The Life and Times of Prince Charles Edward Stuart*, 2 vols (London: Chapman and Hall, 1875), ii. 27–33; Frank McLynn, *Charles Edward Stuart* (London: Routledge, 1988), 257.

18. See Murray Pittock, 'Charles Edward Stuart', *Études écossaises* 10 (2005), 57–71; M. Hook and W. Ross, *The 'Forty-Five* (Edinburgh: HMSO, 1995), 110.

Chapter 6

1. Letter of Uriel Dann to the author, 18 January 1989.

2. John R. and Margaret M. Gold, '"The Graves of the Gallant Highlanders": Memory, Interpretation and Narratives of Culloden', *History & Memory* 19/1 (2007), 5–33 (13–14); Neil Ramsay, 'Reframing Regicide: Symbolic Politics and the Sentimental Trial of James Hadfield (1800)', *Journal for Eighteenth-Century Studies* 36/3 (2013), 317–34 (318).

3. Simon Schama, *Landscape and Memory* (London: HarperCollins, 1995), 467; Murray Pittock, *Material Culture and Sedition* (Basingstoke: Macmillan, 2013), 146; Corrine Harrol, 'Whig Ballads and the Past Passive Jacobite', *Journal of Eighteenth-Century Studies* 35/4 (2012), 581–95 (589–90).

4. David McCrone, Angela Morris, and Richard Kiely, *Scotland the Brand* (Edinburgh: Edinburgh University Press, 1995), 194.

5. *Sir William Burrell's Northern Tour, 1758*, ed. John G. Dunlop (East Linton: Tuckwell Press, 1997), 97.

6. *Tours in Scotland, 1747, 1750, 1760 by Richard Pococke*, ed. Daniel William Kemp (Edinburgh: T. and A. Constable, for the Scottish History Society, 1887), pp. lxix, 105, 108; Thomas Pennant, *A Tour in Scotland 1769* (Chester, 1771), ed. Brian D. Osborne (Edinburgh: Birlinn, 2000), 103.

7. James Boswell, *The Journal of a Tour to the Hebrides with Samuel Johnson* (London and Edinburgh: Thomas Nelson & Sons, n.d [1785]), 109; John Leyden, *Journal of a Tour...in the Highlands and Western Islands of 1800*, ed. James Sinton (Edinburgh and London: William Blackwood and Sons, 1903), 216; *The Oxford Edition of the Works of Robert Burns: Commonplace Books, Tour Journals, and Miscellaneous Prose*, ed. Nigel Leask (Oxford: Oxford University Press, 2014), 149, 383 n.

8. Ronald Black (ed.), *An Lasair* (Edinburgh: Birlinn, 2001), 180; John and Margaret Gold, '"The Graves of the Gallant Highlanders"', 5; *A Century in Atholl* (Blair Atholl Estates, 1990); Ann Rigney, *The Afterlives of Walter Scott: Memory on the Move* (Oxford: Oxford University Press, 2012), 130; Sanja Perovic, 'The French Republican Calendar: Time, History and the Revolutionary Event', *Journal for Eighteenth-Century Studies* 35/1 (2012), 1–16 (11); Murray Pittock, *The Invention of Scotland: The Stuart Myth and the Scottish Identity* (1991; London: Routledge, 2014), 99, 103, 108.

9. Marion Löffler, *'A Book of Mad Celts': John Wickens and the Celtic Congress of Caernarfon 1904* (Llandysul: Gomer Press, 2000).

10. John and Margaret Gold, '"The Graves of the Gallant Highlanders"', 22–4; Iain Gale, 'From the Archive: The Irish Stone at Culloden, 1963', *In Trust* (Spring 2012), 74.

11. Tony Pollard, 'Capturing the Moment: The Archaeology of Culloden Battlefield', in Pollard (ed.), *Culloden: The History and Archaeology of the Last Clan Battle* (2009; Barnsley: Pen & Sword, 2011), 130–62 (153).

12. John and Margaret Gold, '"The Graves of the Gallant Highlanders"', 26–7.

13. Elspeth Masson and Jill Harden, 'Drumossie Moor', in Pollard (ed.), *Culloden*, 203–17 (214–16); McCrone, Morris, and Kiely, *Scotland the Brand*, 192; information from Ross Mackenzie, NTS Manager, Culloden Battlefield, 1992–2002.

14. John and Margaret Gold, '"The Graves of the Gallant Highlanders"', 27, 29–32; *Cùil Lodair/Culloden* ((Edinburgh: National Trust for Scotland, 2007), 69.

15. John and Margaret Gold, '"The Graves of the Gallant Highlanders"', 8; Alison Landberg, *Prosthetic Memory: The Transformation of American Remembrance in the Age of Mass Culture* (New York: Columbia University Press, 2004).

16. Andrew McKillop, in *Cùil Lodair/Culloden*, 13–15.

17. Pittock, *Invention of Scotland*, 127, 130, 134–44 (135–6, 138); Pittendrigh Macgillavray, *Memories of the '45* (Edinburgh, 1911), 3, 4, 9.

18. John and Margaret Gold, '"The Graves of the Gallant Highlanders"', 18. See Andrew Henderson, *The Life of William Augustus, Duke of Cumberland*, ed. Roderick Macpherson (1766; London: Pickering & Chatto, 2010), p. xxiv for a different interpretation.

19. See https://www.youtube.com/watch?v=HR_ltIlAeYA.

20. See http://www.bbc.co.uk/history/scottishhistory/union/trails_union_culloden.shtml.

21. See http://www.educationscotland.gov.uk/scotlandshistory/jacobitesenlighten mentclearances/culloden/.
22. See https://www.youtube.com/watch?v=RF16VwNCOek.
23. Colin McArthur, 'Bleeding Wallace', *Scottish Review of Books* 1/4 (2005).
24. http://www.undiscoveredscotland.co.uk/inverness/culloden/.
25. http://www.tartansauthority.com/tartan/the-growth-of-tartan/the-batle-of-culloden/.
26. https://www.youtube.com/watch?v=PrIUwo_GgmE.
27. Stephen McGinty, 'Soap Statue Won't Wash in Culloden', *Scotland on Sunday*, 8 July 2012; HeraldScotland (http://www.heraldscotland.com/), 27 December 2005.
28. Murray Pittock, ' "To See Ourselves as Others See Us": The Scot in English Eyes Since 1707', *European Journal of English Studies* 13/3 (2009), 293–304 (301–2).
29. http://lallandspeatworrier.blogspot.co.uk/2012/02/study-reveals-average-snp-member-is.html, 12 February 2012.
30. http://www.scottishjacobites.co.uk/banks/salmond.htm.
31. McCrone, Morris, and Kiely, *Scotland the Brand*, 195.
32. See https://www.youtube.com/watch?v=5Fs2nEKCT10 and https://www.youtube.com/watch?v=VCrx8l5YFMQ.

BIBLIOGRAPHY

Primary MS Sources

Aberdeen City Archives
L/L/2

Angus Archives
A1/1/1–2: Arbroath Town Council Minutes, 1727–66
B1/1/2: Brechin Town Council Minutes, 1713–59
F 1/1/4: Forfar Town Council Minutes, 1737–58
M 1/1/7: Montrose Town Council Minutes

National Library of Scotland (NLS)
NLS ACC 5039
NLS Adv. MSS 23.3.28
NLS Adv. MSS 82.4. 1, 2 (Gask Papers)
NLS MS 3142
NLS MS 3787 (Order Book of Appin's Regiment)
NLS MS 17505
NLS MS 17514
NLS MS 17522
NLS MS 17523
NLS MS 17525
NLS MS 17527

National Records of Scotland (NRS)
NRS GD 14/98
NRS GD 26/9
NRS GD 95/11
NRS RH 15/201

Perth and Kinross Archives
PKC B59/30
PKC B59/32

The National Archives (TNA)
SP 54/26
SP 54/35
SP 54/37
SP 54/38

Primary Printed Sources

The Albemarle Papers, ed. Charles Sanford Terry, 2 vols (Aberdeen: New Spalding Club, 1902).

Allardyce, James (ed.), Historical Papers Relating to the Jacobite Period 1699–1750, 2 vols (Aberdeen: New Spalding Club, 1895).

Balmerino, Arthur Elphinstone, 6th Lord, True Copies of the Papers Wrote by Arthur Lord Balmerino (London, 1746).

Black, Ronald (ed.), An Lasair (Edinburgh: Birlinn, 2001).

Bland, Humphrey, A Treatise of Military Discipline (London: Buckley, 1727).

Boswell, James, The Journal of a Tour to the Hebrides with Samuel Johnson (London and Edinburgh: Thomas Nelson & Sons, n.d. [1785]).

Burns, Robert, The Oxford Edition of the Works of Robert Burns: Commonplace Books, Tour Journals, and Miscellaneous Prose, ed. Nigel Leask (Oxford: Oxford University Press, 2014).

Burrell, William, Sir William Burrell's Northern Tour, 1758, ed. John G. Dunlop (East Linton: Tuckwell Press, 1997).

Campbell, John Lorne, Highland Songs of the 'Forty-Five (Edinburgh: J. Grant, 1933).

A Copy of a LETTER From a GENTLEMAN in London To His FRIEND at Bath (Bath, 1750).

Cordara, Padre Giulio Cesare, 'Commentary on the Expedition to Scotland Made by Charles Edward Stuart, Prince of Wales', Miscellany of the Scottish History Society, 4, ed. Sir Bruce Seton Bart (Scottish History Society, 3rd ser. 9; Edinburgh: Constable, 1926), 1–174.

Defoe, Daniel, A Tour through the Whole Island of Great Britain (1724–6), ed. Pat Rogers (Harmondsworth: Penguin, 1971).

Elcho, Lord David, A Short Account of the Affairs of Scotland in the Years 1744, 1745, 1746, with a Memoir and Annotations by the Hon. Evan Charteris (Edinburgh: David Douglas, 1907).

Forbes, Robert, The Lyon in Mourning, ed. Henry Paton, 3 vols (Edinburgh: Edinburgh University Press/Scottish History Society, 1895).

Geddes, Alexander, Some Account of the State of the Catholick Religion in Scotland during the Years 1745. 1746. & 1747, ed. Fr Michael Briody (Moodiesburn, n.d.).

The Gentleman's Magazine and Historical Chronicle, 16 (1746).

Graham, Dougal, A Full Particular and True Account of the Rebellion in the Years 1745–1746 (2nd edn, Glasgow: Dougal Graham, 1752).

Henderson, Andrew, The Life of William Augustus, Duke of Cumberland (1766), ed. Roderick Macpherson (London: Pickering & Chatto, 2010).

Hughes, Michael, *A Plain Narrative and Authentic Journal of the Late Rebellion* (London: Henry Whitridge, 1747).

Jarvis, Rupert C. (ed.), *Collected Papers on the Jacobite Risings*, 2 vols (Manchester: Manchester University Press, 1972).

Johnstone, Chevalier de, *A Memoir of the 'Forty-Five*, ed. Brian Rawson (London: Folio Society, 1958).

Lang, Andrew (ed.), *The Highlands of Scotland in 1750* (Edinburgh and London: Blackwood, 1898).

Leyden, John, *Journal of a Tour in the Highlands and Western Islands of Scotland in 1800*, ed. James Sinton (Edinburgh and London: William Blackwood and Sons, 1903).

Macpherson, James, *Original Papers: Containing the Secret History of Great Britain*, 2 vols (London: Strahan and Cadell, 1775).

'March of the Highland Army, in the Years 1745–1746, Being the Day Book of Captain James Stuart, of Lord Ogilvy's Regiment', in *Miscellany of the Spalding Club*, i (Edinburgh, 1841), 275–344.

Maxwell of Kirkconnell, James, *Narrative of Charles Prince of Wales' Expedition to Scotland in the Year 1745* (Edinburgh: Maitland Club, 1841).

Mercy the Truest Heroism... (London: M. Cooper, 1746).

Memorials of John Murray of Broughton, ed. Robert Fitzroy Bell (Scottish History Society; Edinburgh: Constable, 1898).

A Panegyric; INTITLED, The POOR MAN's honest Praises and Thanksgiving To His ROYAL HIGHNESS WILLIAM DUKE OF CUMBERLAND (London: Cooper, 1746).

A Particular Account of the Battle of CULLODEN. April 16, 1746 (London: T. Warner, 1749).

Pennant, Thomas, *A Tour in Scotland, 1769* (Chester, 1771), ed. Brian D. Osborne (Edinburgh: Birlinn, 2000).

Pococke, Richard, *Tours in Scotland, 1747, 1750, 1760 by Richard Pococke*, ed. Daniel William Kemp (Edinburgh: T. and A. Constable, for the Scottish History Society, 1887).

Prince, Thomas, *A Sermon Deliver'd at the SOUTH-CHURCH in Boston* (Boston, 1746; repr. Edinburgh: R. Fleming, 1747).

Rae, Peter, *The History of the Late Rebellion* (2nd edn, London: A Miller, 1746).

Ray, James (attrib.), *A Journey Through Part of England and Scotland Along with the Army Under the Command of His Royal Highness the Duke of Cumberland* (London: Osborne, 1747).

Ray, James, *A Compleat History of the Rebellion* (Bristol: Farley, 1750).

St Fond, B Faujas de, *A Journey Through England and Scotland to the Hebrides in 1784*, trans. and ed. Sir Archibald Geikle, 2 vols (Glasgow: Hugh Hopkins, 1907).

Warrand, Duncan (ed.), *More Culloden Papers*, 5 vols (Inverness: Carruthers & Sons, 1930).

Secondary Sources

Abrams, Lyn, *Oral History Theory* (London: Routledge, 2010).

Assmann, Jan, 'Collective Memory and Cultural Identity', *New German Critique* 65 (1995), 125–33.

Assmann, Jan, 'Communicative and Cultural Memory', in Astrid Erll and Ansgar Nünning (eds), *Media and Cultural Memory: An International and Interdisciplinary Handbook* (Berlin: Walter de Gruyter GmbH & Co., 2008), 109–18.

A Century in Atholl (Blair Atholl Estates, 1990).

Bastian, F., *Defoe's Early Life* (London and Basingstoke: Macmillan, 1981).

Bate, Jonathan, *The Song of the Earth* (London: Pimlico, 2000).

Black, Jeremy, *Culloden and the '45* (1990; Stroud: Sutton, 2000).

Black, Jeremy, *Eighteenth-Century Europe* (1990; 2nd edn, Basingstoke: Macmillan, 1999).

Brundage, Anthony, and Cosgrove, Richard A., *British Historians and National Identity* (London: Pickering & Chatto, 2014).

Caldwell, David H., *The Scottish Armoury* (Edinburgh: William Blackwood, 1979).

Carswell, Allan, '"The Most Despicable Enemy That Are": The Jacobite Army of the '45', in Woosnam-Savage (ed.), *1745*, 29–40.

Chambers, Robert, *History of the Rebellion of 1745–1746* (1827; London: W. & R. Chambers, 1929).

Churchill, Sir Winston, *A History of the English-Speaking Peoples*, 4 vols (New York: Dodd, Mead, 1956).

Clark, Jonathan, *From Restoration to Reform: The British Isles 1660–1832* (London: Vintage, 2014).

Colley, Linda, *Britons* (New Haven and London: Yale University Press, 1992).

Collins, Peter, *Who Fears to Speak of '98: Commemoration and the Continuing Impact of the United Irishmen* (Belfast: Ulster Historical Foundation, 2004).

Corp, Edward, *Jacobites at Urbino* (Basingstoke: PalgraveMacmillan, 2009).

Corp, Edward, *The Stuarts in Italy, 1719–1766* (Cambridge: Cambridge University Press, 2011).

Craig, Cairns, 'Introduction: Race, Scripture, Science', *Journal of Scottish Thought* 2/1 (2009), 1–33.

Cruickshanks, Eveline, *Political Untouchables: The Tories and the '45* (New York: Holmes & Meier, 1979).

Cubitt, Geoffrey, *History and Memory* (Manchester: Manchester University Press, 2007).

Cùil Lodair/Culloden (Edinburgh: National Trust for Scotland, 2007).

Dalgleish, George, and Mechan, Dallas, *'I Am Come Home': Treasures of Prince Charles Edward Stuart* (1986; Edinburgh: National Museum of Antiquities, n.d.).

Davidson, John, *Inverurie and the Earldom of the Garioch* (Edinburgh and Aberdeen: Douglas, 1878).

Davidson, Neil, *Discovering the Scottish Revolution 1692–1746* (London: Pluto Press, 2003).

Dobson, David, *Directory of Scots Banished to the American Plantations 1650–1775* (Baltimore: Genealogical Publishing, 1994).

Dobson, David, *The Jacobites of Angus, 1689–1746*, 2 vols (St Andrews, 1995).

Ducros, Louis, *French Society in the Eighteenth Century*, trans. W. De Gryer with a foreword by J. A. Haggs-Walker (London: G. Bell and Sons, 1926).

Duffy, Christopher, *The Military Experience in the Age of Reason* (London and New York: Routledge & Kegan Paul, 1987).

Duffy, Christopher, *The '45* (2003; London: Phoenix, 2007).

Durie, Alastair J., *Scotland for the Holidays* (East Linton: Tuckwell Press, 2003).

Edwards, David, Lenihan, Pádraig, and Tait, Clodagh (eds), *Age of Atrocity: Violence and Political Conflict in Early Modern Ireland* (2007; Dublin: Four Courts, 2010).

Edwards, Owen Dudley, 'Margo', *The Drouth* 48 (2014), 19–31.

Emerson, Roger L., *An Enlightened Duke: The Life of Archibald Campbell (1682–1761) Earl of Ilay 3rd Duke of Argyll* (Kilkerran: humming earth, 2013).

Ewald A. C., *The Life and Times of Prince Charles Edward Stuart*, 2 vols (London: Chapman and Hall, 1875).

Faiers, Jonathan, *Tartan* (Oxford and New York: Berg, 2008).

Findlay, J. T., *Wolfe in Scotland in the '45 and from 1749 to 1753* (London, New York, and Toronto: Longmans, 1928).

Fiske, Roger, *English Theatre Music in the Eighteenth Century* (London: Oxford University Press, 1973).

Fortescue, Sir John, *History of the British Army*, 13 vols (London: Macmillan, 1899–1930).

Gale, Ian, 'From the Archive: The Irish Stone at Culloden, 1963', *In Trust* (Spring 2012), 74.

Geertz, Clifford, *The Interpretation of Cultures* (1973; London: Fontana, 1993).

Glaser, Konstanze, *Minority Languages and Cultural Diversity in Europe* (Clevedon: Multililingual Matters, 2007).

Gold, John R., and Margaret M., '"The Graves of the Gallant Highlanders": Memory, Interpretation and Narratives of Culloden', *History & Memory* 19/1 (2007), 5–33.

Gray, W. Forbes, and Jamieson, John H., *A Short History of Haddington* (Edinburgh: Neill & Co., 1944).

Gray, W. Forbes, et al., *The Book of the Old Edinburgh Club XXVII* (Edinburgh: T. & A. Constable, 1949).

Guy, Alan, *Oeconomy and Discipline* (Manchester: Manchester University Press, 1985).

Guy, Alan, 'King George's Army, 1714–1750', in Woosnam-Savage (ed.), *1745*, 41–56.

Hall, Jacqueline, 'Loyal Societies in Ireland, 1690–1790', in James Kelly and Martyn J. Powell (eds), *Clubs and Societies in Eighteenth-Century Ireland* (Dublin: Four Courts, 2000).

Hallam, Henry, *The Constitutional History of England*, 3 vols (1827; London: John Murray, 1867).

Harris, Bob, *Politics and the Nation* (Oxford: Oxford University Press, 2002).

Harrol, Corrine, 'Whig Ballads and the Past Passive Jacobite', *Journal of Eighteenth-Century Studies* 35/4 (2012), 581–95.

Herrman, Luke, *Paul and Thomas Sandby* (London: Batsford, 1986).

Hill, James Michael, *Celtic Warfare* (Edinburgh: John Donald, 1986).

Hirsch, Marianne, 'Connective Histories in Vulnerable Times', *PMLA* 129/3 (2014), 330–48.

Home, John, *The History of the Rebellion in Scotland in 1745* (Edinburgh: Peter Brown, 1822).

Hook, M., and Ross, W., *The 'Forty-Five* (Edinburgh: HMSO, 1995).

Houlding, John, *Fit for Service: The Training of the British Army, 1715–1795* (Oxford: Clarendon Press, 1981; repr. Sandpiper, 2000).

Hunter, James, *On the Other Side of Sorrow: Nature and People in the Scottish Highlands* (Edinburgh: Mainstream, 1995).

Iggers, George G., Wang, Q. Edward, and Mukherjee, Supriye (eds), *A Global History of Modern Historiography* (Harlow: Longman, 2008).

Ingram, Mary, *A Jacobite Stronghold of the Church* (Edinburgh: Grant & Son, 1907).

Kansteiner, Wulf, 'A Methodological Critique of Collective Memory Studies', *History and Theory* 41 (2002), 179–97.

Kelvin, Martin, *The Scottish Pistol: Its History, Manufacture and Design* (London: Cygnus Arts, 1996).

Kenyon, John, *The History Men* (London: Weidenfeld & Nicholson, 1983).

Klein, Kevin Lee, 'On the Emergence of Memory in Historical Discourse', *Representations* 69 (2000), 127–50.

Landberg, Alison, *Prosthetic Memory: The Transformation of American Remembrance in the Age of Mass Culture* (New York: Columbia University Press, 2004).

Langford, Paul, *A Polite and Commercial People* (Oxford: Clarendon Press, 1989).

Lawrie, John, *The History of the Wars in Scotland from the Battle of the Grampian Hills in the Year 85 to the Battle of Culloden in the Year 1746* (Edinburgh: W. Darling, 1783).

Lenman, Bruce, *The Jacobite Clans of the Great Glen* (London: Methuen, 1984).

Lindsay, Thomas B., 'Highland Dress', in *Scottish Weapons, Scottish Art Review Special Number* 9/1 (1963), 6–10, 33.

Löffler, Marion, '*A Book of Mad Celts': John Wickens and the Celtic Congress of Caernarfon 1904* (Llandysul: Gomer Press, 2000).

McArthur, Colin, 'Bleeding Wallace', http://scottishreviewofbooks.org/index. php/back-issues/volume-1/volume-one-issue-four/198-bleeding-wallace-colin-mcarthur.

McCarthy, Justin, *A History of the Four Georges*, 4 vols (London: Chatto and Windus, 1890).

McCrone, David, Morris, Angela, and Kiely, Richard, *Scotland the Brand* (Edinburgh: Edinburgh University Press, 1995).

McDonnell, Frances, *Jacobites of 1745 North-East Scotland* (n.p., n.d.).

Macfarlane, Charles, and Thomson, Thomas, *The Comprehensive History of England*, 4 vols (Oxford: Blackie, 1861).

Macgillavray, Pittendrigh, *Memories of the '45* (Edinburgh, 1911).

MacGill-Eain, Somhairle, 'Tha na beanntan gun bhruidhinn'/'The mountains are speechless', in MacGill-Eain, *An Cuilithionn 1939: The Cuillin 1939 & Unpublished Poems*, ed. Christopher Whyte (Glasgow: Association for Scottish Literary Studies, 2011).

Macinnes, Allan, 'The Aftermath of the '45', in Woosnam-Savage (ed.), *1745*, 103–13.

MacIvor, Iain [Revd Doreen Grove], *Fort George Ardesier* (1988; Edinburgh: Historic Scotland, 2009).

MacLeod, Christine, *Heroes of Invention: Technology, Liberalism and British Identity 1750–1914* (Cambridge: Cambridge University Press, 2007).

McLynn, Frank, *France and the Jacobite Rising of 1745* (Edinburgh: Edinburgh University Press, 1981).

McLynn, Frank, *The Jacobite Army in England: The Last Campaign* (Edinburgh; John Donald, 1983).

McLynn, Frank, *Charles Edward Stuart* (London: Routledge, 1988).

Maxwell, Stuart, 'The Highland Targe', in *Scottish Weapons, Scottish Art Review Special Number* 9/1 (1963), 2–5, 33.

Michel, Francisque, *Les Écossais en France/Les Francais en Écosse*, 2 vols (London: Paternoster Row, 1862).

Murdoch, Alexander, *British History 1660–1832: National Identity and Local Culture* (Basingstoke: Macmillan, 1998).

Nicholas, Donald (ed.), *Intercepted Post* (London: Bodley Head, 1956).

Nora, Pierre, et al., *Realms of Memory: The Construction of the French Past*, ed. Lawrence D. Kritzmann, trans. Arthur Goldhammer, 3 vols (New York: Columbia University Press, 1991).

O'Brien, John, *Harlequin Britain* (Baltimore: Johns Hopkins University Press, 2004).

Olick, Jeffrey H, *The Politics of Regret* (New York and London: Routledge, 2007).

Owen, John B., *The Eighteenth Century 1714–1815* (London: Nelson, 1974).

Ozouf, Mona, *Festivals and the French Revolution*, trans. Alan Sheridan of *Les Fêtes révolutionnaires* (Cambridge, Mass: Harvard University Press, 1988).

Pascoe, Judith, *The Hummingbird Cabinet* (Ithaca, NY and London: Cornell University Press, 2006).

Penman, Michael A., 'Robert Bruce's Bones: Reputations, Politics and Identities in Nineteenth-Century Scotland', *International Review of Scottish Studies* 34 (2009), 7–73.

Perovic, Sanja, 'The French Republican Calendar: Time, History and the Revolutionary Event', *Journal for Eighteenth-Century Studies* 35/1 (2012), 1–16.

Pincus, Steven, *1688: The First Modern Revolution* (New Haven: Yale University Press, 2009).

Pittock, Murray, *The Myth of the Jacobite Clans: The Jacobite Army in 1745* (1995; Edinburgh: Edinburgh University Press, 2009).

Pittock, Murray, *Jacobitism* (Basingstoke: Macmillan, 1998).

Pittock, Murray, *Celtic Identity and the British Image* (Manchester: Manchester University Press, 1999).

Pittock, Murray, 'Historiography', in Alexander Broadie (ed.), *The Cambridge Companion to the Scottish Enlightenment* (Cambridge: Cambridge University Press, 2003), 258–79.

Pittock, Murray, 'Charles Edward Stuart', *Études écossaises* 10 (2005), 57–71.

Pittock, Murray, '"To See Ourselves as Others See Us": The Scot in English Eyes Since 1707', *European Journal of English Studies* 13/3 (2009), 293–304.

Pittock, Murray, *Material Culture and Sedition, 1688–1760* (Basingstoke: Macmillan, 2013).

Pittock, Murray, 'What is a National Gothic?', in Mary-Ann Constantine and Dafydd Johnston (eds), *Footsteps of Liberty and Revolt: Essays on Wales and the French Revolution* (Cardiff: University of Wales Press, 2013).

Pittock, Murray, *The Invention of Scotland: The Stuart Myth and the Scottish Identity* (1991; London: Routledge, 2014).

Pittock, Murray, and Mackay, Pauline, 'Highland Mary: Objects and Memories', *Romanticism* 18/2 (2012), 191–203.

Plank, Geoffrey, *Rebellion and Savagery: The Jacobite Rising of 1745 and the British Empire* (Philadelphia: University of Pennsylvania Press, 2006).

Plumb, J. H., *England in the Eighteenth Century* (Harmondsworth: Penguin, 1950).

Pollard, Tony (ed.), *Culloden: The History and Archaeology of the Last Clan Battle* (2009; Barnsley: Pen and Sword, 2011).

Pollard, Tony, 'The Archaeology of Scottish Battlefields', in Edward Spiers et al. (eds), *A Military History of Scotland* (Edinburgh: Edinburgh University Press, 2012), 728–47.

Prebble, John, *Culloden* (1961; London: Pimlico, 2002).

Quinault, Roland, 'The Cult of the Centenary', *Historical Research* 71 (1998), 303–23.

Ramsay, Dean, *Reminscences of Scottish Life and Character* (1857; 14th edn, London and Edinburgh, 1920).

Ramsay, Neil, 'Reframing Regicide: Symbolic Politics and the Sentimental Trial of James Hadfield (1800)', *Journal for Eighteenth-Century Studies* 36/3 (2013), 317–34.

Reid, Stuart, *Highland Clansman 1689–1746* (1997; Oxford: Osprey, 1999).

Reid, Stuart, *The Scottish Jacobite Army 1745–1746* (Oxford: Osprey, 2006).

Reid, Stuart, *Culloden 1746* (2005; 2nd edn, Barnsley: Pen and Sword, 2011).

Reid, William, 'Walter Allan, Armourer in Stirling', in *Scottish Weapons, Scottish Art Review Special Number* 9/1 (1963), 16–21.

Reid, William, 'The Heart-Butt Pistols of East Scotland', in *Scottish Weapons, Scottish Art Review, Special Number* 9/1 (1963), 26–30.

Rigney, Ann, 'The Dynamics of Remembrance: Texts Between Monumentality and Morphing', in Astrid Erll and Asgar Nunning (eds), *Cultural Memory Studies* (Berlin and New York: Walter de Gruyter, n.d.), 345–53.

Rigney, Ann, 'Plenitude, Scarcity and the Circulation of Cultural Memory', *Journal of European Studies* 35/1 (2006), 11–28.

Rigney, Ann, 'Embodied Communities: Commemorating Robert Burns, 1859', *Representations* 115 (2011), 71–101.

Rigney, Ann, *The Afterlives of Walter Scott: Memory on the Move* (Oxford: Oxford University Press, 2012).

Rogers, Nicholas, 'Popular Protest in Early Hanoverian London', *Past and Present* 79 (1978), 70–100.

Rossington, Michael, and Whitehead, Anne (eds), *Theories of Memory: A Reader* (Edinburgh: Edinburgh University Press, 2007).

Schama, Simon, *Landscape and Memory* (London: HarperCollins, 1995).

Scott, J. G., 'Basket-hilted Swords of Glasgow Make', in *Scottish Weapons, Scottish Art Review Special Number* 9/1 (1963), 22–3.

Simpson, Peter, *The Independent Highland Companies 1603–1760* (Edinburgh: John Donald, 1996).

Sloane, Hamish, and McKay, James, 'Scottish Pistols-4', *Dispatch* (1983).

Smith, Annette M., *Jacobite Estates of the Forty-Five* (Edinburgh: John Donald, 1982).

Southey, Robert, *The Life of Horatio Lord Nelson* (1906; London and Toronto: J. M. Dent/Everyman, 1925).

Speck, W. A., *Stability and Strife: England 1714–1760* (London: Arnold, 1977).

Speck, W. A., *The Butcher* (Oxford: Basil Blackwell, 1981).

Stevenson, David, *Alasdair MacColla and the Highland Problem in the 17th Century* (Edinburgh, 1980).

Stevenson, David, *Highland Warrior: Alasdair MacColla and the Civil War* (Edinburgh, 2003).

Summerfield, Penny, 'Culture and Composure: Creating Narratives of the Gendered Self in Oral History Interviews', *Cultural and Social History* 1/1 (2004), 65–93.

Szechi, Daniel, *Jacobitism and Tory Politics 1710–1714* (Edinburgh: John Donald, 1984).

Szechi, Daniel, 'The Jacobite Theatre of Death', in Eveline Cruickshanks and Jeremy Black (eds), *The Jacobite Challenge* (Edinburgh: John Donald, 1988), 57–73.

Szechi, Daniel, *1715* (New Haven: Yale University Press, 2006).

Szechi, Daniel, 'Jamie the Soldier and the Jacobite Military Threat, 1706–1727', in Allan Macinnes and Douglas Hamilton (eds), *Jacobitism, Enlightenment and Empire* (London: Pickering & Chatto, 2014), 13–28.

Tomasson, Katherine, *The Jacobite General* (Edinburgh: Blackwood, 1958).

Tomasson, Katherine, and Buist, Francis, *Battles of the '45* (London: Batsford, 1962).

Trench, Charles Chevenix, *George II* (London: Allen Lane, 1973).

Trevelyan, G. M., *History of England* (3rd edn, London: Longmans, 1952).

Turner, Roger, *Manchester in 1745* (Royal Stuart Society Paper 49; London, 1997).

Walsham, Alexandra, *The Reformation of the Landscape* (2011; Oxford: Oxford University Press, 2012).

Weir, David, 'Tontines, Public Finance and Revolution in France and England, 1688–1789', *Journal of Economic History* 49/1 (1989), 95–124.

West, Christina, 'Memory—Recollection—Culture—Identity—Space: Social Context, Identity Formation, and Self-Construction of the Calé (Gitanos) in Spain', in Peter Meusburger, Michael Heffernan, and Edgar Wunder (eds), *Cultural Memories: The Geographical Point of View* (London: Springer, 2011), 101–19.

Whatley, Christopher A., 'Order and Disorder', in Elizabeth Foyster and Christopher Whatley (eds), *A History of Everyday Life in Scotland 1600–1800* (Edinburgh: Edinburgh University Press, 2010), 191–216.

Whatley, Christopher A., 'Reformed Religion, Regime Change, Scottish Whigs and the Struggle for the "Soul" of Scotland', *c.*1688–*c.*1788', *Scottish Historical Review* 92 (2013), 66–99.

Whitworth, Rex, *William Augustus, Duke of Cumberland* (London: Les Cooper, 1992).

Williams, Basil, *The Whig Supremacy 1714–1760* (Oxford: Clarendon Press, 1939).

Withers, Charles W. J., *Urban Highlanders: Highland–Lowland Migration and Urban Gaelic Culture, 1700–1900* (East Linton: Tuckwell Press, 1998).

Woolf, Daniel, *The Social Circulation of the Past* (Oxford: Oxford University Press, 2003).

Woosnam-Savage, Robert (ed.), *1745: Charles Edward Stuart and the Jacobites* (Edinburgh: HMSO, 1995).

PICTURE ACKNOWLEDGEMENTS

1. © PAINTING / Alamy
2. © Murray Pittock
3. March of the Guards to Finchley, 1750, by William Hogarth. The Foundling Museum, London, UK / Bridgeman Images
4. © Murray Pittock
5. © Murray Pittock
6. © Murray Pittock
7. © Murray Pittock
8. © Murray Pittock
9. © Murray Pittock
10. © Murray Pittock
11. © The Trustees of the British Museum
12. An Incident in the Rebellion of 1745, c.1745–85, by David Morier (attr. to) / Royal Collection Trust © Her Majesty Queen Elizabeth II, 2015 / Bridgeman Images
13. The Harlequin Portrait of Prince Charles Edward Stuart. c.1745, by John Worsdale. Private Collection / Photo © Philip Mould Ltd, London / Bridgeman Images
14. The Abdication of Mary Queen of Scots (1542–87) in 1568, c.1765–73, by Gavin Hamilton. The Hunterian, University of Glasgow, Scotland / Bridgeman Images
15. © Calum Colvin

map 1. Courtesy the private collection of Roy Winkelman. FCIT
map 2. Reproduced by permission of the National Library of Scotland
map 4. A Plan of the Battle of Culloden, 16th April 1746, by Thomas Sandby. Royal Collection Trust © Her Majesty Queen Elizabeth II, 2015 / Bridgeman Images

INDEX